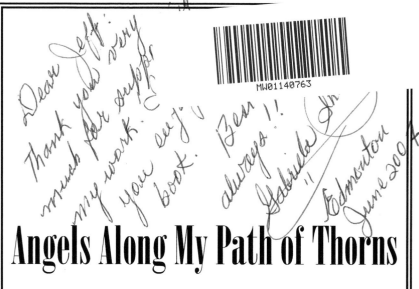

Angels Along My Path of Thorns

An Autobiography

By

Gabriela A. Folgar de Shea

Note for Librarians: A cataloguing record for this book is available from Library and Archives Canada at www.collectionscanada.ca/amicus/index-e.html
ISBN 1-4120-9656-1

Printed in Victoria, BC, Canada. Printed on paper with minimum 30% recycled fibre. Trafford's print shop runs on "green energy" from solar, wind and other environmentally-friendly power sources.

Offices in Canada, USA, Ireland and UK

Book sales for North America and international:
Trafford Publishing, 6E–2333 Government St.,
Victoria, BC V8T 4P4 CANADA
phone 250 383 6864 (toll-free 1 888 232 4444)
fax 250 383 6804; email to orders@trafford.com
Book sales in Europe:
Trafford Publishing (UK) Limited, 9 Park End Street, 2nd Floor
Oxford, UK OX1 1HH UNITED KINGDOM
phone 44 (0)1865 722 113 (local rate 0845 230 9601)
facsimile 44 (0)1865 722 868; info.uk@trafford.com
Order online at:
trafford.com/06-1412

10 9 8 7 6 5 4 3

Introduction

I have written my autobiography of my childhood and adolescence for several reasons: first, to bring hope to those who suffer adversity through no fault of their own that tenacity and a positive outlook accomplishes much; second, to share my story with family and other people who know something about what I had to suffer but who do not know many of the details.

Guatemala is a small and very complex country composed of many ethnic groups and numerous indigenous languages. I was born and grew up in a region called by the locals, "the East." This region lies southeast of Guatemala City, south of the main highway from Guatemala City to the Caribbean Sea, and borders Honduras and El Salvador. I cannot venture to say that the customs described in my story are representative of Guatemala, since I am not familiar with many other regions. In addition, I cannot say that the application of the law is the same now as it was in the nineteen–fifties and sixties. I immigrated to Canada in 1974 and have made only three short trips back to my country of birth since that time, and the purpose of these visits was to visit my family, not to make intensive studies of Guatemala's politics, regions and customs.

I have not been able to find adequate or correct English translations for many of the social customs and objects mentioned in this book. In order to aid the reader I have included many standard Spanish, Guatemalan dialectical Spanish, and local Mayan indigenous words with their English translation. More often than not, I could not even find the academic Spanish word for many indigenous words used by all Guatemalans of all races. Many photographs and maps are interspersed throughout the book to enable the reader to visually follow the text and to mentally enter into an unknown region of the world.

I wish to add one last note: most of what has been written and portrayed about Guatemala in the English language media the past thirty years revolves around political problems and I fear that this narrow reporting could skewer the reader's perceptions and subsequent interpretations of my story. This is simply a story of one adolescent girl caught up in a dysfunctional family and judicial system, a male dominated society, and, on many occasions, being in the wrong place at the wrong time.

Gabriela A. Folgar de Shea

Acknowledgements

The first person I wish to thank is my husband, David Shea. As soon as I told him my complete story more than three decades ago he suggested that I write a book. And once I had started to write he was the one to talk to me and to console me when the memories became too overwhelming and I was ready to quit. He also has been my writing assistant, editor, photographer, computer assistant and final book layout person.

Next I wish to thank a good friend and work colleague, Marlaine Sitch, who also encouraged me to write my story. It was her enthusiasm that finally pushed me to start. She also was one of my proofreaders.

I wish to acknowledge and give special thanks to the people who assisted me with my writing: Sandra Maygard, Laura Patterson and María Luisa Rodas, who proofread the manuscript and gave me excellent suggestions; to Lavonne Hailes, Barry Greenspan and to many other colleagues for their support.

My sister, Señora Piedad Eneida Folgar de Castellanos, has been a wonderful help. She is a schoolteacher in Guatemala City and has taken the time to research and to find items of interest. She has made numerous trips to San Pedro Pinula and other towns on my behalf to get information that would have been impossible for me to find.

My cousin, Señor Ramiro Folgar, who used to live and farm in San Pedro Pinula, was a great source of information. I visited him on a recent trip to Guatemala and he provided details about the personalities and history of several key people in my story. He also was help in a geographical sense. With his information I was finally able to learn the names of places along with their locations where important events in my life took place.

I wish to thank Lic. Victor M. Cruz Rodriguez, a lawyer in Guatemala City, who provided me invaluable information about the law, regional application of the law, and local customs in Guatemala. His information has helped clear up many mysteries of why the police and justice system acted in the way they did during the course of my ordeal in 1964.

Dedications

To my deceased mother, Manuela Josefa Lucero and to all of the angels who helped me and saved my life and who are now deceased. I was never in the position to thank them when they were alive in this world.

Memory Eternal

To our children: Merle, Michael, Norman, Walden and Elva. To Mr. Milton Wong. To my aunt, Sra. María Teresa Menendez de Buckley. To my sister, Sra. Piedad Eneida Folgar de Castellanos. Lastly, to two of my friends from my school days in Chiquimula: Sras. Soila Elizabeth Guerra de Santos and Marta Estela Solís de Martínez.

May God Grant Them Many Years

Guatemala, Central America

Part I

Through A Child's Eyes:

Childhood and Adolescence

Gabriela A. Folgar de Shea
Gabriela in the Central Plaza in El Progreso Guastatoya, town of birth–2005

Chapter 1
Beginnings

Like all humans, I do not remember my birth. By the time we wake up too our-selves, we are little children... We live like latecomers at the theatre: we must catch up as best we can, divining the beginning from the shape of later events.
–Diane Setterfield–

The night was similar to any other night. I went to bed, the sound of my mother's sewing machine was humming like a lullaby, lulling me to sleep. Even at five years of age I was a light sleeper, waking up every time my mother opened the door to the patio to see if my father was coming home and waking up for sure when my father came home and knocked on the door. But on this particular evening I did not hear him entering the house. Suddenly, I awoke to the sound of his voice. I could tell right away that this was not an argument with my mother. His voice was different—more like a desperate cry.

"Chepita, where is the gun, I am finished, I am lost and I don't want to live anymore!"

I heard my mother trying to calm him down. "Carmelino, be quiet you're going to wake up the children, please tell me what has happened?"

"No, don't ask me questions, just give me the gun, where is it? I want to die!"

She pleaded once more, "Please, Carmelino, remember the children are sleeping. Please tell me what happened? Maybe I can help."

"No, nobody can help me. No, I can't tell you. It's horrible. It is the worst. I might even lose my job. I want to die. Please give me the gun. Where is it? I want to kill myself. Where's the gun? Please, tell me, where…is… the… gun?"

"Shhh, Carmelino, don't talk so loud," she said in a hushed tone, "tell me what happened and then I will help you look for the gun."

Their conversation quieted and I was no longer able to hear, for now they were whispering. Then my mother came to my bedroom where a wooden trunk with a lock was kept. Through the transparent mosquito net I watched her. She placed the kerosene lamp on a table and then opened the trunk. I could hear my father in the living room crying uncontrollably. I knew what my mother kept in that wooden trunk. Every time she sent me to deliver the dresses she had made she took from me the money I had collected and went immediately into the bedroom. A few times I peeked and observed her putting some of the money in the trunk.

She went back to the living room and approached my father saying, "Here Carmelino, this is all I have, maybe you can go to San Pedro Pinula (my father's family home) tomorrow morning and try to borrow some money or sell some of your horses in order to make up the difference. I will keep this money here until you come back."

The next morning my mother's eyes were swollen from crying and she told us that my father had gone to San Pedro Pinula.

Several years later when I questioned my mother about this incident she told me what had happened. "Your father had gone to Guatemala City to collect his monthly salary together with the monthly salary of some or all of the teachers who worked at the same school with him. After he had returned to El Progreso, instead of going straight home, he went to gamble and lost all the money. This was not the first time your father had the thought of killing himself after having lost money by gambling. That's why I had hidden the gun from him in the first place."

Even though I was only five years old I had guessed the source of the problem long before my mother's explanation because I had been awakened several times previous to this incident (and afterwards too) by the noise of their arguments. The arguments always revolved around the same issue—my father's gambling. I was unable to understand what gambling meant at that time. I only knew that it was related to some kind of money matters and that it was a constant source of sadness in our home.

My baptismal name is Gabriela Antonia Folgar–Lucero, the Lucero part of my name is my mother's family name and the Folgar part is my father's family name. I was born on November 7, 1948 in the small provincial town of El Progreso Guastatoya, in the province (*departamento*) of El Progreso, Guatemala–Central America. El Progreso Guastatoya is situated approximately one hundred and fifty kilometers southeast of Guatemala City and due to the winding roads it takes about one and a half hours to travel there from the capital. The town is very hot, for it sits in a valley, and as I remember, the people were very friendly. It had one very large and beautiful school, *ESCUELA FEDERAL DE EL PROGRESO*. This is where I attended grade one in 1955 at the age of six until the beginning of grade two when I was seven. This school was a boys' school in the morning and a girls' school in the afternoon. Our school uniform was white and blue, symbolizing the colours of the Guatemalan flag. The town also had a beautiful colonial Catholic church. I am using the past tense to describe this town here because, unfortunately, it was situated on top of the epicenter of the horrible fourth of February earthquake in 1976 and was totally destroyed with a great loss of life.[*] Only two buildings were left intact, the elementary school and the church on the main plaza (minus its vaulted roof). On a recent visit I observed that the town has been completely rebuilt and it looks better than it did before.[*]

I am the second child of Luis Carmelino Antonio Folgar and

---

[*] This earthquake (7.6 Richter) caused 22,000 killed, 5,000 missing, 74,000 seriously injured and over one million homeless in Guatemala.

[*] Please refer to the map on page thirty (30) to locate the towns mentioned in this chapter.

Manuela Josefa Lucero. People in Guatemala are often classified by their racial make-up—Indigenous, European or *Ladino* (mixed-*mestizo*). People of pure European blood make up a very small percentage of the population, although they are quite often in positions of power. About fifty percent of Guatemala's population is of pure Mayan Indian decent. *Ladinos* make up most of the remaining population. Some *Ladinos* have the European features of the people of Spain, which is the case in my mother's family and others have more Indian features, which is the case in my father's family.

My father was much older than my mother. He had been hired to be her home–schooling teacher. He told me that he fell crazily in love with her. My mother, on the other hand, told me that she needed to get out of her mother's house and it was a good opportunity to do this by marrying him. She was seventeen years old and he was forty-one.

In 1955 our family moved from El Progreso Guastatoya to Sanarate, another town in the province of El Progreso. I finished grade two at the boys' school where my father was the principal. In the beginning of 1957 my father was transferred again, this time to his hometown of San Pedro Pinula (San Pa̲y-dro Pee-noo-la), a town in which he always had wanted to teach. He was the principal of the boys' elementary school and as a result, I was allowed to attend this school for grades three, four and five. My father was my teacher in grade four.

A casual outside observer of my life in El Progreso, Sanarate and San Pedro Pinula, from birth to age eleven in 1959, would have said that I was living a normal and uneventful life. But the reality of my world was quite different. At a very early age I realized that the relationships between my parents, between my brothers and me, and between my parents and all of their children were not the type of relationships I was observing in other families. My earliest observations in this regard were that other children were allowed to play, had toys and enjoyed treats. I observed that other children went out and socialized with both of their parents. None of this was part of my life in my early years. Of course, at that age I was not able to draw conclusions or to connect these observations to family dynamics.

As far back as I can remember I thought that I was not being treated fairly and had to defend myself, mostly around the differences of expectations between boys and girls. Whenever I saw inequality between my older brother and me I would always challenge it and ask why. I recall questioning my father when I was as young as six years of age, "Why do I always have to do the dishes? Is my brother a king? Where's the crown on his head? Why doesn't he sweep?"

My father would then become very angry and tell me that I had a big mouth and was insolent. I was never disrespectful toward my father. He became angry with me because he just could not handle my logic. My mother always tried to smooth things over by advising me, "Just do your chores quietly."

Since I was the only girl attending a boys' school, I was in academic competition with boys and, therefore, at a quite young age I was in a position to see that I was on an equal intellectual footing with them. I was a keen observer of human behaviour, a thinker, an excellent student and especially, a talker. My struggle with my father and Guatemala's cultural preference for all things male would be a defining battle in my life. I could never accept, beginning at a very early age, that I was inferior and less capable just because I was a girl. The struggle for fairness and equality was the crucible where the combative part of my personality was refined. My stubbornness and fearlessness to speak up to injustice would be one of the causes of the many troubles I was to suffer in the future. However, this stubbornness also gave me the strength to survive horrible events and to later achieve my greatest personal victories.

My mother was a very nice looking woman possessing a beautiful body. Every time we went out men would look at her and make comments to her, comments that I did not understand at that time. When this happened she started walking very rapidly and say to me, "Hurry, walk faster."

Sometimes I asked her, "Why do men look at you and say

things when you pass by?"

She always only answered, "They're just retarded."

I spent most of my free time with my mother, up to the time my parents separated when I was almost eleven years old. I was what she called, "her right arm." Since she was always busy with  her sewing, I was the one to take care of the cooking, cleaning, washing and ironing of the clothes. I also helped her with minor things in her sewing business such as doing button holes, attaching buttons to dresses, hemming sleeves and skirts, and keeping the charcoal iron ready and hot at all times. I ran all the errands to buy the notions and sewing supplies. She would write me a list and I would show this paper to the store clerk. Quite often I had to make four to six trips to the fabric store to exchange notions and sewing supplies until I brought home the right ones. I also delivered the dresses to her customers. My mother gave me ten percent of the total bill for doing this work. With this money I helped my mother with her expenses by buying my own socks and shoes. I started doing these chores before reaching the age of six. I loved helping my mother with the sewing, but I was so tired from all of the other work I had to do in the house that many times I fell asleep while doing my schoolwork. When this happened I had to get up at five o'clock in the morning in order to finish before leaving for school.

My mother used to sing while she was sewing. I learned quite a few Mexican rancheros by listening to her. Sometimes we sang together. She made beautiful dresses for me and I believe I was probably the best-dressed girl in the elementary school. She made these dresses from the fabric remnants her customers left her. Many times I wanted to learn how to operate the sewing machines but she never really had the time to teach me.

My mother was caring, but not affectionate. I cannot remember her ever hugging any of us children. When I was sad or hurt and came to her for some comfort she just pushed me away saying, "Stop that mushiness." She was very physical when she disciplined her children. Whenever my brothers or I did something wrong she took a belt and hit us very hard. She not only hit the child who was at fault but every one of us as well. Her reasoning was, "When you spank only one child, the other ones laugh. In order to prevent that, you have to spank them all together." She and my father had quite a few arguments due to her ways of disciplining us. My father did not use the belt, but made us pay for our mistakes with chores. If we did not do the chores as soon as he had told us to do them, then the number increased.

In spite of her harshness when punishing us children, my mother had sympathy for the needs of a child and she tried to provide us, within her limited means, with treats such as the occasional ice cream or candy, items my father would never dream of spending money on. My mother genuinely loved her children, even if her ways of demonstrating this love were limited.

When I was six years old I passed by a store on my way to and from school where a most beautiful doll was on display in the window. Every day I stopped and took a few minutes to admire this doll. It was clothed in a beautiful green dress and was placed in a seated position. From the doll's neck hung a tag that read, Q5.00. Five Quetzals was a lot of money in those days. It was the equivalent of five American dollars. Possessing only a rudimentary idea of mathematics at my age, I had no notion of wages and prices of items. The only thing I knew was that my mother was charging one Quetzal for each dress she made and this would take her more than a half a day to finish. I had an idea, therefore, that the doll was very expensive, but at my age I was only looking at how beautiful it was and wishing that Santa Claus would bring it to me for Christmas. Every evening I went to bed thinking about the doll and dreaming about having it in my arms.

I do not recall all the conversations I had with my mother about the doll prior to Christmas. I only remember talking about the doll and constantly pestering her about it. She always told me that it was too expensive to buy. This is when I started to figure out that Santa Claus did not exist. If he did exist, I thought, he only brought toys to rich children.

The last day of school was on Friday, October 21. On this day I took extra time coming home from school, stopping at the market to look at the doll. I knew it might be my last opportunity to see it, because I was no longer going to be walking past the store now that school was finished. Of course, when I got home my mother was very worried. My father, who usually arrived after me, was already home and very upset.

"What happened to you, where have you been?" she asked.

With tremendous excitement I replied, "I stopped at the market to look at the doll."

My mother looked at me sympathetically and said, "You really like that doll, don't you?"

My father then interrupted, "So, I guess you're not hungry now...you got full by looking at the doll."

"Why do you have to open your big snout?" My mother angrily shot back at him.

Later that evening I was sitting by my mother's side while she was sewing and I asked her, "Why does Santa Claus never bring us toys for Christmas? Is Santa real?"

She did not want to destroy that magic of my fantasy world, but I knew the answer when she looked at me with teary eyes and told me, "Tomorrow, you will deliver some dresses I have just finished. If the people pay right away, we'll go to the market and look at that doll. Maybe we can buy it."

I now knew that my mother was my Santa Claus.

When I delivered the dresses I made sure I told the people that my mother needed the money right away and when I returned home she and I went to the market. She bought me the doll and told me that it was my birthday gift. My seventh birthday was only a few days away on November the seventh.

Sadly, the magic and excitement of the doll lasted only as long as our return journey to the house from the market. That doll caused a huge argument between my mother and father because my mother had spent money on "something so superfluous," as my father put it.

I do not remember how many times I played with that doll,

not many. Each time I played with it there was a fight between my parents. After a few days I sat the doll on top of my father's radio and never played with it again so as to not cause problems between the two of them. When we moved to other houses and towns I again sat the doll on the radio. Many years later my sister Eneida became the owner of that beautiful doll and as far as I know my father never had a problem with her playing with it.

San Pedro Pinula is approximately two hundred and fifty kilometers from Guatemala City, situated at a high elevation. The temperature in the early morning and in the evening after sunset is usually around fourteen degrees Celsius, requiring a sweater to keep warm. By noon the hot sun pushes the temperature up as high as thirty degrees and one can walk around with shorts. Most of the town's people were, and still are, farmers and ranchers. One might conclude from the surnames that this town to be populated by only five families, one of them being my father's family. The two most popular names were Sandoval and Portillo. My father's last name, Folgar, was also popular, but it took third place. It seemed to me like everyone in this town was related to everybody else.

San Pedro Pinula has a high percentage of indigenous people who live mostly in surrounding small villages where they do their farming. When I lived there most of the pure Mayans wore the typical and colourful dresses for which Guatemala is famous. On a recent visit, I observed that not much has changed, except in dress—now many of the Indian people wear western clothing. Most of the Indian population who live in the country still speak their native tongues, *Pocomán* in and around San Pedro, and have very limited Spanish. The men usually speak more Spanish than women. The people living inside the town of San Pedro Pinula are mostly mixed—*Ladino.*

A country town like this, with its close family relationships, might appear the ideal place to live; a place where everyone gets along with everyone else very well—but that was not the situation. There were many animosities among the families (clans) and people even fought within their immediate families. The issue was almost always about land and family honour. I remember hearing stories of brothers not talking to each other and of fathers not talking to their daughters or sons. People in this town knew the complete life history of everyone else. At that time people from other cities or towns referred to the people in San Pedro Pinula as *macheteros* (people who fight with machetes, which is not a flattering term). Every man walked around the town, the farm or ranch carrying some sort of a weapon. Some carried guns, others had knives or machetes and some carried all three items.

Although the people in the town were very friendly and everyone knew each other, one learned at a very young age that the town had many dark secrets. Judging by the stories I heard, these secrets seemed to be always related to inter-familial fights. Many of these fights occurred when people had taken the law into their own hands, seeking revenge for the harm done to a brother, sister, father, or some other relative.

The concepts of revenge and defending one's honour (blood feuds) loomed very large in the mentality of the people of this region. I remember my father telling me stories about someone who had killed another person in the town. Everyone knew who had committed the crime, including the victim's family, but nobody would take the step to go to police or to seek justice in the right way. They would wait for the opportunity to avenge the death of their relative or loved one. I recall my father and other people mentioning the names of people from whom it was best to keep one's distance. In those days, people in this town preferred to personally deliver justice to their enemies. Another way to personally see that *justice* was done was to bribe officials of the justice system. This still happens today. In Guatemala, justice is not available to everyone and is quite often not impartial. If one has money and can afford a good lawyer, one will usually prevail in court. Also, the justice system in Guatemala is not regionally uniform; it is often influenced by local and regional customs.

This region had another unsavory custom—the kidnapping of girls to become brides. My father told me stories of women in the town who were forced to marry the men who had kidnapped them. From where this custom came, Spain or indigenous cultures, I do not know. This is how it worked: a man would kidnap a girl from her family, take her out into hiding, have forced or consensual sex with the girl and then force the girl to become his wife. This happened especially when a girl's family did not consider a certain man as a suitable partner for their daughter. After the kidnapping, the girl's family, more often than not, would acquiesce to the arrangement when the couple reappeared, since the daughter was no longer a virgin and quite often pregnant. I was told that the husband of one of my aunts had kidnapped her because her mother (my grandmother) was against their relationship. My father also told me that one of my uncles also had kidnapped his wife.

This is what happened to one of my cousins. She fell in love with a man who was her first cousin (first cousin relationships are, unfortunately, still common in rural Guatemala). Her father and mother totally disliked this fellow and in order to stop the relationship they managed to get her to become involved and engaged with a young man of whom they approved. On the day of her wedding while she was walking to the church wearing her wedding dress, her ex-boyfriend arrived on horseback with some of his friends. They snatched her from the entrance of the church, hoisted her onto a horse and disappeared into the countryside. Nobody dared to do anything. Eventually, the kidnapper and the girl were married, but my uncle never again spoke to his daughter or to his son–in–law and never met his grandchildren. It is amazing to think that an event such as this can still take place in the twentieth century. One might think that it could only occur in a gothic–romance novel or in a western adventure film.

It was also common for a woman to elope with her sweetheart when one or both families disapproved of their children's chosen mate. Sadly, these practices also are still happening in certain areas of Guatemala, including the region around San Pedro Pinula.

❧

In San Pedro Pinula we lived in my paternal grandmother's

compound. With the word "compound" I am referring to a very large house that is divided into separate living quarters for the extended family. If this house were located in the country or on a farm it would be called an *hacienda*. The house was built in a rectangular shape with a courtyard in the middle. My grandmother's house contained sixteen separate residences or apartments. It was situated on the main plaza of the town and was probably as old as the colonial period in Guatemala. My father's part of the house faced the main plaza where the Indian-indigenous farmers brought their crops to be sold during market days on Thursdays and Sundays. The Municipality Building was situated on the north side of the plaza. On the west side were the two schools, one for boys and one for girls. On the south side there were two large houses, my grandmother's compound and Mr. Ernesto Wong's store and house. On the east side was the old colonial and historic church of Santo Domingo. This was a very pretty church built by the Dominicans in the seventeenth century. I always remember its big clock with Roman numerals. The plaza had an open area and a park–like area. In the park area, right in front of the church, there was a pretty gazebo for concerts. On the plaza right next to the south side of the park there was a fountain in the open area (please see a plan of the central plaza area on page 118).

Mr. Wong's store & house (left) and my grandmother's house.

My Grandmother's compound and Mr. Wong's house abutted each other, the two houses occupying the complete street block on the south side of the plaza. Her house was much bigger than Mr. Wong's, but it was not as pretty or as new. When you viewed the compound from the street it resembled a fort. The only thing one would see was a wall pierced with doors and windows. The outside walls were whitewashed and the whitewash had to be reapplied at least once every other year. But when one walked inside the compound through the main gate, he entered into a big courtyard, adorned with a colonial fountain (*pila*) and with tall, large trees. The sixteen apartments were of various sizes and each one had its own individual kitchen. These apartments surrounded the courtyard, motel style. There was only one outhouse having two stalls and a shower room, also with two stalls. Toward the west side of the house there was a big wooden door (*portón*) approximately four meters wide and six and half meters in height. A large, wooden, sliding bolt latch secured the door. Family members arriving home by horse or donkey used this door. My aunts and uncles also used this door when they were transferring the harvest, furniture and their families from the farm (*majada*) back to the town.*

Inside the compound, along the south wall, was a very large piece of empty land, which was used to grow vegetables during the dry season. Several species of fruit trees such as pomelo, orange, pomegranate, mango, along with a large *matasano* tree, were growing inside the compound. The word *matasano* means "killer of the healthy" in Spanish and I am sure that this name is not the correct Spanish name for the fruit, but it is no wonder that people gave it this name—the flavor of the fruit is so awful. However, the tree provided wonderful shade in the courtyard and a good place to tie the horses.

All the attached apartments of this big house were occupied and would eventually be owned by my aunts and uncles on my father's side of the family after my grandmother's death. My father owned the last apartment and it abutted against Mr. Wong's house.

The region of Jalapa (pronounced: Ha-l<u>a</u>-pa), of which San Pedro is part, is mainly ranching country. It has two seasons like the rest of Guatemala. The rainy season is from May to October and the dry season extends from November to April. As a result the population in the compound fluctuates during the year. During the rainy season the farmers leave their homes in the town

---

* Please refer to a diagram of this house on page thirty-one.

and move their families to their farms to cultivate the land. People usually live on their farms from the middle of May until the middle of December when they return to the town with their crops, either for their own consumption or for selling. At that time they also bring their cows to secondary pastures closer to town, and even into town for milking.

᠊ᢕ

My grandmother was a very strange person. Some people in the town thought that she was crazy, calling her *Chon Loca* (Crazy Chon). Chon is a nickname for Concepción. If she was not insane, she was definitely eccentric. She made life very difficult for all of the daughters–in–law who were living in the apartments of the compound, accusing them of not being good wives to her sons. She would customarily get up at four in the morning and go from house to house waking everyone up. When everyone was up, working and going about his or her affairs, she would then go back to bed. My mother and all of the other daughters–in–law absolutely detested her.

My grandmother was pencil thin and always wore skirts that reached to the ground. At anytime, in front of anyone, and anywhere, she would spread her legs and urinate. Only when she started walking again did one notice the puddle. We children found this quite humorous. Was this craziness, senility or just weird behavior? I do not know.

Living in this housing complex was fun for a seven to ten year old. During the six months of the dry season all of my uncles came back to the city from the farms and when my father was not around I was able to play with my cousins and get into mischief.

One of my aunts, Aunt Florinda, became very ill with cervical cancer. The family fixed up the apartment on the southwest corner of the compound and that was the place where she spent her last six months of life. It is very common in Guatemala for the relatives of someone who is terminally ill to prepare things ahead of time, especially the coffin. My aunt's coffin had already been purchased and was kept in the same room where the grain silos were located. The children were not allowed to go in there except when they needed to scoop some beans or corn from the large bins—one of my grandmother's nonsensical rules.

Our favourite game was hide–and–seek. We played this game almost every evening. One day when we were playing this game I thought:

I want to find a good place to hide, because I am the first one they always find and then I have to be the one to search for everybody else.

I went into the forbidden room, opened the coffin and climbed inside. Usually, when someone had hidden herself very well and the others could not find her, the hidden person had to give some signals such as making little noises or whistle. I could hear my cousins looking for me and calling me, "Gaby, Gaby, Nena, Nena," and they could not find me. I heard steps coming into the forbidden room and I thought that I would make my little noises or whistle very softly to give them a clue and help them. I was doing this when someone approached the coffin and abruptly opened the lid. It was also part of the game to say, "wow", in order to scare the people who had been looking for you. When I did this, my mother screamed and almost fainted. I never dreamed that it would be my mother who was going to open the coffin.

My mother was pregnant in 1957 when I was nine years old. As I mentioned before, I was very observant and curious about any changes happening around me and I asked questions. This is when I discovered how prudish she was. I could not ask her simple questions about the mysteries of life that all children wonder about, such as: "Why do women have breasts? Why do some women have big stomachs? Why don't men wear bras?" I noticed her stomach growing bigger and bigger and I noticed her legs developing varicose veins. One day I asked her, "Why is your stomach getting so big? Why are your veins so thick and blue?"

She looked at me nervously and responded, "It is because I hang around your aunt."

One of my aunts was suffering from dropsy and she also had a very bad case of varicose veins. Since my mother and this aunt were always together, I believed her story. I also knew that my aunt was dying and therefore concluded that my mother was soon to die too.

The next afternoon I was sitting by the water fountain at my grandmother's house when my father came and asked me, "What is going on? What's with you?"

"Mamá is going to die," I replied.

My father looked startled and with his usual blunt manner of speech he said, "Of course she's going to die, we all die; you're going to die too. At the moment we enter this world we sign our death sentence."

I did not understand what all that meant and I started to cry, tears flowing in torrents.

My father's face took on a very serious look; he firmly looked at me and asked, "Who told you she's going to die? Where did you get such an idea?"

"I know it because she has the same disease that my aunt has," I said with an air of surety.

"And who told you that?" He still had a puzzled look on his face.

"My mother said that the reason her stomach is so big and her veins are so thick and blue is because she always gets together with my aunt."

My father jumped up and went straight to my mother and a big fight ensued immediately between them. Later, when he tried to explain to me about my mother's pregnancy, my mother prevented him from telling me. The only thing he was able to tell me, and at the same time keep peace with my mother, was that I was going to have a baby sister or brother. He realized that I was of the age to start learning some facts of life. Eventually, he explained to me in a very elemental way the way humans multiply, but not in my mother's presence.

❧

I was doing well in the boys' school, at the top of the class, along with one of Mr. Wong's boys. I won many awards in the school, especially in the language arts. Poetry reading and recitation are very important in Spanish culture. I was able to memorize and recite, with excellent voice and diction, very long poems at student assemblies. I was also my father's helper in recording his students' marks in the official records and helping during school registration day. I was the child my father could rely on to get things done; I was the child to go shopping because I always brought back the correct change; I was the child to cook and keep things clean; I was the child to deliver messages correctly; but he still did not allow me to play, even during recess at school. There was never praise for a job well done or any other kind of reward. My father just seemed to expect a good performance from me. I observed, however, that he did not expect the same performance from my brothers and that really bothered me.

None of this meant that I was not happy. My personal rewards came from the friendships I had made with the students and my cousins, along with the respect I received from my mother, teachers, and from the priest, in spite of my pranks in the church. This is what carried me through the negative atmosphere and arduous labour in the house.

My father's belief that I should not play took bizarre turns. As an example, one day my cousin Carmencita noticed that I did not have toys and that I did not play with my doll. Feeling sorry for me, she gave me a squash to play with. This squash had a human form and even had arms formed from miniature squashes growing from the sides. I dressed the squash and played with it just as if it were a real doll. I also had a collection of corncobs, which I pretended to be children. I made clothes for them too.

One day my father saw me playing with the squash and abruptly grabbed the *doll* and threw it on the ground on the patio, smashing it into a thousand pieces. I cried and cried. I do not think that I had ever cried so much. I was inconsolable. This squash in the shape of a woman was so precious to me, not just because it was my only toy, but mainly because it was a gift from someone who cared for me. My mother became really angry with my father and a there was a big argument between them. Eventually, he bought me a miniature tea set, probably to keep peace with my mother. He even played house with me with this tea set. As I see it now, even this action had an aspect of control attached to it because he would always say, "Alright, I will play with you if you don't go to play at other girls' houses. I want you to stay here." This was the only toy he ever bought me during my entire childhood.

It was nice when my father went away on a trip, for then my mother would allow me to play and to have some fun. I went swimming as often as possible to *Los Chorros*, a swimming area formed from natural pools of water, and to *Agua Tibia*, another water and swimming attraction. During school holidays I also enjoyed going to the farm with my uncles, taking care of the calves and milking the cows.

My sister, Piedad Eneida, was born in 1957 when I was nine years old. I noticed immediately that my father acted differently toward her. He appeared to be more caring toward her than to me. When talking to his friends or to my mother he did not say the mean and awful things about having daughters or about girls in general as he did in my presence. He always said that he preferred boys, but I was really thinking that he had something against me and it was not just because I was a female. Although my outward demeanor suggested a happy and competent girl, the inward reality was quite different. Many times, between the ages of seven to ten, when I was studying alone very late at night by candlelight, I broke down and started crying, thinking:

Why does he treat me in the way he does? Am I really my father's daughter?

I was not very popular among my peers in the school because of my young age and studious ways. Most of the students in my classes were much older than I and not much interested in books. My friends were always the most dedicated students. My lack of popularity, however, was mostly due to my father being the principal of the school. This was not an enviable position for one to be in from a social point of view.

The Guatemalan school system, as I knew it, did not promote

students according to age. Students had to pass the exams and if they did not, they were held back. As a result, one would find twelve to fifteen year olds in grade three. This happened especially in farming–rural areas where young people would often leave school during the harvest season, causing them to fall behind in their studies. However, I did have good relationships with my girl cousins and a few other girls.

I was excellent in finding ways to keep busy and, at times, make some money. For example, I made wreaths to sell for All Souls' Day on the first of November. This is a very big day in Latin American countries and it is a custom to go to the cemetery on this day to remember the deceased in one's family. The wreaths sold very well to the Indian people on market days. I made quite a bit of money on this project, even after having paid my father for the cornstarch I used.

Church in this small town was another major activity in my life. I was baptized and brought up in the Catholic faith. I was confirmed by the bishop and received first communion at the age of seven. As far back as I can remember I was attending Mass. Church was very important for my mother, so it was natural that it was a big part of my life as well. Women wore either a hat or a *madrileña* (an oblong or triangular head covering, usually made of very fine lace) in church. My mother bought me beautiful *madrileñas*.

The parish church in San Pedro is very beautiful and dates from the earliest colonial times. It was built in the Spanish colonial style, which is so typical of many of Guatemala's churches. The outside is white with statues of Jesus and the saints placed in niches on the front façade. The church's bells are placed in several rows on top of the church. These bells not only announce church services but also the time of day, ringing every half hour.

In the interior the ceiling is vaulted over the nave and a dome rests over the transept. The decor is very plain—too plain. The vaulting and dome are painted stark white, as are the walls. In my opinion, the classic architecture of the interior of the church cries for some paintings and frescoes, especially around the dome. I guess San Pedro Pinula is too poor for that. The nave of the church is long but not wide, having one central aisle with pews seating perhaps eight people each on each side of the aisle. In contrast to the general austerity of the interior, the altar is beautiful and elaborate. It is tiered, with statues positioned on each level, and was carved from wood with wonderful craftsmanship.

One day at church I was paying particular attention to the four letters INRI inscribed on the cross above Jesus' head and I asked my mother, "What does that mean?"

"I have no clue," She replied frankly.

I kept asking her to find out what the inscription meant. Finally, she took me to the priest, whom we found in the sacristy, to ask him the question. Father Magin rubbed my head and said, "That is a good question. It means, JESUS OF NAZARETH KING OF THE JEWS.

This knowledge gave me the opportunity to brag in front of my mother's clients. Sometimes she would ask some of her clients if they knew the meaning. When they answered no, she gave them the information and I would proudly interject, "She knows this because I asked the priest."

I was a mischievous little girl in the church. One day, prior to

my first communion, I went to catechism studies in the church and I brought a balloon to class. I inflated it and went behind the priest who was teaching catechism to the older children and released the air, which blew on the back of his head. All of the other children laughed at the joke and at the priest because his very thin hair was now ruffled up and looked very funny. He kicked me out of the church and told me, "Out of my temple; don't ever come back!" For many days I did not go to catechism lessons and I gave my mother several false excuses. Eventually, she went to the church and spoke with the priest. When she came back home I was expecting the worst, but all she did was to ask me to take my copybook and to write three hundred times, *I will not be disrespectful to Father Magin Hawrrieta.* Was this my mother's or the priest's idea? I do not know.

Strangely enough, after this incident, I became a very good friend of this priest; he turned out to be kind. He trusted me, called upon me to help him, and relied on me to the point of becoming his assistant to teach other children the catechism—I was only eight years old at the time. I have never forgotten this priest's name to this day, especially not after having written that line three hundred times.

It was not too long after having moved to my grandmother's house in San Pedro Pinula when I was eight that I encountered a really BIG PROBLEM and that problem was my grandmother's husband Felícito or Don Licho (lee-cho) as we called him. He was my grandmother's second husband and therefore, not my grandfather or the father of any of my father's sixteen or so brothers and sisters. He was quite a few years younger than my grandmother and he never allowed any of the children in the house to call him grandfather.

One day I was sitting at the table placed on our patio doing some embroidery when I saw one of my cousins, who was about my age or perhaps a little older, walking toward the east area where the wood storage room and the big baking oven were located. I called out to her, "Hey, where are you going? You know we're not supposed to go in that room!" But she did not seem to hear me.

I noticed that Don Licho was heading in the same direction and I became a little curious. I waited a few minutes to see if my cousin was going to come back toward her house with some firewood, and when I did not see her or Don Licho I became even more curious and decided to investigate. I went to the area by the wood storage room and was unable to see either one of them. Now my curiosity was on fire: *Where did they hide that I cannot find them? Are they playing hide–and-seek?* I noticed that the door to the wood shed, which was always kept closed and locked, was now partially open and I heard some voices coming from inside. That did not seem right to me. We children never went into that room, and besides, it was always secured with a padlock. This room was the wood storage room for Don Licho's carpentry shop and we were told that there were scorpions, spiders and snakes lurking in the piled up wood. The room was dark and dirty and some of my cousins said it was haunted. I got closer to the room. I recognized Don Licho's voice and wanted to hear what he was saying. His voice was in a whisper and I was not able to understand. Then I heard my cousin's voice softly pleading, "No, no, no Don Licho!"

Now I was no longer just curious but suspicious. I pushed the door open with some force and saw my cousin lying down on the dusty floor with Don Licho on top of her. He looked at me and immediately got up, pulling up his pants at the same time. My very first thought was that he was killing her. Everything happened so fast. When he stood up he turned around, completely exposing his genital area to me before turning his back to me again. He was working feverously on fastening his pants and closing his belt. My cousin jumped up and ran out of the room, not saying anything or even looking at me. I could not move and I did not know what to think, but I knew instinctively that what I had just witnessed was something not good at all.

Don Licho called to me in a rough voice, "Come over here! I need to talk to you. I'll give you some money if you don't say anything."

I was very frightened and started walking backwards away from the door, silently, watching to see if he were going to come after me. He was looking at me with glazed-over eyes, and then, raising his hand and pointing his index finger at me, he growled, "If you open your mouth, you'll pay for it."

I turned and ran off, shaking, crying, feeling cramps in my stomach, and having a sensation of diarrhea and of wanting to throw up. At my age and innocence I could not figure out what I had just seen and I knew I had to tell someone and that person had to be my father.

"You are just making this up," my father said.

"No, Papá, I saw everything I told you," I insisted.

"You just have a big imagination."

"No, Papá, you have to believe me!" I pleaded.

"Don Licho has been like a father to me since the death of my father," he scolded, "and if you tell stories about this you could send someone to jail. You'll get into big trouble, especially if the story isn't true. Don't you ever tell anybody about this!" he said, pointing his finger at me. "Do you understand?"

It was then I knew that what I had witnessed was something terribly serious and awfully wrong and I became even more scared.

Even before our move to my grandmother's house I never liked Don Licho and I never liked to be around him. There was something about him, something about the way he looked at me. Many times I noticed him looking at my female cousins in a way that also made me feel extremely uncomfortable.

My grandmother would say things such as, "Don't talk or get close to Felícito. Between his legs he has something different than what you have and he'll use it if you give him the opportunity. "*Si se fían, ese hombre las coge* (That man will fuck you if you let your guard down)."

None of that made any sense to me. So I went to my mother and father and asked, "Why does Mamita say, 'Stay away from Felícito. If you take your guard down, he'll fuck you'".

My father replied in a dismissive way, "Your grandmother is just old and old people say a lot things that make no sense. Don't pay attention to her senile statements."

I had no trouble connecting my grandmother's crazy statements and my fear of Don Licho's constant starring at my cousins and me to the scene I had witnessed in the wood storage room. I became more vigilant than ever when visiting my grandmother or when moving around the compound. Now I was noticing that Don Licho was looking at me in an even more strange way, a way that gave me the feeling that I was walking around naked. He had an intimidating and fearful stare.

Not long after I had caught him with my cousin he started exposing himself to me wherever I went; on my way to the vegetable garden, when I walked to get charcoal for my mother's iron, or when I went to fetch water from the fountain. I do not know how he appeared everywhere. My grandmother's compound was big, but it seemed as if he knew where I would be at all times.

He started to call me, "*pajarita* (pa–ha–r<u>ee</u>–ta)," which means "little bird." I knew his calling me *pajarita* was not right. I realized this because in front of my father, my mother or any of my cousins he took care to call me by my proper name. The compound had a big oven situated on the east side adjacent to the wood storage room and Don Licho was constantly there pretending to be cleaning the oven. When I passed by he would turn and expose himself to me. This happened countless times because there was no other route for me to take. I had to pass by the big oven each time I left my house to go anywhere else in the compound.

One time I went to get some corn at the vegetable garden situated at the south side of the house and I saw him standing in front of me just as I was leaving. He tried to grab me but I evaded his grasp. As I was running away he threatened me that if I said anything he would tell my grandmother that I was stealing corn.

There was another occasion when I was going to the outhouse around six in the evening, right after nightfall. The outhouse had two stalls, but with no signage indicating male or female. I do not know if Don Licho was spying on me or if he happened to be in the second stall just by coincidence. The wall between the stalls was so thin one could hear everything from one stall to the other. I heard him breathing very fast, faster and faster, as if he were running. Then, in a low and creepy voice he called to me,

"*Pajarita*, I have something to show you, go to the wood storage room. I have something for you. Don't say anything to anyone if you don't want anything to happen to you. Remember your cousin? She liked what I showed her. You will like it too."

I ran out of the outhouse even before I had finished my business. As soon as I ran into our house I felt that I was going to throw up; I was at the point of fainting. My heart was racing. My whole body was shaking. I was out of breath. I sat down, trying to calm down, trying to get some air into my lungs. *I have to tell someone, I have to tell someone. Oh God, this is horrible.* I was thinking.

However, once I had settled down a bit, the need to talk quickly left me. *What's the point? My father did not believe me when I told him about my cousin and he's definitely not going to believe me now.*

I do not know if my father informed my mother about what I had told him concerning my cousin, or if she had been observing Don Licho's weird behaviour around me and my cousins, or if she had previously known about his perverted predilections? One day, however, my father wanted to send me to my grandmother's place to deliver some food that my mother had cooked, but my mother intervened, "Don't go there alone; take your brother with you when you go to visit your grandmother." Some other times she would send my brother instead of me or she would fulfill the errand herself rather than have me go there alone.

Don Licho's behavior never stopped. The only time I felt totally safe in the compound was when he went back to the farm in May, not to return until the end of October and sometimes until mid-December.

The problems between my mother and father persisted in San Pedro Pinula due to my father's gambling and stingy ways with the family. Adding to this stressful situation was my mother's sadness about having to endure my grandmother's cruelty toward her. In January of 1959 my father was transferred again. This time he was transferred to a school in Ipala (Ee-pa-la), a town in the province of Chiquimula (Chee-kee-moo-la), about sixty kilometers distance from San Pedro Pinula. My mother was born in Ipala and her extended family still lived there. When my father was transferred my mother begged him to take us with him. She did not like living at my grandmother's house, especially when my father was away. My grandmother would then become even nastier toward her. I do not know if my father ever believed the stories my mother told him about my grandmother's mean ways, but in any case, he refused to take us with him to Ipala. One of his excuses was that the houses in Ipala were very expensive to rent while in San Pedro Pinula we had a free house. He returned back home to visit us almost every weekend and once in a while every other weekend.

Next to our apartment lived a woman, Doña Catalina Beteta, who operated a small restaurant in her rented accommodations. When she became ill from terminal cancer my mother helped her a lot. She had two sons, Antonio and José. José lived in El Salvador, but during the time when his mother was sick he came to stay with her in San Pedro Pinula. José Beteta and my mother became very good friends and he spent lots of time with her when my father was away teaching in Ipala.

One evening, right after sunset, I was taking out the garbage when I heard a noise in one of the trees. I became startled and I was about to scream when suddenly a man fell from the pomelo tree. Initially, I thought it was a ghost because there was the never-ending rumor that my grandmother's house was haunted. Before I could scream I saw that it was my father, "Shhh, keep quiet," he whispered, "Don't say anything—go to the house and leave the living room door open." I did as he requested. I knew that he was spying on my mother, but I was not sure why. I knew that my mother was spending a lot of time with José Beteta and my father had previously asked me if I had seen her around this man. I always denied this because of the secretive manner in which he asked the question. I did not know what kind of relationship my mother had with José Beteta and I did not want to get involved in things I did not understand.

Father

My father had decided to separate from my mother, and initially, he wanted to do this without telling us the truth. He told us that my mother was ill and that she was going to have to leave the house for a while. However, this explanation did not make sense to me. So, using my sneaky ways to listen to their conversations, I was able to put the pieces together.

One morning, we were having breakfast and I blurted out, "I know something. Mamá is not going to the hospital; papá and mamá are going to separate and we are going to stay with our father."

My father became nervous and with a stuttering voice accused me of all of the usual things—having a big mouth, being an ungrateful brat and a pest. My mother started to cry hysterically. Later, I learned that the complete plan was for my mother to go away, pretending to be ill, and then after a few months my father was going to tell us that she had died.

Now that the truth was out in the open my father insisted that he would take the boys and me and leave the baby with my mother. I had already made up my mind that I wanted to go with my mother. When I told my father this he was very upset with me and told me that if I chose to live with my mother I had better forget that I ever had a father. He told me that it was best for Eneida to go with my mother because she was still a baby and he could not take care of her while teaching school. He warned me that I would starve to death with my mother since he was keeping the sewing machines and was not going to help her financially.

He also attempted to influence my decision by trying to make me hate my mother by telling me that she was an adulterous woman. When I told him that I did not understand what that meant, he said, "Your mother is something like a prostitute." I knew what that meant. In spite of my father's threats and manipulations, I still wanted to go with my mother.

My father allowed my mother to remain in the house for three more weeks until I had written my school exams. Then the day came when we had to leave. I got on the bus with my mother and sister, along with some of our essential belongings. Just before the bus was to depart, my father came to the window where I was sitting and whispered in my ear, "Remember this, today you have just buried me, and today I have buried you".

"I don't know what you mean by saying that," I said.

"That means that you'd better forget that you ever had a father!"

I understood the meaning of those words and they were very painful; they plunged into my chest like a knife. I became very angry and told him in a very loud and stressed voice, "Why on earth do you want me to stay with you? You never wanted to have a daughter. You told me so. You said that girls aren't even capable of keeping the family name. Don't you remember how many times you told your friends, and who knows who else, that you wanted to exchange me for a dog because a dog could at least guard the house? Well, now you will be happy with your two sons and without me you can afford to get a dog for the house."

Everybody in the bus looked at me as if I were the most insolent child they had ever heard. Some of them made derogatory comments, rolled their eyes and shook their heads. Of course, the people on the bus could not hear the hateful things he was whispering in my ear. To them he was the aggrieved parent, the loving father, and the honourable professor.

My mother, sister and I left San Pedro Pinula for the town of Ipala. This was such a sad time in my life. I was separated from my brothers. I was moving to a town where I only knew some uncles from my mother's side of the family and to a school where I would not know anybody. But the worst thing was my having to leave my cousins and good friends in San Pedro Pinula. Even at the age of ten (almost eleven) I could feel that I was heading into a very uncertain future; but I could never have imagined the tragic and remarkable role that San Pedro Pinula was going to play in my life only four and a half years later.

A torn jacket is soon mended; but hard words bruise the heart of a child.
–Henry Wadsworth Longfellow–

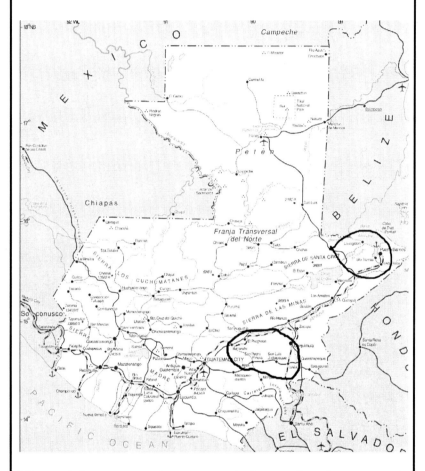

The circled areas are the regions of Guatemala where most of my story took place: the Jalapa–Chiquimula area and the Livingston area on the Atlantic coast.

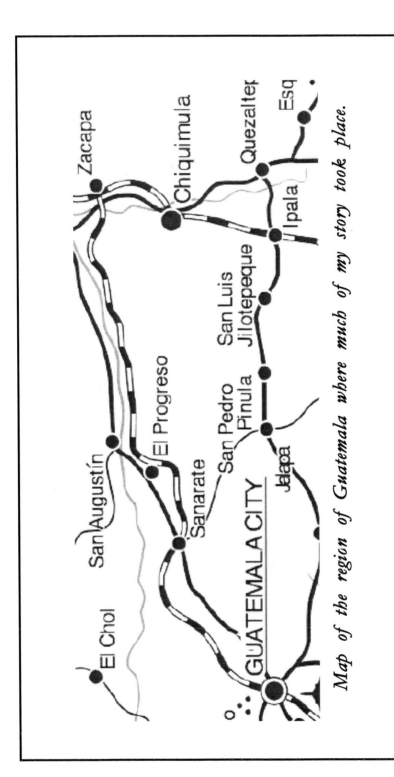

Map of the region of Guatemala where much of my story took place.

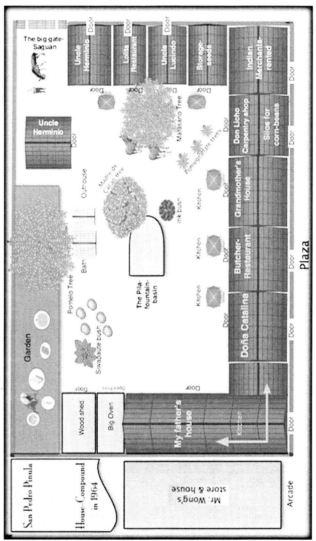

My Grandmother's House

Chapter 2
The Little Mother

I don't think of myself as a poor deprived ghetto girl who made good, I think of myself as somebody who from an early age knew I was responsible for myself, and I had to make good.
–Oprah Winfrey

My mother took us to live in Ipala with one of her brothers. We had been there for only a month when my father came to the house with a court order granting him custody of my baby sister and me. In order to get custody of all of the children he used the grounds that an adulterous woman loses all her rights. In Guatemala a woman who commits adultery commits a criminal offence, at least that was the way it was in 1960. But, not surprisingly, this law did not apply to men. If an adulterous person was a man he was seen as being macho and to be doing something very natural and within his rights.

On the day my mother had to say goodbye to Eneida and me she was crying so much that she could barely talk. She took my face into her hands as if she wanted to memorize it forever and in between her sobs she said,

"Please don't forget about me, I will always be thinking about you, your sister and your brothers. Please take care of your little sister, for she is going to need you a lot. I will write to you quite often. Remember your aunts in Pinalito (pee-na-leé-to) and if you ever need anything, just go to them because they are very nice people."

The bus for San Pedro was leaving and my mother was left standing at the bus stop crying and waving her hand goodbye to me.

Soon after I had moved into my father's care I knew immediately what was in store for me—I was to become the eleven–year old mother of the house. My father explained to me the situation: "You know we no longer have your mother and there is nobody to do the cooking, the laundry, the cleaning, the shopping and to take care of Eneida."

He did not say the words, but I knew that it would be my job to look after my brothers too.

"I cannot hire someone," he continued, "I have no money."

I felt sorry for him. I was fearful that he would not have enough money for food or other important things. I had no choice but to accept this demanding job of housekeeper and babysitter. I also knew from past experience that he would expect me to keep up with my studies and do well in school. I did all of the cooking, cleaning and laundry in the house. I had no time left for myself. To do the laundry we had to walk to the river on Saturdays. I stood in the water and used the rocks to scrub the clothes. We spent the whole day at the river: I washed the clothes and my brothers played.

As soon as my father had been granted custody of my sister and me we left Ipala for the two months of school holidays (November and December) to stay in my grandmother's house in San Pedro Pinula. This was my real initiation into the life my father had prepared for me. He established the routine on the very first day. In the morning, I prepared his and my brothers' breakfast. He put some money on the table so that I could go to the market to buy food for lunch and supper and then he left the house. Some days he came home for lunch, but usually he did not return to the house until it was time for supper. In the meantime, I had to clean the house, cook, iron the clothes and take care of the baby. After supper, he departed again and did not return until I went to get him at the bar very late at night.

San Pedro had only one bar and it was one block and a half from our house. This is where my father spent most of his time, playing billiards. I do not believe he drank very much, maybe a few beers, for I never saw him drunk. He just loved billiards and gambling—those were his vices.

The doors to the house had no locks; instead, one had to secure them from the inside with wooden rods, pushing one end of
the rod into a groove on the inside of the door and placing the
other end into a crack or into an opening between the bricks of
the floor. When my father arrived, he knocked and I removed the
rod and let him in. Therefore, I had to keep myself awake, waiting for him. When I felt tired and could no longer stay awake I
left the house and went to the bar to get him, leaving the door
closed, but not secured.

The town had no electricity in 1960, which meant that we
were mostly in the dark. From six o'clock in the evening until we
went to bed we had some light provided by a kerosene lamp or
by candles. Almost every night I had to walk alone after midnight
through very dark streets to the bar and beg my father to come
home. Sometimes the Wong family kept their gasoline generator
for their store going late at night and that provided some outside
lighting, but this was rare. When it did happen, however, it was a
real treat. When I was in the bar some of the patrons and the wife
of the owner told my father, "*Profe* (short for *professor*), go home,
take your child." My father's reply was, "Just one more," and that
one more turned into another game and then another. A few
times I sat on the floor in the bar and fell asleep until he awakened me when he was ready to go.

Sometimes I had to take my sister with me because she was
awake and crying and I did not wish my brothers to wake up, or
worse, to alert Don Licho that we were alone in the house. I was
still wary of his perverted behavior and sexual advances. Thank
God, I was always in the company of my brothers and sister or
too busy to leave the house to visit my grandmother and my
cousins. He rarely, if ever, saw me alone around the compound.
When I was alone with my brothers and sister in our house I always secured the door. My biggest fear was that he would find
out that we were alone every night and would try something at
that time. I think that he did not know that my father went out
every night, for he never came close to our door. Sometimes, after dark, I heard steps outside our bedroom. I peeked through the

crack in the old wooden door and with the little light provided by the moon I glimpsed Don Licho's silhouette. He was walking around the courtyard, cigarette in mouth, possibly doing a security check or possibly waiting for me to go to the outhouse.

Taking care of my baby sister was a very difficult job for me. I tried to do everything that my mother had taught me before we were separated. This, however, did not prepare me to deal with everything. One day my sister got very sick; she was vomiting, had bloody and mucus–laden diarrhea and registered an extremely high fever. I did not know what to do. It looked as if she were dying. My father came home for supper and immediately went to the pharmacy for advice and medicine. The pharmacist advised him to take Eneida to the hospital in Jalapa. When my father returned to the house there was news that Dr. Arturo Wong was visiting his parents next door. The doctor came to the house and after a short examination of my sister he immediately inserted an I.V. Dr. Wong had a worried look on his face and said, "We must bring the fever down and stop the dehydration. She's vomiting and has diarrhea. If we can stop this, she will live."

I wiped Eneida with wet towels. I helped Dr. Wong by holding my sister steady. My father, however, just stood aside and started blaming me for her sickness. He threatened me that if Eneida were to die I would be sent to jail. His words so terrified me that I started praying to God even more fervently to save her life. I loved my sister so much. During the whole ordeal my father kept on berating me in front of Dr. Wong,

"If she dies, it will be your fault. You will never forget that you killed your sister. You should have taken better care of her."

I thought I had done everything well. I did not know what had happened. My father spied a banana peel and started claiming that I had fed her a green banana, causing her to become ill.

As Dr. Wong was preparing the I.V. he corrected my father, "Profe, I don't even know what is exactly wrong with your little one. Besides, your daughter Gabriela is too young to have the responsibility of looking after a child." Sternly looking at my father and pointing his finger toward him, he emphasized, "That is the responsibility of the parents."

I looked upon Dr. Wong not as a man, but as an angel sent by God. I felt a great relief that I was not going to go to prison. I never forgot his words and I would use these words again to defend myself whenever my father blamed me for doing something wrong, especially in the area of taking care of my siblings.

I stayed up all night taking care of Eneida. It was December and very cold at night in San Pedro Pinula and I had to go outside to the *pila* at three o'clock in the morning to wash diapers. I was shivering; for in my desperation to save Eneida's life I went out wearing only a short-sleeved blouse. In fact, I did not even own a sweater. My sister's life was in balance for ten critical days, but she eventually recovered. To this day I have no idea what was wrong with her.

In January 1960, after the school holidays, we returned to Ipala to start the new school term, grade six for me. I went to the same school where my father was teaching. To my surprise, my mother was nowhere to be found in the town. Neither my father nor any of my mother's relatives even mentioned her name around us children.

The life I had to endure in San Pedro Pinula continued after our return to Ipala. I was having difficulty studying, going to school, and managing the house at the same time. Sometimes I resented my father for working me like a slave. Other times, I felt sorry for him because he always sadly complained that he had no money. In order to help him save some extra money I took care of mending my brothers' clothes, especially their pants, which they ripped every time they wore them. Money was so tight that I did not get a new dress for Christmas, as I did on every previous Christmas when my mother was with us. I wanted and needed to have new clothes, but I knew I could not ask my father to buy me anything.

One day, I approached my father and asked if he would buy material so that I could make a dress myself. At first, he looked at me with disbelief and questioned my ability to sew, which was understandable, since I had never really sewn a complete dress. However, I had a very good idea how to do it by watching and helping my mother. A big surprise—he went out to buy material. My surprise was even greater when he brought home a whole eleven meters, what remained of the bolt. And then I became even more astounded when he told me, "I bought enough material for more than one dress, so you can practice. Don't worry if you ruin the material."

Gabriela at eleven years of age
I am wearing the first dress that I made (read below).
This is my only extant photo from my childhood; all others were lost in the 1976 earthquake.

I was very happy and immediately I started making my dress. The first dress was a success, although it was very simple. I used up the rest of the material by making four more dresses for myself, all in different styles. This was one of the few times my father praised me and felt proud enough of me to brag to other people. "She made that dress," he proudly pointed out to people when I went out with him.

My father was having difficulties of his own, mainly in finding a way to take care of my sister during school hours. He took her to the classroom in order to be able to watch her. This raised many concerns with the students' parents and they subsequently complained to his supervisor. He almost lost his job and it was only because he had former students who were now placed in high educational positions that he was able to preserve his position. He then knew that he could no longer cope and he hired a lady to take care of Eneida during school hours.

My father had the financial means to have a maid to take care of all of the household needs, for maids were not expensive in Guatemala. Any professional person could afford to have one or two of them at home. He had his salary as a teacher, income from his portion of the family farm near San Pedro Pinula, and in addition, he sold lottery tickets. If my father truly did not have enough money to hire a full-time maid, it was not due to lack of income.

In spite of the hardships I did well in my last year of elementary school, but I knew that significant changes were going to happen once I graduated to grade seven. Ipala did not have a middle school and that meant that I would have to go to a larger town to continue my education. In January of 1961 my father decided to send me to a very prestigious girl's college in Jalapa, a departmental capital, about twenty-two kilometers from San Pedro Pinula. His only sister, Aunt Chus, lived in Jalapa and the plan was to send me there along with my two brothers and sister to live with her. He had rented two bedrooms from her so that I could take care of them and attend school. Aunt Chus was to take care of my sister when my brothers and I were in school. I took the responsibility of taking care of Eneida when I came home from school and on the weekends. I was back into the same routine, cooking for my brothers and my sister, doing the laundry and trying to study when I could. This arrangement worked very well for my father who remained teaching in Ipala, about eighty kilometers away.

Life in my aunt's house was hell. She was not a very kind person. I think that she was very angry with my mother and projected this anger onto me. I was so busy being a twelve-year-old mother to three children that I became exhausted after no more than a month of this ordeal. Several times I fell asleep in class. I did not complain or even try to talk to my father about this because I knew what his answer would have been:

"First of all, I did not want you to go to college. I need you to help me take care of your brothers and sister at home. Since you wish to attend college you have to make a sacrifice because I do not have the money to send you to college and hire someone to help me around the house with your brothers and sister."

As far back as I could remember my father made it very clear that, in his opinion, sending girls to study beyond elementary school was not as important as sending boys to acquire their education. His standard lines to me were, "Spending money to send girls to school is like throwing salt back into the sea; some of them get pregnant before they graduate or get married, others get married and as soon as they graduate their diplomas become nothing more than a wall decoration. Women should be trained to be good wives, to serve their husband and to take care of their children. That is all they should know anyhow." He repeated this so often it resembled a chant. This talk made me all the more determined to prove him wrong.

I loved the college in Jalapa and when I was in school I could forget for a short time the ordeal I was suffering in my aunt's house. I felt important at this school. It had a high reputation, the teachers were wonderful and I instantly made lots of friends. I felt so good when I was getting ready to go to school in the morning.

The school uniform was beautiful. It had a white blouse with the school crest on it, a necktie, and a beautiful blue pleated skirt that went to just below the knee In addition, the uniform came with a jumper and a blue sweater, because Jalapa can get cold in winter. The material of the uniform was of extraordinary quality, and the sweater even had the school crest emblazoned on it. Oh, how wonderful I felt when I put on this uniform. I was so proud of myself and I felt like I was really going somewhere.

During my last year of elementary school in Ipala, before going to middle school in Jalapa, I was constantly begging my father to take me to this town to write a government scholarship eligibility exam. This exam had written and oral components and up to fifty thousand students throughout Guatemala took it. The number of scholarships awarded each year numbered between two to three hundred. Since I was only eleven years old at the time I was officially too young to write the exam; only students thirteen and up were allowed to do this. However, I learned that children of teachers were permitted the privilege of writing the test at a younger age if their marks were above ninety. It was a huge struggle to get my father to allow me to compete. It was becoming obvious that it was not important to him that I get a good education, but I pestered and pestered him and finally he relented. I had to travel to Jalapa to take the exam. My father accompanied me on the bus.

After writing the exam, I felt that I had done well. My father's words were discouraging, however, when he told me that he thought the trip was a waste of time and money and that I had no chance of winning. As time passed I started to believe that he was right in his prediction. The school year in Guatemala runs from January to October with the month of October reserved for testing. I wrote the test around the middle of April of 1960 and when the 1960 school term had finished in October I had not yet received any reply from the government. I wanted to win this scholarship so very much because the government would then pay for my food and lodging at a boarding school along with my books and uniforms. It also meant that I would not have to live at my mean aunt's house and would not have to carry the enormous load of taking care of my sister and two brothers. I knew that if I did not get the scholarship I was not going to be able to physically cope with all the work and would eventually have to drop out of school.

Aunt Chus was providing some sort of supervision to my *motherly* work, but she was better with criticism than with real help. Many times I wished that she had said, "Go…study, and I will cook your and your brothers' dinners." That never happened. After one month in Jalapa I was completely worn out. I had given up my hopes for a scholarship and started making plans to leave school, probably never to return.

❧

I was in class one Monday morning in early February, almost falling asleep due to a full weekend of chores, when the loud speaker interrupted the classroom announcing, "Miss Gabriela Folgar, please report to the principal's office." When I heard this announcement I started to shake. I thought I was going to be expelled because of my dozing off in class too many times. I was so afraid I did not even want to get up. I stayed sitting, glued to my desk, totally paralyzed.

The teacher looked sternly at me and said, "Miss Folgar, did you hear? You are being called to the principal's office?"

I slowly got up and dejectedly walked with my head down to the principal's office. The principal was sitting at her desk and was smiling at me when I entered. She rose from her chair. It was then that I noticed that she had an envelope in her hand.

"Congratulations! You have been selected to attend school in the province of Chiquimula on a government scholarship."

When she handed me the envelope I thought I was dreaming. I hugged the letter on my chest. I wanted to scream, I wanted to cry with happiness, but nothing came out of my mouth.

God loves me; yes, yes. God loves me! Thank you God for answering my prayers.

I had been praying for this to happen every night before I went to bed. Even as I was falling asleep I kept praying and praying. Every day I felt that I was dying living in that house.

The principal obviously noticed my agitation, but she continued speaking in her official voice,

"Miss Folgar, I must inform you that the letter instructs that you are to report to EL INSO *(INSTITUTO NORMAL PARA SEÑORITAS DE ORIENTE* in Chiquimula by the end of this week. You have very limited time and you must hurry or you will lose your scholarship. Go and retrieve all your belongings and feel free to leave as soon as you are ready. You are a good student, you deserve this scholarship, and we are going to miss you at this school."

I wanted to send a telegram to my father right away to ask him to come to Jalapa as soon as possible, but I had no money. I would have to ask my aunt for money to pay for the telegram.

Aunt Chus became very upset when I told her about the scholarship. "You should think twice before going to Chiquimula. Your poor father without a wife and with his full time job is not going to be able to take care of your brothers and sister. You're a very inconsiderate and ungrateful child. If I tell your father not to send you to Chiquimula, he will listen to me and that will be the end to all of this nonsense."

My anger was boiling: *How dare she try to wreck my future.* I was tempted to scratch her face and run away, but I knew better to do that. I regained my composure and talked to her calmly, "Aunt Chus, my father promised me that if I won a scholarship, he would allow me to attend a boarding school, just as the government scholarship system is set up. He told me that if I go to a boarding school paid by the government, it would save him money and then he could hire a maid to help him with the housework. So, if my father doesn't keep his promise, he knows that I'll start looking for my mother and I'll go and live with her."

"You ungrateful creature," she screeched, "how could you think of such a thing? How could you leave your brothers and sister with your father? You're so selfish, only wanting to look after yourself."

I had enough of her trying to make me feel guilty for trying to better myself and exploded. For the first time since my parent's separation I found the courage to unload onto someone my great resentment surrounding the unfairness of the custody situation. I told her everything I had heard that horrible day in Ipala when my father was given custody of my sister and me.

"Aunt Chus, when my parents separated I went to live with my mother and I was happy living with her. My brothers stayed with my father. My wish was and always had been to live with my mother and my father knew it. My sister and I were sitting in the next office and I heard what took place in the judge's office. I heard my father tell my mother, 'Chepita, (my father's nickname for my mother), I refuse to pay child support for what you did. I want to take the girls because I know that Gabriela wants to attend college and you have no financial means to fulfill her dreams beyond elementary school.'"

As I was talking my aunt's face was turning beet–red from anger, but I continued, "I begged my father to let me stay with my mother and he told me, 'If you wish to stay with your mother, it will be your choice. Just remember, I won't give your mother one penny for anything you or Eneida may wish or need. I also want you to remember that if you decide to choose your mother instead of me, you'd better forget that you ever had a father. On the other hand, if you come to live with your brothers and me, I will send you to college for anything you wish to study.'"

While I was telling this story my two brothers were constantly pulling on me and pleading, "Nena (my nick name until I was fourteen), be quiet! You're going to be in trouble. Let's go inside our rooms and close the door. Nena, please." Eneida was crying and screaming. I took her in my arms and we closed the door. I knew that I had cooked myself for now and I could never ask Aunt Chus to lend me money to pay for the telegram. I went to bed crying as much as I had cried on the day my father and mother separated and as much as I had cried on the day my father took me away from my mother's side. Now I was going to lose the scholarship and I would have to leave school—age twelve, education finished. "Oh Christ my God, help me!"

The next morning I awoke and got ready to go through the same routine I had been doing since coming to live at my aunt's house. I dressed in my blue uniform, fixed breakfast for my brothers and sister and went to school with heavy feet and with very swollen eyes from crying.

The principal was astonished to see me back at school and

called me to come into her office. I explained everything to her. She came close to me, put her arm on my shoulder in a loving manner and asked me to sit down. She then went to her desk and took out a piece of paper and started writing. I sat quietly, not knowing what to think. She opened a drawer in her desk, took out a five Quetzal note and said, "Here, go to the post office, and deliver this telegram to your father. Go ahead, you may read it." I tentatively took the paper and read it:

MR. FOLGAR, COME URGENTLY TO DISCUSS GABRIELA'S SCHOOL AND SCHOLARSHIP.

It was difficult to believe that anyone could be as kind as this principal; I looked upon her as my rescuer and as an angel of God sent by the holy Archangel himself, Saint Gabriel, my namesake and protector. I did not know it then, but she was to be one of many angels who would be appearing to rescue me at critical moments in my life over the next six years.

I sent the telegram at about eight-thirty in the morning and then went back to school. As I was returning home from the afternoon session I saw the bus from Ipala stopping in front of my aunt's house. When I entered the house, I saw my father standing in the large room waiting for me. He greeted me and before I could return his greeting, he started asking me questions.

"Do you know why I am here?" he said with in a stern voice.

Aunt Chus kept looking at me with angry slanted eyes as I smartly chirped, "Yes, I won a scholarship and the principal wants to talk to you."

My father smiled and he looked happy. That was a great relief. However, his smile did not last very long when I added, "My scholarship requires that I attend college in Chiquimula and I must be there by the last day of class of this week."

Of course, I understood the reason he had made a face. He was happy for me, but he was wishing that the scholarship had been granted for the school in Jalapa. I knew that my father was concerned about my brothers and my sister and he was asking himself how he would manage to take care of them without my help. My going to Chiquimula also meant that if my father did not want to hire a housekeeper, he had to start teaching his boys how to cook and do some of the housework—a concept totally foreign to them. After all, "cooking, sweeping, washing dishes and any housework is not a boy's chore but a girl's responsibility," as he never tired of repeating.

I was as happy as a robin after a rain when I got on the bus the next morning. During the long trip to Chiquimula I was thinking about nothing else but my new and brighter future. I also had a sense of deep satisfaction:

Now I've proven to you that girls can do things. You never believed in me and now you will have to eat your words.

I had proven to my father that I, and by extension all girls, are worth something, and I was determined that I was going to continue proving him wrong. I loved my father and I wanted him to wish the best for me, to be proud of me, and to love and treat me as a daughter. Since he was a teacher, I thought that by doing well in school was the best way to accomplish this.

The bus traveled from Jalapa, through San Pedro Pinula, across the mountain, through San Luis Jilotepeque, and then through Ipala on its way to Chiquimula (map: page 30). As the bus passed through each of these towns, with their more often than not bitter memories, I felt as though all of my family troubles were now falling behind me with every kilometer. An immense feeling of calm displaced my initial feeling of trepidation of going to a boarding school where I would not know anybody.

Aunt Chus's house in Jalapa

Instituto Normal Centro Americano Para Señoritas
(INCAS) *in Jalapa*

Chapter 3
New Hope

No one can make you feel inferior without your consent.
–Eleanor Roosevelt–

Chiquimula is a medium–size provincial capital city situated in a valley about half way to the Atlantic Ocean from Guatemala City. It is hot and dry for much of the year—a desert region, with cactus and irrigated farming. I remember traveling to this city with my mother to visit her relatives before my parents' separation. It is only about forty kilometers from Ipala, the town where my father was teaching at the time.

Chiquimula was a lively city compared to Jalapa. It was, and still is, the agricultural trading and financial centre of the region. But Chiquimula's main significance for me now was that it was also a centre for education. It had several prestigious private schools and two outstanding public schools that attracted students from all over the eastern area of Guatemala. One of these public colleges was for boys and one for girls, the school I was to attend— *EL INSTITUTO NORMAL PARA SEÑORITAS DE ORIENTE* (THE EASTERN NORMAL INSTITUTE FOR YOUNG LADIES).

It is difficult to describe the immense euphoria I felt upon arriving in this city in February of 1961. I had just turned twelve years old and for the first time in my life I felt I could breathe freely. Although I had no personal spending money, I felt free. I could now study without having to worry about domestic matters. I had food and a bed in the school dormitory. I was living as a normal child and student, not as a maid and mother. I had no worries about whether my father was late from his billiards or whether he had gambled away all of his money. I no longer had to hear the awful things he kept repeating about my mother. I was certainly worried about my siblings whom I had had to leave behind in Jalapa, especially Eneida; she was always in my thoughts. I knew, however, that it was not right that my father expected me to give up my dreams in order to become the mother of the family when he could have afforded to hire a maid or nanny, if he had only stopped gambling his money away. At first I was wondering how I was going to fit in at this school. A lot of the students came from wealthy families and from regions I had never visited and from schools I had never attended. Unlike the college in Jalapa, where I knew quite a few girls from my elementary school, here I did not know one person. However, It did not take me long to be accepted by my classmates. Since shyness was never part of my personality, I did not have any trouble making friends. It felt wonderful to have friends with whom I could freely associate, real friends my own age. Before this, my only friends were my girl cousins. As the school year progressed I met people who thought well of me, who told me that I was intelligent and pretty. I met people who enjoyed my company and people who gave me respect. I was able to do normal teenage activities and have fun. But more than anything else, I was very proud of myself because I was doing very well in school.

The one school uniform my father bought me was not sufficient. This school, as all schools in Guatemala, was very strict about cleanliness, dress and decorum and an absolutely clean and pressed uniform was *de rigueur*. Having only one uniform meant that I had to wash and iron it every day. During the day at school I had to be extra careful that it did not become soiled. The uniform at INSO was not as elegant as the one I had worn in Jalapa, mostly due to the climate. It did not have a matching sweater and jumper. The collar of the blouse was open and there was no necktie. On top of that, the uniform that first year was just plain ugly. The skirt was cotton cloth with black, red, and white checks. The blouse was white cotton with the school monogram attached to the left side by snaps. Students from other schools called us "the tablecloths." The school uniform for my second year was much nicer, having a pleated green skirt, but the material was still lightweight and wrinkly cheap cotton.

For the first few months at INSO I lived with all of the other out-of-town students in the government boarding school dormitory. However, in June of 1961, after only four months at this school, the government no longer wished to continue this arrangement and decided to introduce the initiative of Student Boarding Houses *(Bolsas de Studio)*. What this meant was that the school dormitory was being shut down and the out-of-town students now had to find their own accommodations. My father had to shop very hard to find a home he really trusted and would feel comfortable for me to live in. He found a boarding house owned and run by a lady named *Señorita* Elvira Cordón. It was not long after having moved into this house that I knew I would be living in another home during the next school year since my father was not happy with the arrangements. Miss Elvira had decided to take in male students and my father immediately envisioned a threat to my wellbeing.

At INSO–age thirteen.

The next boarding house, where I was to live for the next two school terms, in 1962 and 1963, was the home of *Señor* and *Señora* Belisario y Romelia de Diaz. All of the girls in her house called *Señora* de Diaz "Doña Rome". She had sixteen girls as boarders.

Most of the girls at the school came from wealthy or middle class backgrounds and money was not a problem for them, but it sure was for me. My father expected my scholarship to cover everything. I started out with only one school uniform, no books and no money for personal items such as sanitary pads, deodorant and cosmetics. I had to become very innovative. I was able to go on the school's excursions free or at a reduced charge by volunteering for the coordinating committees. In the boarding house I was also able to earn some money. The little knowledge of sewing that I had learned during the days when I was helping my mother with her dressmaking became very handy. Doña Rome allowed me to use her sewing machine and I did a lot of mending for many of my classmates. I also made the lazy students' beds, for a fee. In other words, I became a maid again, but this time I did not mind because it was of my own volition and on my terms. The money I earned was my salvation. With this money I paid for some entertainment such as going to the movies, buying sweets, and going out once in a while to eat with my friends and class-mates.

My father did not give me money to buy schoolbooks either. He told me that he expected me to borrow books from other students—incredible as this reads. As an explanation for this odd behaviour he told me, "This is what my mother did to me when I attended college." This might have been true, but I never be-lieved for one second that this was real reason for his penny pinching on my books. Doña Rome helped me to get around this difficulty, as she did with many other problems. She received twenty-four Quetzals a month from the government to cover my room and board, but she only charged me eighteen and did not tell my father. In that way I was able to buy my schoolbooks and an extra uniform in my second year.

Very quickly I became friends with many girls at the boarding house. Many of these friendships have lasted until now, even though I left Guatemala and immigrated to Canada in 1974. There was one girl in particular, Marta Estela Solís, who became my closest friend. She came from a fairly wealthy family, at least by my standards. On the weekends one of her brothers drove to Chiquimula to pick her up and drive her to her family's farm. Sometimes she invited me alone, and at other times all of the other girls in the boarding house, to her family's hacienda. I en-joyed the times I spent there with her. Everyone in her family was friendly and everything seemed so normal. When it was time to return to school I did not want to leave. Her mother was excep-tionally wonderful and loving with me. Marta Estela and I be-came so close that on one occasion she asked me to let her family adopt me—she wanted me to become her sister and I knew that she was sincere. I wonder now what would have happened to me if I had accepted and my father would have agreed—certainly my life would have taken a different turn. But at thirteen I could not entertain such thoughts. All I could do was to enjoy the moment, to enjoy the carefree and peaceful life at her family's house; something I had never experienced with my own family.

It was on the bus from Chiquimula to Ipala where I met a boy, José Esteban Villeda Sagastume. Many times we traveled together on the same bus; he was going to visit his parents, brothers and sisters and I was going to visit my own family. José Esteban or, Canche, as I called him (because of his blonde hair) was three years older than I. He also was two years ahead of me in his studies. He was attending a private school, *LICEO FRANCÉS*. During our travels together to Ipala we had a great time, as the bus was always filled with students who were traveling to different towns on weekends and holidays to visit their families.

By May 7, 1962, the anniversary of the college, our friendship had grown into teen dating. This was my second year in Chiquimula. Canche was now attending a different college from when I first met him—a public school, the *INSTITUTO NORMAL PARA VARONES DE ORIENTE* (INVO), (EASTERN NORMAL INSTITUTE FOR BOYS). Conveniently, his new college was located just across the street from mine.

My father almost had a heart attack when I told him that I had a boyfriend, for I had just turned thirteen years old. He started again with his worn-out and tiresome sermon about girls, "Isn't it what I always told you, sending girls to school is like throwing salt back into the sea. That's why I never wanted to send you to college. I hope you finish your school without bringing a surprise to me."

I understood immediately to what he was referring; he thought that I would be having sex with Canche sooner or later, probably sooner, and getting pregnant before graduating. Apparently, he had no trust in me and I could only conclude that this was due to my being a girl. I had never done anything in my life to cause him to fear that I would do something to embarrass the family or myself.

Canche was my first love. Our love was pure, innocent and filled with a lot of dreams. Even as young as we were we talked about getting married when we both had finished school. We built all these castles in our heads and we thought that our love would have no end. We had a lot of fun together. If he finished his classes before I did, he waited for me at the corner of the college and we walked together to where I lived. If I finished my classes before him, I waited for him at the park in front of the college and then we would walk together to Doña Rome's home. At the school dances he always danced with me. We went everywhere together—to the movies, to the cafeteria, to the park.

My father very reluctantly agreed to meet him, if only to take the opportunity to tell him that he was not worthy of me and that I was too young to think about boys. In that area he was probably right, although he married my mother when she was only seventeen. But more than anything else my father wanted to tell him to keep away from me. In contrast, Canche's father came to meet me and to take the opportunity to express his and his wife's approval and happiness. He gave us good advice in relation to how to keep up with our studies and what not to do in order not to jeopardize our schooling. His father also expressed his concerns about our young ages and he, as well as my father, did not wish for us to do anything crazy. I know that our parents' concerns were legitimate in view of the custom of early marriage in Guatemala. Many girls in school, ages fifteen to seventeen, were already engaged and just waiting to finish their schooling to get married.

My father eventually, very much against his will, agreed to let Canche visit me at my boarding residence. As a trade-off, he stipulated that Canche and I would not see each other outside of the house. My father knew that he could not stop our seeing each other and figured that it was better to arrange supervised visits. This type of supervised visiting in the home by a boyfriend, or even a fiancé, was another hoary Latin American custom. Canche was considered my *novio official*. In Guatemala, this means a boy has permission from the girl's father to visit his girlfriend at her home, as if they were engaged. After the girl turns fifteen, a formal engagement would be allowed, if marriage were in the offing.

Needless to say, my father's silly and futile mechanizations did not deter us from seeing each other. How could it be otherwise? We were in love. We met after school, at school dances, at the movies, in the park, and at any place where he and I, *just by accident*, would happen to meet. It was fun to flaunt the rules. Many times I got into trouble with Doña Rome when she found out that I had gone to the movies or had been at the park with him. She became angry because she had promised my father that she would closely supervise me.

In Jalapa, when I broke the news about my scholarship, I thought that my father was displeased about my going to Chiquimula only because he now had to take care of his children. Even at that time, however, the extent of his sourness was still somewhat enigmatic since Chiquimula was only an hour away from where he was teaching in Ipala and my living in that city would give me the opportunity to visit him and my siblings quite often. Besides, I would be studying on a scholarship, which meant that he did not have to worry about my food, lodging, uniforms and many of my books. Saving money, especially on my education, was very important to him.

I was not in Chiquimula very long, though, when this mystery was solved in a surprising way. One day I was called to the principal's office and to my astonishment my mother was waiting for me. I was shocked to see her, for I had no idea to where she had disappeared. I had not seen nor heard from her for more than a year. My heart was starting to pound and I felt my blood starting to run quickly through my arteries. She had tears in her eyes as she walked toward me and then she hugged me. This was surprising because she was not usually this affectionate, even though I knew that she loved me. This hug was one of the very few I ever received from her, and it was the sweetest.

She was wiping away tears from her eyes and said, "Gabrielita (as she sometimes called me), just by accident I found out that you were attending this college and I couldn't wait any longer without seeing you."

I threw myself in her arms. We stood embracing each other, crying together, until the principal interrupted, "If you wish you can take a couple of hours off and go to the park across the street." When we were leaving the school I examined her because she looked different: heavier and paler. There were considerably more wrinkles on her face

We crossed the street to the park and sat down on one of the benches. My mother kept talking, "I found out about you from a daughter of one of my co-workers. When I heard her mentioning your first and last name, I thought that it couldn't be a coincidence that there were two girls with the same first and last name. I asked this girl what you looked like and after she had told me I knew then that she was talking about you. And here I am. I've missed you. I've suffered without you and now my prayers have been answered"

"Mamaita, I'm so happy to have found you too," I said, shaking and with tears flowing from my eyes.

I tried to lighten the atmosphere by asking about her family in Chiquimula, "Mamá, have you seen any of my uncles and aunts? I remember that some of them live here. I'd love to reconnect with them. What about Aunt Teco, where is she now? I haven't seen her for so many years and I would like to visit her. I have been so cut off from my relatives here."

"She is now living on the coast, in Livingston. She graduated from INSO and is teaching there."

Aunt María Teresa Menendez (Teco is a nickname) was only eleven years older than I. In the past, when we visited Chiquimula to see my mother's relatives, Aunt Teco was the person I best related to. I was disappointed to learn that she was no longer in Chiquimula.

"Mamaita, where did you go after   papá took Eneida and me? Why didn't you write to me as you had promised?" I asked softly.

She did not answer. She just sat on the bench, crying and crying. To make her feel better I took her hands in mine and told her, "I am not angry with you." But she continued crying and did not answer any of my questions.

After that first meeting in Chiquimula, my mother and I agreed to continue seeing each other behind my father's back.

A few days later we were sitting together again in the park and she handed me a package of letters without saying anything. I looked at them and saw that they were the letters that she had sent to me, but which had been returned to her. Each letter bore what looked like my father's handwriting across the envelope: RETURN TO SENDER. I became so sad, and angry. She did not have to explain anything, for I figured out what had happened. My father was hiding my mother's letters from me, and then returning them to the post office. All the while he and his family were telling me that my mother had abandoned us.

He told me several times, "Look, your mother doesn't even write!"

Eventually, my father found out that my mother and I were seeing each other and he became furious. He then ordered her to stay away from me. We continued to see each other secretly anyway, but much less frequently

In 1961, my father was still teaching in Ipala and traveled quite often from Ipala to Chiquimula, but not to visit me. I found out about these trips from my classmates who had spotted him standing at the bus stop or walking about in the centre of town. I questioned him about this when I went to Ipala one weekend. He told me that all of these trips were to attend interviews in order to arrange an exchange of positions with another teacher in a different town or city. He said that he wanted to go to a town where no one knew about my mother's infidelity.

From mid-June to mid-July I did not travel to Ipala due to mid-term exams. One day toward the end of July Aunt Teco traveled to Chiquimula to see her boyfriend and having heard that I was now studying at her old school she came to visit me. It had been many years since I had last seen her.

"You must be happy," she said excitedly, "that your father is now teaching in Livingston at the boys' school."

"What?" I exclaimed. "But he hasn't written and said anything to me about this."

"Really, you don't know that he's moved? He's living with us at my father's house, and he's living there with your mother!"

I was astounded, for I had been talking to my mother regularly and she never mentioned anything about this either.

"You have to be kidding," I said, in a manner that suggested that this had to be a practical joke. "And my brothers and sister are there too?"

"Yes," she replied, still with an incredulous look on her face. "It's hard to believe you didn't know this. They are living with us for now. Housing is in very short supply in Livingston since the fire. You probably don't know about that either. There was a big fire in the town last year and many houses and businesses were completely destroyed."

I knew for sure that I had to travel to Livingston soon to find out what was going on. I was happy to know that my parents were re-united but devastated that I had to find out about this from a third person.

Am I so unimportant to my parents that they could not tell me something as important as this?

The Parrish Church and market–Chiquimula

El Instituto Normal Para Señoritas de Oriente–INSO in Chiquimula

Gabriela & Aunt María Teresa Menendez (Aunt Teco)—2005

Gabriela, Canche & Finy—1962

School Outing At Los Chorros

1962- on a school outing to San Pedro Pinula. In the first photo- Gabriela is at top right and Marta Stella on the bottom row, second from right. Second photo Gabriela is on the bottom and Marta Estela is on the top row—middle.

Reunion

Marta Estela & Gabriela in Guatemala City, Dec. 2005.

Marta Estella's Family Hacienda.
The farm was located in Padre Miguel near Esquipulas.

The Municipal Building in Chiquimula

Chapter 4
Happiness and Sadness

It is a wise father who knows his own child.
–William Shakespeare–

In the middle of July, midway through my first year at INSO, after finishing my mid-term exams, I made plans to visit my reunited parents in Livingston. I had never been to that town before and I was unsure what was waiting for me there. I did not have to arrive in Livingston for adventure to find me though, for on my first trip I experienced one of the most terrifying events in my life—at least up to that time.

My father had telegraphed Miss Elvira Cordón to put me on a bus to Puerto Barrios, which is the main port city on the Atlantic Coast of Guatemala and is one and a half hours from Livingston by boat. I arrived in Puerto Barrios at about one o'clock in the afternoon. The boat on which my father and I were supposed to travel to Livingston was to leave Puerto Barrios at six o'clock and arrive in Livingston at about seven–thirty. He telegraphed Miss Elvira to tell me that I was to wait for him at the train station. He also instructed Miss Elvira to give me the exact amount of money I needed for the bus transportation to Puerto Barrios. When I arrived I had no money for lunch or for a porter to carry my luggage from the bus station to the train station, and to my surprise, the two stations were not located close to each other. It was very difficult to haul my luggage in the coastal heat.

I waited and waited at the train station, hours and hours. This was not a very good area of the city. There were quite a few bars around the train station and there were many prostitutes strolling around with their customers, all of them staring and leering at me as if I were a prostitute, even though I was obviously a child and wearing my school uniform. I became very, very frightened.

Six o'clock passed and I knew that the boat to Livingston had left and my father had still not appeared. I did not know what to do, I felt completely lost, I thought I was going to be killed or attacked by the scruffy people mingling around in the streets. I did not even know what time it was because my father had never bought me a watch. Night descended; the heat was suffocating me. I sat on my belongings, watching the activities around the numerous bars, hoping my father would arrive soon. The juke-boxes in the bars were playing the current hit tune, seemingly non-stop, and at times, in unison. The name of the song was, *Y Qué Hiciste Del Amor* ("And What Have You Done With The Love"). During the hours I was sitting outside the train station I heard the song so many times that to this day I have never forgotten the words.

Finally, I heard the whistle of a train. *Maybe my father is on this train?* When it stopped I watched with excitement as the passengers got off, standing on my tiptoes, craning my neck, examining every passenger, but my father did not appear. I now became desperate and frightened.

I approached one of the passengers leaving the station. "Excuse me, sir. Can you tell me the time and where the boat to Livingston is docked?"

"It's seven thirty but the boat to Livingston has already sailed, it left at six. The pier is about four blocks from where we are standing," he said, pointing in one direction.

I thanked him and the man walked away, leaving me alone—alone except for the creepy men and prostitutes walking to the bars and the brothels. The station was now almost empty. I sat down on my belongings and started crying—bawling, wailing—louder and louder, with tears streaming down my face and falling onto my skirt.

A woman who had disembarked from the train came up to me, bent her head down, and asked in a kindly voice, "What is wrong? Why are you crying, my dear girl?"

"I am waiting for my father," I replied, wiping the tears that were still running down my cheeks. "He was supposed to meet me here and then take me to Livingston on the boat."

"This was the last train for today," she said. She turned to walk away, but turned around suddenly and with decision in her voice said, "You're coming with me—to my house and I'll make sure you get on the first boat to Livingston tomorrow morning."

I was not sure what would be more dangerous, to go to a stranger's house or to stay where I was. I was afraid to go with this lady but I knew that I had to make a fast decision and I chose to go with her. That had to be better than staying where I was, with no food or money, suffering in the heat, surrounded by the oppressive darkness and in danger from the creepy looking men.

The lady had a car parked near to the station and she drove me to her house. When we were in her house she went to her husband and spoke to him in a whisper. Then she went to the kitchen to prepare some food and invited me to eat.

"Down that way is the bathroom and shower," she said.

While I was showering she fixed up a bed next to the bed of one of her two daughters. "Everything is going to be just fine," she consoled and assured me. And it was.

The next morning the nice lady woke me up and fed me breakfast. Around quarter to ten she gave me some money and instructed her maid to take me to the pier where the boat to Livingston was docked. I cannot recall this lady's name and unfortunately, I was never in a position to seek her out and to thank her again. The only thing that I was sure of at the time was that she was another angel that St. Gabriel had sent to help me when I needed it the most.

I boarded the boat, found a seat and looked around, taking in my new surroundings. This was my first time I had been on the coast. It was a beautiful day and the scenery was exotic, at least for me: the lushness of the vegetation, the smell of the ocean, the large freighters entering the harbour, strange birds soaring overhead and others gliding just above the water. I was not able to appreciate these things for long, however, because I had never been at sea before and I became seasick, even before the hawsers were loosened. The churning in my stomach, which was aggravated by the anger I had toward my father, was the only thing I could think about during that first voyage.

My father was waiting for me at the pier in Livingston. I was so upset with him that instead of greeting him, I started haranguing him about his neglectfulness, stinginess, and the danger he had just put me through. He tried to explain to me that he had

missed the two o'clock boat to Puerto Barrios. I then calmed down a little. However, when we arrived at Aunt Teco's house, where he and my mother were living, Aunt Teco told me that my father had been playing the slot machines and that was the reason he had missed the boat. He never even inquired as to where I had spent the night in Puerto Barrios. This was enough for me to start telling him hurtful things that maybe, as a daughter, I should not have told him. I was angry and his lying and nonchalant attitude toward my predicament infuriated me even more. That was the first day of a most horrible time at my parents' house.

I experienced a similar frightening situation three months later on my second trip to Livingston. I was traveling there for the main end–of–year school holidays, which ran from the end of October 1961 to mid-January of 1962. My father's instructions for my travel were a little different this time. I was to travel to Puerto Barrios by train and he would meet me at the train station. Again, he instructed Miss Elvira to give me only enough money to pay for the transportation.

Before boarding the train in Chiquimula I had learned that it was not scheduled to arrive in Puerto Barrios until after six o'clock in the evening. I already knew from my first trip that the second and last boat to Livingston from Puerto Barrios sailed at six o'clock. This information gave me a very uneasy feeling, but I had to trust my father that he would meet me at the station and take care of things. I had no other choice.

The train pulled into Puerto Barrios on time at seven-thirty and again my father was not at the station. As the station emptied I sat on my belongings, crying and thinking about what I was going to do. I did not want to wait around at the train station for as long as I had done before. I remembered the lady who had previously helped me and I started to walk in the direction to where I thought she might live, dragging along the street my heavy luggage.

Train Station in Chiquimula

As I was leaving the station the man who had been sitting close to me on the train and whom I had already noticed was watching me as I paced around the station approached me and said, "I saw you on the train. Are your lost?"

"My father was to meet me here, but he's not here and I have no money and nowhere to go," I answered.

I tried to put forward a brave face but I was more scared and even more desperate than I had been three months previously.

"I'm going to a hotel and I'll take you there, that is, if you wish to come with me," said the man.

"I do have one quetzal," I replied, "but how can I afford to stay at a hotel?"

"The rooms at the Hotel Los Arbolitos are cheap and we can share a room," he replied.

I was very afraid to go with this stranger but I was even more afraid of the neighborhood around the train station. Puerto Barrios was a big city and it was still strange to me, so I went with him to the hotel. He was kind enough to help me with my luggage.

The hotel appeared to be very old and rundown, even scary looking. There were weird looking women and men entering and exiting. The stranger went to the front desk and talked to the lady managing the hotel. She looked at me, nodded okay and took us to a room.

We were not in the room very long when the lady from the front desk came to our floor. I think that she was looking for me. I saw her first and asked, "Where are the bathrooms?"

She showed me the bathroom and then inquired in a hushed voice, "Little girl, where are you from and what are you doing here in Puerto Barrios?"

"I'm from Chiquimula and I am going to Livingston. My father was supposed to meet me at the station, but he was not there," I answered smartly, trying not to show my fear.

"Oh, I thought that man you're with is your father."

"Oh no," I answered crisply, "the man saw me crying by the train station and since I have only one Quetzal he brought me here to this hotel to share a room." Then in quieter voice I continued, "I don't want to share a room with him. Could you rent me a single room for one Quetzal?"

Los Arbolitos Hotel
It is no longer a hotel. The building looks the same today as it did in 1960

"How old are you," she asked suspiciously and with her eyes examining closely.

"I'm turning thirteen next week."

In a firm voice she said, "Well, I don't have a room available for that price and I won't have you staying in that room either. You can sleep downstairs in a space behind the desk. I will watch out for you."

Taking me by my hand, she led me down the stairs while saying, "Don't worry, you will be safe here with me."

I do not know if the stranger had bad intentions toward me, or if he truly was trying to help me. I suspected at that time, and learned for certain later on, that men took prostitutes to this hotel, although it was not a brothel. In Guatemala, prostitution is legal, but it is strictly controlled. Prostitutes must be registered with the government and have regular medical check-ups. I think that the lady came to check on me because she could see that I was a minor and of course, that would have meant big trouble with the police if I were seen in the hotel with a man.

There was so much activity in the hotel during the night; the bell kept ringing, announcing new guests; there were loud conversations accompanied by a constant pounding of footsteps. All of this commotion, combined with my worries, did not let me get very much sleep. When morning arrived the kind lady prepared me a breakfast and afterwards, accompanied me halfway to the pier. She did not ask me for my one Quetzal. As I watched her walking away I had to pray, "Oh Holy Saint Gabriel, thank you for sending another angel to help me. Guard her and keep her safe."

I paid my fare and boarded the Santa Marta for Livingston. As soon as the boat had left the dock I again became seasick. I put my head down in my lap, trying not to throw up. When my stomach had calmed a bit and I was half–asleep I heard someone call my name. I looked up and saw my father, standing right in front of me.

"Nena, here you are!" he exclaimed.

I was so startled seeing him in front of me that my nausea went away. "Papá, why weren't you at the train station?" I asked, now awake and with my eyes wide open.

"I got busy," he replied in a too calm and off-handed manner for my liking, "Where did you stay?"

"A wonderful lady helped me and put me up at Los Arbolitos. If it weren't for her I would've had to stay in a room in a very creepy hotel with a strange man I had met at the train station."

This answer did not seem to shake my father up at all—his face was expressionless, placid, as if I had just told him that I had stayed overnight with a trusted relative.

"That's a bad hotel. I was staying in a hotel just beside the one you were staying in."

This type of answer, or rather, non–answer from my father always stirred up intense anger in me, but I thought it best to bite my tongue until we had left the boat. I never liked making a public display of my anger.

As soon as the boat docked and the people dispersed I looked at my father and in an angry voice asked, "Have you any idea of what danger you put me in? Don't you care what happens to me?"

"I knew that you'd make out okay," was his only reply.

"Papá, I'll go to the police and tell them and everybody else, including your colleagues, about what happened if you don't agree right now that in the future you will give me enough money to cover the bus fare, hotel, taxi, food and boat fare, no less the ten Quetzals, when I travel to Livingston. I'm serious," I threatened.

My father did not reply to my threats. However, I am sure that they made him reflect. I never had any more problems after this. He always sent me the required money for my trips, enough that I never had to use all of it, and he met me at the place we had agreed to meet. Of course, he would then ask me to give him back the change.

I never found out what he was doing in Puerto Barrios that day, that he was not be able, or forgot, to meet me—gambling, lottery business, visiting a prostitute?

Livingston is a peninsular town situated along a beautiful bay on the Atlantic Ocean, one and a half hour boat ride from Puerto Barrios. The local people call it an island because there is no connection with any other town or port unless one travels by boat. When I arrived I found the town to be so different from any other town I had experienced in Guatemala. Most of the popula-

tion were black and made their living by fishing. They also spoke a different language, a language called Garífuna, which I believe is a mixed language derived from American indigenous languages, African languages, English, and Spanish. Of course, most of the adults spoke Spanish as well, and some had a smattering of Caribbean English since the country of Belize, formerly British Honduras, is very near.

The buildings and houses in the town were constructed of untreated wood with corrugated metal roofs. The whole ambiance was of a relaxed and carefree nature. In the 1960s there was very little crime, no drugs and none of the intra and extra-familial problems involving vendettas that plagued the region around San Pedro Pinula. Even the music was different. In place of Mexican mariachi music, Latin trios, salsa and marimba music I was now hearing calypso and reggae. I enjoyed Livingston. My aunt took me to all the places around town and I quickly made new friends with all the girls and boys.

My first visit to Livingston was around the end of July of 1961. That was the time of the first horrible experience at the train station in Puerto Barrios. I went to Livingston hoping to enjoy once more the home I had lost twenty months before. Once having arrived, I tried to forget the Puerto Barrios problem and hoped to enjoy my stay. However, things did not start very well. My mother and father were constantly fighting and I could not study. When my father was not fighting with my mother she was either crying or just remaining quiet. She barely talked to me the whole time I was there. Finally, after a couple of days of this I told my father that I needed to concentrate and study for my final exams and I was going to leave and return to school. I knew that I would return at the end of October for the annual school holiday and at that time be able to examine the family situation more closely.

I returned again to Livingston in early November (the time of the second scare in Puerto Barrios) and I stayed there until the middle of January when the new school year started. My parents, brothers, and sister were living in a very large rented house along with Aunt Teco and her father. My aunt took the time again to take me around the town. She was like the older sister I never had. At other times, I thought she acted toward me like a very affectionate mother. I did not realize it at the time how much she protected me. I now know that many times she took me away from the house because she did not want me to observe what was really going on between my parents.

During those two months I barely spent any time in the house with my parents. I was so busy meeting people, going to the beach, going to dances. I became an important part of Aunt Teco's school theatre group. Every year around Christmas this group put on a show to raise money for the school. I was having too much fun to pay much attention to my parents' fighting. Once in a while, Aunt Teco and I talked about my parent's situation and she told me that my father was not a kind man to my mother. She told me that her father had already asked my father to move out because he was not able to tolerate the things my father was doing to my mother.

One day Aunt Teco overheard my parents' conversation and she later relayed it to me, "Chepita, remember that our agreement was that you were to come to live with us only as a maid. Based on what you did, you have no rights over the children. You are lucky I did not pursue criminal charges against you. Don't forget that when a woman commits adultery she commits a crime which can be used against her to take her children away forever."

I was mortified to learn about the true nature of my parents' so-called reconciliation and I now did not want to stay around Livingston any longer than I had to. It was just too painful to witness my father torturing my mother.

Aunt Teco had good taste for clothing and dressed very well. She was young and very slim, and my mother was her dress-maker. When she walked through the streets she was free advertisement for my mother's business. By the end of November of 1961 my mother was so busy with her sewing  that my aunt and I had to help her. My mother paid me with money and she paid my aunt by making her dresses for free. When I returned to school in January of 1962 I had a very nice and large wardrobe and Aunt Teco went back to teaching as impeccably dressed as ever.

During these holidays Aunt Teco and I became very close. Her friendliness, kindness, elegance, up–beat attitude, honesty, and morality, along with her success as a teacher were an inspiration. She was my best friend and my sounding board. She became the only person with whom I was able to confide all that I observed and knew about my parent's separation, reunion and current problems. After I had returned to school in January, we wrote to each other quite often. Since my father tried to read all letters addressed to my mother Aunt Teco came up with the idea of inserting my notes to my mother inside the letters I sent to her. In one of her letters to me, probably around the third week of January of 1962, she told me that my parents had moved out of their house and were now living about a block away. She also gave me the warning that it seemed that things between my parents were even worse than when they were living in her house.

I was determined that this information was not going to interfere with my life, at least for the moment; for I now had my own life, my classmates, my boyfriend, and my success in my studies.

The school's Easter holiday of 1962 fell on the fourteenth of April (my second year at INSO) and I apprehensively left Chiquimula for Livingston. This time I stayed no more than four or five days. The atmosphere in the house was unbearable. I did not know how to cope with my father's constant recriminations toward my mother, mainly about her past unfaithfulness. I also could not stand having to witness my mother's crying for hours and not eating, sleeping or talking to me. Many times I thought that her silence was directed at me, reproaching me for something. With my parents living in their own place I had less opportunity to spend time with Aunt Teco and this was an additional incentive to pack up and leave for school as early as possible.

During this short visit I noticed that my mother had befriended her next–door neighbor Feliciano, who was about twenty-seven years old. I did not know what was the exact relationship between my mother and Feliciano, but I remember during the five days I stayed there I observed this fellow coming to our house and spending many hours talking to her. Some of those visits took place very late at night. I got up and tried to listen to their conversation and what I heard was my mother telling him about her suffering and trials with my father and asking him for advice about what to do. I did not see them doing anything that would be considered inappropriate, but I believed that it was not right for a married woman with children to have a young man visiting her while her children and husband were already in bed.

I went to visit Aunt Teco and talked with her about the situation. She too did not believe that my mother's present behaviour was appropriate. I told my aunt that I did not want to stay in Livingston any longer because of the atmosphere in my parents' house and that I was returning to Chiquimula. She tried to convince me to go to her place and spend the rest of the Easter Holiday with her. I knew, however, that my father would not approve and that would be a cause for another fight.

I had a few words with my parents. First, I spoke with my mother, "Mamá, I don't think it is appropriate for you to have Feliciano over at the house so late at night. You know how jealous and suspicious Papá is."

She looked at me with angry eyes and said, "Why don't you go ahead and tell your father what you are thinking about me again. You told him once and he believed you, and if you tell him again, he will believe you once more."

I could not answer my mother because I had no idea what she was exactly alluding to:

Did my father tell her that I was the one who told him that she was being unfaithful?

Whatever my father had told my mother it would have had to be done after they had reconciled because my mother's attitude before their reconciliation was much friendlier than it was now. More than ever, I knew that I had to leave the house very soon. I tried to talk to my father about the situation, but he was even more hostile than my mother.

On the last evening before my departure, when we were all eating together, I decided this was the time to talk. In a very serious tone I started:

"Papá, Mamá, your decision to get back together was the worst mistake you could have made." And then looking straight at my father I continued, "You are torturing my mother and killing her little by little with your reproaches for what you believe she did." Then, looking at both of them, I said, "You had better think twice before continuing to live together because if I am suffering, my brothers and sister are suffering too."

I do not think that my father was prepared to hear something like this from a thirteen-year-old and he was looking at me with narrow eyes. I felt terrible anger and hatred shooting toward me across the table and this was confirmed when he said,

"I knew that I was not mistaken when I said that God had punished me with giving me a daughter like you. You don't deserve to be my daughter. You are very disrespectful and have a big mouth." He also cursed my future by saying, "You've always had a big mouth it will be your downfall. Eventually, it's going to bring you disgrace if you don't change your ways. If you don't learn to control your mouth, you will end up black and blue on the very day you get a husband. You don't even know what you are talking about. You're just a kid who doesn't even know how to wipe your behind and you dare to tell your parents what they're doing wrong and what they have to do."

This was one of the few times that I thought my father was going to hit me and I was extremely fearful. Despite my fear, I was able to continue, "Don't you see how she cries all the time and it's because she's suffering due to the things you tell her every moment. I also know that when you brought my mother to live with us you told her that she was coming as a maid, not as your wife"

"You're taking sides with your mother," he replied furiously, "without knowing all the facts. I'm sorry for bringing you to live with your brothers and me. It would have been better if I had not reconciled with your mother and had left you with her, even if you had starved to death. I would have peace now, not having to live in this hell around you."

"I would've had a better life with my mother since life with you has been hell," I retorted, lifting my voice. "I don't know if you sought custody of me because you care about me or because you just needed a maid for the house!" At this point I was almost screaming.

My father came very close to me again, pointed his finger very close to my nose and said, "I don't even think that you're my daughter. A daughter of mine would not talk to me like that. Do you know what? You had better pack and go back to school because I don't want to see you and I don't want to have you here. I'm going to disown you."

My mother jumped between my father and me. I think that if she had not done this, my father would have hit me very hard. He was more furious than I had ever seen him before. Eneida was crying and screaming while my two brothers stood quietly and motionless to the side. My mother was having trouble hiding her anger too, but she tried to be sweet and said, "Go and pack, I think it is better if you return to college. Things could get out of hand here."

I left and went to talk to my aunt, to tell her about all that had transpired.

"You shouldn't have talked to your parents like that," Aunt Teco said with some reproach in her voice. "I've had many bad moments with my father and no matter what he said or did I never lifted my voice to him. I think that it is best that you leave and return to college before Easter."

"I have already been thinking about doing that," I replied dejectedly. "I can't handle this situation any more."

Unfortunately, I now had to ask my father for money to pay for the boat and bus fare. But now he did not want me to go and ordered, "You have to stay here until the holidays are finished and your school starts again. What are you going to do in Chiquimula? The school is closed and there will be no students around."

I had to think of something. If I had to stay in Livingston, it would mean one more week of hell. I would surely die.

"Papá, I'm behind in my studies and I need some peace and quiet to study."

He finally relented, gave me money for the trip, and took me to the pier at five o'clock that very next morning.

On the way he started berating me again, *"Caramba!* You just come here to disrupt our peace and now you go back as if you had done nothing. Yes, go back. You're better off in Chiquimula and we're better off without you here in Livingston."

I was crying when I left Livingston. I did not get a hug from my mother, nothing unusual about that, but I didn't get one from my father either. He simply turned his back and did not even wave good-bye. I cried during the hour and half on the boat and I continued crying during the four hours on the bus back to Chiquimula. I was hurting, for I loved both of my parents so much.

In January of 1962, at the start of my second year at INSO, I changed boarding houses and I was now living with Doña Rome and was much happier there. I was more involved than ever in all of the school committees and in the band as a majorette. There were school dances to organize, socials, and excursions—I practically lived at the school. I was thirteen and semi–independent on a scholarship. On short holidays and on many weekends I went with Marta Estela to her family's hacienda or to the homes and farms of a few of the other girls. There was also my boyfriend, Canche, whom I was now madly in love with. There were no really big worries; I had only visions of a good career in the future and eventual marriage to my love. In addition, this was my best year as a student. Life was a blast.

For the rest of the 1962 school term my father did not come and visit me or even communicate with me in any manner. I have to admit that this did not bother me too much because I was so busy in school.

In July of 1962 Aunt Teco came to Chiquimula to visit her boyfriend and, as always, she gave me the latest news (gossip) from Livingston and her news this time was really big. The inevitable had happened—my parents separated again in July of 1962 and my mother was now living with her and her father in Livingston. I thought that it was very insensitive that nobody, including my parents or brothers, notified me about this. But the really, really big news was that my mother was pregnant.

When the end of October arrived and school was finished for the 1962 term I did not want to go home. I wanted the happiness that I was enjoying at school and at Doña Rome's house to continue. I did not know what I was going to do. It was depressing to think about returning to Livingston: back to arguments and fights.

What is going to happen to me there? My parents are separated and I will be living with my father and brothers being their cook and maid again, just as I was in Ipala two years ago.

I even asked Doña Rome to hire me to work in her grocery store over the holidays. She wanted to hire me since she needed a reliable person to help her. I was a minor, however, so she and I needed my father's approval. She wrote to my father regarding this matter and received back a curt one–sentence telegram: PUT GABRIELA ON A BUS AND SEND HER HOME.

When I arrived in Puerto Barrios toward the beginning of November of 1962, close to my fourteenth birthday, my father was not waiting for me at the pier. However, the horrible experiences in Puerto Barrios had taught me a lesson and I had prepared myself. I made my own arrangements for transportation and I had money. Aunt Teco had told me in one of her letters that my father had bought a house in Campoamor, a hamlet about a kilometer and a half from Livingston. Campoamor was a neighborhood where mostly Garífuna–speaking black people lived and it was also a place where one could buy a very cheap house. My father bought a house with a big yard, which he used as a vegetable garden. He called his house *mi rancho* (my farm).

Aunt Teco was waiting for me at the pier in Livingston and took me home with her. On the way to her house she explained to me, "Your mother wants you to stay with her. Her baby is due at the end of November and she is going to need a lot of help. I'm traveling to Chiquimula to marry my fiancé and I can't stay to help her."

I stayed at my aunt's house with my mother. My father did not appear until two days later, very upset because of my decision to stay with my mother. It was another argument, almost as big as the one we had the previous April.

"Papá, I don't want to live with you all the time. I know you will use me the same way you have always used me; to cook, clean, wash clothes and iron. I want to spend some time with you and with my brothers and sister and I want to help around the house, I just don't want to become a full–time maid."

I saw in my father's face that he was really getting worked up, but I continued, "Papá, with my mother I can make money, the money I need, the money you won't give to me. Remember the watch you had promised to buy me since I was in the fourth grade? Well, every year you think of some excuse not to buy it. I am the only girl in the school without a watch."

"You're so ungrateful," he fumed, "I'm going to take you out of my will and give your portion to your brothers."

This was another one of his threats when he was really angry with me.

He never agreed to what I had proposed, but I did what I wanted to do anyway and stayed with my mother. I had to work with my mother to earn the money I needed for school. I helped her with her sewing, with the house chores and with the baby once it was born. With my mother I was able to get new clothing, shoes and other things that young girls like to have—deodorant, cosmetics, nylons and spending money. These things I would have never acquired if I had stayed with my father. I kept my promise, however, and did all the chores at his house two days a week.

My father was so angry with me that he started announcing around town that I was an ungrateful daughter because I had de-cided to live with my mother who was "a woman who is pregnant with her lover's child while I'm slaving away to support Gabriela in school," as he put it. "My daughter isn't even grateful for all the help and support I've given her with her schooling."

When I heard this I became sick and I went around town telling everyone the truth: "the government is paying for my expenses at school, not my father. He's angry at me because he does not want me to have any contact with my mother."

When my father heard about my truth-telling activities around town there was a huge explosion. "Why do you have to go around with your big mouth, blabbing nonsense?" he shouted. "You should honour your father, just as the Bible says."

"Why do you go around telling people that you're putting me through school when I'm on a scholarship?" I replied coolly.

"I should disown you!" He thundered. "You have no respect for your father. You're a disgrace and an awful daughter; God should send down lightning and cut you in half."

This particular statement about God sending down punishment was always his ultimate threat. Nevertheless, lightning or no lightning from God, I could never put up with his telling stories about me or about my mother. He was not going to gain respect in the community at my expense. It is true, I had a big mouth, but I felt that I had no other means to cope with his lying, manipulative behaviour and cheap ways.

When I went to Campoamor to help my father with the cooking and cleaning my brothers did not talk to me or show me any kindness—but they ate the food I cooked, and wore the clothes I washed and ironed. Not once did they ever thank me. Every time I went to the house to do the housework they treated me as if I were the maid, and my father did nothing to defend me or to correct the situation. Nothing was more valuable to him than his sons. He called them his left and right arms.

During the two and a half months from November of 1962 to mid-January of 1963 I never saw my brothers coming to visit my mother. I brought Eneida to visit her a few times behind my father's back. Eventually, he found out about this and threatened to take me, his own fourteen-year old daughter, to court over this issue. At the end of November he took Eneida back to San Pedro Pinula and left her with one of my older cousins. I concluded that he did this to prevent me from bringing her to visit our mother.

My sister, Norma Noemí (Naomi in English), was born around nine o'clock in the evening on the twenty-seventh of November 1962 and surprisingly, my mother allowed me to be present and to assist the midwife during the birth. This was surprising because she had never discussed anything about sex, the menstrual cycle, or the reproductive process with me during my pre-adolescence and afterwards.

After Noemí's birth my father immediately broadcast all over town that she was not his child. He never claimed custody as he had done with the rest of us. He would not have been able to take care of her even if he had wanted custody. He could not even take proper care of Eneida, who was now five.

I then did something really cheeky. I was able to find my father's identity card (*Cédula de Vencindad*), took it to the Municipal Building in Livingston and registered the baby with my father's surname (Folgar). I got away with this by telling the registrar that my father was busy and he had sent me. I did not tell my father that I had done this, but somehow he found out about it before I had left Livingston to return to school. I was expecting the worst from him but to my surprise, he was not particularly angry with me. I could never predict his reactions. He and I both knew that he had a window of forty days to renounce his fatherhood and remove his name from the child, but he never did. We were now five children in total: Carlos Aníbal, the oldest; Jesus Carmelino; Piedad Eneida; Norma Noemí (Mimí) and I, Gabriela Antonia.

Aside from the problems with my father and brothers, something I always anticipated and was prepared for, the holidays in Livingston that year turned out to be a happy time. Since I was living with my mother I was able to celebrate Christmas for the first time in my life. We had never celebrated Christmas before in the house because my father, who believed in God but was not a regular churchgoer, considered Christmas a waste of time and in particular, a waste of money. I was very busy helping my mother. I also had enough time to do many activities with my friends and attend some of the dances in the town.

My mother and I worked very hard sewing dresses. When the time came for me to return to school in January for the 1963 term I had many new dresses, shoes, cosmetics, a second school uniform and enough money for my transportation.

When I went to Campoamor to tell my father that I was planning to return to Chiquimula, he said sarcastically, "Ah! I bet you're just coming now to ask for money to return to school?" "No, I came to say good-bye, I already have enough money to return to school. I made money while helping my mother with her sewing," I replied proudly. My father appeared to be very surprised when he heard my answer.

I do not know what stories my father had told my brothers about me, but they did not even say goodbye to me. As I was going out the door one of them said, "Why don't you go once and for all and when you come back again from Chiquimula… just go to that mother of yours and never come back to this house."

I thought that my father would say something on my behalf. But on the contrary, he turned, locked his gaze on me, placed his right arm across his chest, and swept his left arm toward my brothers in a gesture of innocence and vindication saying, "Don't you see what you've done? Even your brothers have seen the injustice done to me. That's why they don't want you around. They're the ones who stay at my side; they're the ones who help me with the little farm and keep me company." Turning toward me and poking his finger at me, he added angrily, "You, on the other hand, have been brainwashed by your mother."

Early in the school year in 1963 my father traveled several times to visit me in Chiquimula to see if I was still dating Canche. On one of these visits he told me, "I've made up my mind, next year I'm going to take you out of this school and send you back to Jalapa to live with my sister Chus."

My father's decisions always came as a surprise, and as frequently was the case, his thinking made no logical sense to me. The thought of leaving my school and good life in Chiquimula terrified me, but it was not yet time to panic. I still had almost ten months to think about a way to convince him to let me stay. My sewing skills had greatly improved, thanks to my mother's teaching over the school holidays, and I put those skills to work making more money than ever from my classmates. I did not need to ask my father for money and I told him so. However, for whatever reason, he decided to send me a certified letter once a month with some cash in it. I kept up my correspondence with Aunt Teco and she kept me informed about the situation between my father and mother.

I was also able to write my mother quite often now that my father could no longer control her mail. She wrote to me mostly about her sewing business and about my baby sister, but nothing about her troubles with my father, probably not to worry me. Whenever possible she would send me dresses, perfume and money. My aunt also told me in one of her letters that my mother was planning to leave Livingston because she could no longer tolerate my father's constant harassment, criticism, put–downs and the embarrassment from the nasty rumours that he was spreading around town.

During the 1963 school term my best friend, Marta Estella, was no longer at INSO and the trips to her farm ended, but everything else remained the same. I was more active than ever in the school. My studies were going great and I was still in the school band, although I was now playing the trumpet instead of twirling a baton as a majorette.

I was now travelling to Livingston to visit my mother and my aunt almost every major school holiday. By this time I knew how to travel back and forth between Livingston and Chiquimula and I had my own money to supplement the expenses. In addition, my mother and my aunt were helping me with money and my father was now sending me a little spending money, in spite of his anger with me.

On one of the trips to Livingston I made a comment to Aunt Teco, "My father is sending me enough money to go to Livingston for short holidays, something he has never done before."

She started laughing and said, "Your father is not happy with your dating that boy from Ipala. He would rather pay and have you spend your short or long holidays here in Livingston rather than your staying in Chiquimula spending time with your boyfriend. I don't know if you know it or not but your father would love for you to date one of his colleagues here in Livingston, a man who is single and who approached your father asking to be a possible suitor for you."

"How do you know that?" I inquired.

"I'm a friend of the teacher your father likes for you," she continued, "and actually he's very nice. He told me that he would wait until you graduate from college so you can marry him."

At first, I thought my aunt was joking with me until one evening in Livingston my father took me to a dance. Before we reached the dance he gave me instructions: "There will be a man at the dance, actually a teacher at the school, who would be a good person for you to marry. I would like for you to dance with no one else tonight."

As soon as we were in the dance hall he introduced me to the teacher and left me alone with him. We danced and conversed a little and at one point I told him that I had a boyfriend in Chiquimula.

My father must had been listening to the conversation and he suddenly butted in, "She's not dating anyone. She only met a boy at school who has nothing to offer her for her future."

"But Papá," I answered, "I do have a boyfriend at school and I like him very much."

Actually, I found this teacher to be very nice but I had no interest in him and he showed little interest in me, especially after I said that I had a boyfriend. Later, after the dance, my father and I had a small conversation about what had happened.

"I know what's best for you, and if you marry a man I disapproved of, I will never help you if things don't work out. On the other hand, if you marry someone I approved of, I will be by your side at any moment, even if the marriage doesn't work."

So, if I were now to date someone my father approves of, my young age is not an obstacle. How interesting.

My father still had not learned that his manipulative ways were not working with me. I could never understand why he was not able just to be content and proud with my successes, why he always had to meddle when things were going well. After this conversation I rehearsed my vows: "I will never give up resisting; I will never abandon my ambitions just to please him; I will maintain as much independence as possible over my own destiny.

In May of 1963 I started to suffer some pain on the right side of my abdominal area. Sometimes it felt as if my leg would cave in and I was not able to walk. In June of 1963 I became very ill and was constantly throwing up. I had very high fever and the abdominal pain on my right side had intensified to an unbearable degree. Doña Rome took me to the hospital and the staff told her that they could not do anything for me. They suspected that my appendix had ruptured and that it was too late to treat me in Chiquimula because the hospital was not fully equipped to perform the procedure.

Doña Rome summoned my father by telegram. When he arrived she told him what the doctors suspected. My father did not check my temperature or pay attention to my complaints of stomach pain or to the rest of the symptoms. When he saw me throwing up he became alarmed and started questioning Doña Rome about my daily routines and life, constantly alluding to the possibilities that I was sexually active.

I was half-conscious when he asked me, "Tell me the truth. Did you have sex with your boyfriend? Are you pregnant?"

I did not answer. I was in a lot of pain, and was feeling a true and deep rage toward my father. I was in danger of dying and he was more concerned about my being pregnant.

He took me back to the hospital and the doctor told him that if he did not take me to Guatemala City immediately, I would die within hours. The doctor then gave me an injection to put me to sleep.

We boarded an express mini–bus to Guatemala City. Dr. Labbé was my father's friend and ex–school classmate, the only doctor he would trust in handling this delicate matter. My father told Doctor Labbé to be honest with him and tell him what exactly was wrong with me. I was in and out of consciousness, but I heard Dr. Labbé tell my father that my appendix had ruptured and that an operation had to be performed immediately. Even after hearing this my father had the nerve to ask him, "Is my daughter a virgin? I need to know if she had preserved her purity since she has been going out with a no–good guy."

"Carmelino, are you nuts? This is not the time to ask questions like that." Dr. Labbé replied with incredulity in his voice. "What kind of a heart do you have? Your daughter is deathly ill and you have not even asked me if she is going to live or die. What on earth has happened to you? However, the answer is yes, she is a virgin, but you should be concerned about her medical situation. It is very serious. She can't go to a general hospital. She must be treated in a private hospital where she can have the proper care or she'll die."

My father, however, did not give up and insisted that he see for himself if I were a virgin or not. He watched everything when Dr. Labbé examined me to see if my hymen was broken. I assumed that he did not even trust Dr. Labbé in this matter. I was too sick to be embarrassed.

The private hospital was expensive and my father paid for everything. "I have written down all of the expenses and I expect that when you start working you will pay me back. I wouldn't do this if you were like your brothers. They care about me, but you care only about your mother. I can't understand how you can prefer your mother to your father, knowing that she was the one who destroyed our family and she is the cause of all of you growing up without a mother. Don't you understand that she is an adulterous woman?"

I was totally disgusted and I answered, "Papá, I can't believe that you are saying these things to your fourteen–year–old daughter, especially at this time when I'm so sick. At times I feel ashamed to be your daughter."

❦

My recuperation was long and slow. I missed a lot of school

and my marks dropped significantly. By the end of the school year in October of 1963 I already knew that my father had made his final decision to send me to Jalapa. Canche knew it too. We were devastated. After my father had told me about his decision I became more and more stressed as the end of the school year approached. I failed a subject for the first time and that meant that I had to study and prepare myself during the school holidays so that I could rewrite the test in the second week of January. I would have to pass this exam to be allowed to register at the school in Jalapa.

I begged my father not to send me to Jalapa. Doña Rome also spoke on my behalf telling him how unfair his decision was to me. She told him that I was a good child and that he had nothing to fear about my conduct in relation to Canche. My aunt, my friends, and even my teachers also spoke to him about this, but he was not going to listen to anyone; his decision had been made.

I was suspecting at the time that there was more behind this determination to force me out of my school than his concerns about Canche. I was convinced that he wanted to put a barrier between my mother and me. He knew that it would be impossible for me to travel to Livingston from Jalapa as often as I had been doing for the past three years. Also, I found out that he was having more trouble than ever taking care of my sister Eneida, who was now five years old, and moving me back to Jalapa to live with Aunt Chus certainly would have solved that problem, as it had done once before. At any rate, his desire to move me from Chiquimula solely out of concern for my welfare was totally out of character, especially since I would lose my scholarship and he would have to pay for all of my school expenses.

For the third consecutive year, at the end of October of 1963, I returned to Livingston for the school holidays. My father was still living in Campoamor with my brothers, and my mother was living in a rented house in Livingston. I walked all the way to my father's house once or twice a week to cook, clean and do laundry as I had done the previous year. There was little communication and hardly any arguments. The atmosphere was very cold and I believe our relationship had never been more strained. It was al-

most as if we both knew that we had reached an impasse and that
there would be no benefit to each of us to continue arguing.
Most of the time I stayed with my mother, sewing and taking care
of my little sister Mimí. I distracted myself from my sadness by
socializing with friends, going to dances, spending a lot of time
with Aunt Teco and attending the Christmas and New Year's
events.

I returned to Chiquimula a few days after the New Year to
take the make–up exam for the course I had failed. This time, I
had lots of new clothes, make up and feminine essentials, enough
for the whole school year. And I had considerable money in my
pocket, everything earned by helping my mother sew.

I knew that more difficulties, struggles and fights were on the
way and the good times at school would be suspended for a while
or might be gone forever. There might be delays and many more
bumps on the road, but I was determined to be my own person. I
was older now, and had developed educational, career, and personal goals. I could not surrender and return to the life of menial
servitude that I had lived through prior to going to Chiquimula.
The three years at INSO had opened my eyes to the world and
proved to me that I was capable of being independent and fulfilling my goals. To this very day, I still look back to my years at
INSO in Chiquimula with nostalgia. They were the most wonderful
years of my childhood and adolescence.

INIVO (the boys' school) in Chiquimula.

Chapter 5
Temporary Defeat

Hay derrotas que tienen más dignidad que la misma victoria.
There are some defeats, which have more dignity than a similar victory.
–Jorge Luis Borges–

When I arrived in Chiquimula in January of 1964 to write the make-up exam, Canche was there. He had traveled from Ipala to see me. This was our opportunity to say goodbye to each other, for my father was still firm in his decision to take me away from my school. I felt as if it were the end of my life. Canche and I walked together a long way through the town, talking, crying, trying to figure out a way for me to stay in Chiquimula. At the end of the walk we stopped at the big church on the main square and prayed. All appeared hopeless. He and I were crying in the church. We swore to each other that even if my father were to send me to another city we would continue to write and wait for each other until the day came when nothing and no one would be able to separate us again.

After writing the exam I took the bus to Ipala to visit my uncles. My father knew this and he was in agreement with my plan. He liked my mother's brothers very much. Canche was on the bus with me. In Ipala we had to see each other behind my uncles' backs because my father had already told them to keep a close eye on me and to not allow Canche and me to have contact.

My failing a subject in the third year meant that I had lost my scholarship and that placed me in the situation where I would have to write another test in order to get it reinstated. My father refused to take me to Jalapa to re-apply and to re-write the test. As a schoolteacher he could have used his privilege to apply for more funding on my behalf, had he wanted to. He knew that I would have qualified, but once more, the scholarship would have been assigned to the town of Chiquimula. Without a scholarship, there was absolutely no possibility to remain at INSO. I had to go to Jalapa if I wished to stay in school. I was bending a little and I would have gone to Jalapa with no more argument if I could have lived in a student boarding house, but this would have cost my father more money than if I stayed with my Aunt Chus. He said that he was not prepared to spend any more on my education. And yet, he was willing to throw away scholarship money from the government. I guess he still thought educating girls was a waste, even though I was the only one of his children who was performing well in school.

Every time I thought about living with Aunt Chus I became ill. I was sure that she had not changed and was as mean as ever. I also heard some other disturbing news: Don Licho, my grand-mother's perverted husband, was receiving medical treatment in Jalapa and when he was in town he stayed at Aunt Chus' home. I was not prepared to fend off his advances or listen to his dirty talk any more. It would have been a waste of time to tell my fa-ther about my problems with Don Licho again.

On the twentieth of January I left Chiquimula for San Pedro Pinula to stay at my grandmother's house for a few days. I was very sad and very angry with my father. I thought that he was being very cruel to me. I started to plan how to continue my schooling without having to go and live with Aunt Chus. I knew that I was going to have a big battle with my father, but I thought I would try anything to convince him to send me back to Chi-quimula. I became rebellious, stubborn and decided not to go to Jalapa and register at the school as my father had instructed me to do. Instead, I sent letters to my mother and to Aunt Teresa ask-ing if I could come and live with either one of them, thinking that I could work one year with my mother, helping her with her sewing, save my money and study the following year. I could also help Doña Rome in her store. If this plan worked, I could continue doing this until I finished my schooling and would not need the help from my father. Aunt Teco replied to my letter:

Dear Gabriela,

I am sorry to inform you that your mother left Livingston over a week ago with very little warning. Nobody here has any idea where she has gone. All I know is that she has been complaining that your father has been making life miserable for her with his accusations and degradations of her name and she had been talking about just disappearing to a place where nobody will find her. When your mother disappeared, Feliciano Milian, her rumored boyfriend, disappeared from the town at the same time.

Love from your aunt.

Aunt Teco's letter was written in a business style, quite unlike most of her letters, and she did not express any personal opinions; she knew that I would draw the obvious conclusions.

Now, I felt totally lost. My mother was gone from my life again. There would no longer be an opportunity to stay with her and earn money. My father was more hostile than ever toward me. My scholarship was gone and my schooling was in jeopardy. My boyfriend was gone for now and all of my girlfriends and supports were far away. Everything, everything I had been working for and had accomplished the past three years had vanished in less than two weeks—total ruin. It was impossible to believe that this could have happened. Why? I had so much rage toward my father now that the schooling issue did not matter any more. I decided not to go to Jalapa right away and wait in San Pedro Pinula until my father would give in and allow me to go back to Chiquimula. I was still certain that he would cave in.

I still had some of the money left, the money I had earned while helping my mother with her sewing, but now I had to save it. I was not sure how long I was going to stay in San Pedro Pinula. I also wanted to have some money to call Canche by radio and to go out and have some fun with my cousins. Besides, the town's *fiesta* was approaching and that meant dancing.

❧

While I was waiting for my father's answer I really had nothing to do in San Pedro Pinula except to make it a holiday. I was living in my father's section of my grandmother's house and I visited my aunts from my mother's side of the family, who lived in a small settlement called El Pinalito (small pine forest), as often as possible. This settlement is only two kilometers from San Pedro Pinula. When we were living in San Pedro Pinula as a family, my mother and I visited these relatives quite often. My father never liked these ladies and he never pretended that he did. Every time they came to visit us a fight broke out between my father and mother after they had left. My father said that these relatives were people who only visited us to take advantage of my mother. When they came to visit us my mother did not even offer them a cup of coffee in order not to make my father upset. However, every time we visited them they made us feel at home. They invited us to stay for dinner and they played with us children. When it was time to return home they customarily gave us fruits, vegetables, baked goods and sugar cane candy to take with us. My mother helped them with some mending or remodeling of clothing for free. I guess that is what my father hated, but who really knows, he was just very strange in that way. Four years earlier in Ipala, when my father was granted custody of all the children, my mother's words were: "Don't ever lose contact with your aunts and your cousins who live in El Pinalito." I found them to be as friendly as they had been four years earlier.

I was again having problems with Don Licho and this was another reason to absent myself as much as possible from my grandmother's house. He tried to approach me many times and made gestures that he was going to expose himself to me. But now I made it more difficult for him to get near to me. I always had a friend or a cousin with me. Also, I seldom stayed in the house because I was older and more socially active. I was always at some other relative's house, visiting people or talking to friends in the park or plaza.

When I spent the day in El Pinalito I sometimes helped my aunts with their grocery store and sometimes I sat outside under a shade tree by the well to do my needlepoint. One day a man from San Pedro came to the store to buy cigarettes. I was sitting on a stool across from him when my aunt gave him the cigarettes and took his money. As he was leaving my aunt gazed at him with intensely focused eyes until he was completely on his way down the road.

"I wonder if the cigarettes brought him here or something else," she whispered with a concerned look on her face, "I do not like this man. He was staring at you."

I did not perceive anything strange and I did not see what my aunt had seen.

"I don't like the way he looked at you," she continued, "and I wonder why in the world he would come to buy cigarettes at this little store when he could have bought them in San Pedro Pinula for less money?"

Time was now pressing to register in school but I was still determined to get my way. Sometime in the latter half of January I sent my father a letter stating that I was not going to register at the college in Jalapa and live with Aunt Chus, and if this were to lead to the end of my schooling, that would be okay with me. I thought that my hard line, reluctance and pleading would finally make him bend and he would agree to send me back to Chiquimula. But there was no reply to this letter. I sent him another letter and I promised him that if he would send me to Chiquimula, I would never speak to Canche again. This proposal did not work either. Finally, I had to accept that I was defeated and decided to register at the college in Jalapa after the feast (*féria*) in San Pedro Pinula at the beginning of February. I sent my father a telegram asking him for the money I needed to cover the expenses for uniforms, books, transportation and registration.

In addition to visiting my aunts in El Pinalito, I kept busy by going bicycle riding. I borrowed a bicycle from one of my male cousins. This activity created quite a sensation in San Pedro because no girl had ever ridden a bicycle in public before my arrival in 1964, and no girl had dared to venture in public wearing pants. There were two old maiden sisters, distant aunts living right behind the church, who made the sign of the cross every time they saw me wearing pants, or shorts, or riding the bicycle. Even my uncles criticized me for wearing pants. When I left San Pedro in November of 1959 I was a young schoolgirl just having turned eleven, and now I had become a fifteen–year–old, physically well–developed young lady possessing very citified ways of conducting myself. I was good food for all of the gossips in the town. I have to admit, however, that I took some pleasure in making the gossips wag their tongues.

My other daily activities consisted of swimming with my friends, reading, writing letters, telegramming and two-way radioing my love in Chiquimula. When I went swimming I walked to the river wearing shorts over my bathing suit—another scandal for the town's gossips.

The major public event in San Pedro at this time was the *féria* or *fiesta* of the town, *La Candelaria* (the Feast of Presentation of Jesus in the Temple, or Candlemas as the church day is sometimes called in English) on the second of February. The activities and entertainment for the feast consisted of church services, an outdoor religious procession, carnival rides, bull riding (*jaripeo*) and the crowning of the queen of the fiesta. However, the activities I was most interested in were the two town dances, the *sarabanda* and the formal social dance, *el baile social* where men wore suits or tuxedos and ladies wore evening gowns.

The *sarabanda* was an informal dance open to all. Although there was no admission fee, it was a big money maker for the *féria* committee because, as one of my cousins put it, "Girls paid with a smile and boys paid to dance with the smiling girls." Liquor was not sold at the *sarabanda*. This was to make sure it was suitable for minors. When people wanted to drink or eat anything they went out to the places that sold food or liquor. However, some men had their drinks prior to coming to the dance and there was nothing one could do to stop this practice.

The band was located at the south end of the salon. Benches were placed against the walls all around the salon and the girls sat and waited on these benches for the boys to come and ask them to dance. On the north side of the salon stood two men opposite to each other, each holding one end of a rope stretching the width of the salon. When the band played the two men passed the rope over the heads of the first dancing couple and the male was requested to pay, then the rope went over the second couple and so on. When the male of the last couple, the couple dancing closest to the band, had paid the fee the band stopped playing. Each dance cost five or ten cents, the amount depending on the reputation of the band.

Since I had been away from San Pedro for almost four years I had never attended a *sarabanda,* and therefore had to be brought up to date on the local customs. One of my cousins obligingly instructed me, "Girls are expected to dance with any boy who asks them. It is very bad etiquette to refuse a dance. If someone asks you to dance and you say no, he can and probably will embarrass you on the dance floor. I know some girls who came to the *sarabanda* and refused to dance with a boy. After that, whenever they came to the event nobody asked them to dance."

The place was packed. Lots of boys approached me all at once, asking me to dance. Doing what I was instructed, I did not refuse one dance. I had to assign different turns to each of the boys. I believe I always had good dancing skills and probably that was the reason for my popularity. After I had been dancing for a long time, I finally needed some rest. While I was resting many boys continued to come to ask me to dance and I had to tell them, "Come back later and I'll dance with you."

The boys left and immediately a pest named Jorge Cárcamo came to where I was sitting and politely asked, "Can we dance the next song?" He had been following me around town for days and was the person who came to buy cigarettes in El Pinalito.

"No, thank you, I am very tired," I answered with a sigh.

He repeated his request, "Please, can I have only this one?"

My answer was the same, "No, thank you, I am very tired." I

wanted to tell him that I did not dance with drunks. He smelled of alcohol and showed every sign that he had been drinking heavily. At that moment, another boy came to ask me to dance and I got up to dance with him, leaving the obnoxious pest standing on the dance floor. I could see on his face that he wanted to make me disappear.

The boy with whom I was dancing asked me, "Why didn't you dance with him? He likes you."

"I don't like to dance with drunks." I answered with a look of disgust on my face. "Besides, I was watching him and he doesn't even know how to dance."

This boy dutifully reminded me of the rules with a hint of warning, "Refusing a dance is not right. *For your own sake* you'd better not do that again. You have to dance with everyone who asks you."

Well, these customs did not conform to my independent way of thinking. I believed that I had the freedom to dance with whomever I wished and pleased. I noticed that my friends and cousins were leaving and I asked the boy to walk me to the front entrance where I caught up with them. When we were leaving the salon the creepy pest was standing right by the door. I could see in his eyes that he was very angry and very drunk. As we were proceeding out the door he started spitting ugly and drunken remarks.

"You think you're something big, don't you? You're lucky I didn't spit in your face for embarrassing me on the dance floor. You're lucky there were so many people, otherwise…" While he was spewing these insults my cousins and I started walking faster and faster to get away from him.

On the way back home one cousin lambasted me for not dancing with the drunk. "Jorge is one of the most popular men in San Pedro Pinula. A lot of girls would die to have him ask them to dance. We left because we don't want a scandal."

Then another cousin continued the chastisement, "We told you that if we go to this dance you have to dance with all the men who ask you. You've ruined the party for us and we are no longer going to go with you again."

And they all kept their word.

After the *féria* there was still no answer from my father. I waited and waited and then March arrived. Now it was getting very late for me to register for the 1964 school term. I was so desperate that I decided to use the money that I had saved from my sewing in Livingston to travel to Jalapa with the intention of finding a job to pay for my schooling. I was thinking that I could study in the evening and work in the daytime after school.

I took a bus to Jalapa to look for work, but I did not find a job. Who I did find in that town though was my Aunt Connie, my mother's cousin, who was now married and had moved to Jalapa from El Pinalito. She was willing to take me in as a boarder while I attended school, and she would charge me only half of what I was paying at Doña Rome's boarding house. She promised that she would write to my father. She encouraged me to register at school and stay with her in the meantime to avoid getting more behind in my classes. I knew my father was not very fond of this woman, but he would surely agree with the proposition since it was such a good price. I could accept being in Jalapa if I did not have to live with Aunt Chus. I wrote to my father and presented Aunt Connie's proposal to him. He rejected the idea without explanation.

Now I knew that I had no more options and that I would have to give Aunt Chus another try. I returned to San Pedro Pinula to gather my belongings. Easter was coming and school would soon be out; so, I decided to stay in San Pedro until the Easter holiday had ended. Now, there were only six more days to go before Holy Week was to begin.

Waiting In San Pedro Pinula

I am fifteen, on the front row–extreme left, with my cousins in February of 1964, at the time of the town's fiesta (La Candalaria). The photo was taken on the plaza close to my grandmother's house and was the last photo of me for over three years.

Part II

A Dark Cloud Descends

Good Friday In Guatemala

The afternoon procession with the statues of Christ and the saints. The ladies are wearing madrileñas. Photos were taken in Guatemala City, 2005.

Chapter 6
Good Friday: My Calvary

Throughout history, men have dominated women. This is not because men are more intelligent; not because of their superior sense of logic; and not because of their more highly developed inventive capabilities. It is solely due to their greater physical strength."
–Bertrand Russell (Lord Russell)–

In Guatemala, Lent, Holy Week and Easter are taken very seriously: people fast and in the church the statues of Jesus, his mother Mary, and the saints are covered with purple cloth. School is closed for the complete week before Easter Sunday and the church fills up almost every day. The students who are studying in colleges, away from home, return to spend time with their families. The majority of the stores close, especially on Maundy Thursday and Good Friday. My mother would not touch her sewing machine from the day after Palm Sunday until the Day Of The Resurrection—Easter Sunday.

In San Pedro Pinula, as in many other towns and cities in Guatemala, the Catholic faithful (almost the whole town) re-create every step of Jesus' suffering on his way to Calvary. Volunteers dress up as Pontius Pilate, Jesus' apostles, Simon of Cyrene, and as many of the other biblical characters in the re-enactment of the life of Jesus from Palm Sunday to his capture and Passion on Good Friday. People who had left the town for other places return to San Pedro Pinula for this holiday. My fa-

ther was one of these. He arrived in San Pedro on the day after
school had finished. However, he did not stay for Easter. He left
on Maundy Thursday to return to Livingston.

Good Friday is the busiest day during Holy Week. There are
two processions: one in the morning and one in the evening. Almost the entire town goes to both processions. I told my aunts in
El Pinalito that I was going to town for the procession and after
that I was going to stay at my grandmother's house. I lied to them
when I said that I had my father's permission to go to the funeral
procession in the evening with my cousins.

Early on Good Friday morning I left El Pinalito for San Pedro
Pinula by bus. Around nine o'clock I went to church with my
cousins and friends. This was for the morning procession for

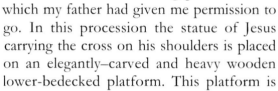

which my father had given me permission to
go. In this procession the statue of Jesus
carrying the cross on his shoulders is placed
on an elegantly–carved and heavy wooden
lower-bedecked platform. This platform is
litted up and carried on the shoulders of fifty or more *penitents*.
The procession leaves the church around ten o'clock in the
morning and winds its way through the main streets of the town.
The procession takes four hours and reenacts the steps Jesus
took on his way to Calvary and to death. It is called, *La Passion de
Cristo*.

Coloured sawdust mosaics are crafted on the ground in the
middle of the street. The men and women who are carrying the
heavy platforms walk over the sawdust patterns during the procession. In order to be a penitent one has to buy a stamp with the
picture of the saint whom one wishes to represent in the procession. Men usually carry the platform with the statue of Jesus carrying the cross, and women carry the platform with the statues of
Mary or of the women weeping at the foot of the cross. The procession stops at twelve different stations—the Stations of the
Cross. These stations represent different events that occurred on
the road to Calvary such as when a woman cleaned Jesus' face
with a cloth. Altars, beautifully decorated with flowers and burning candles, are set up at these stations. Families book the privi-

lege of having an altar placed at the front of their houses almost a year in advance. The lay people accompanying the procession are dressed in their finest clothes. Ladies usually buy a new dress for that day or hire a seamstress to make their dresses. Men dress in their best suits and many wear black tuxedos.

This procession arrives back at the church around two o'clock in the afternoon. After returning to the church a reenactment of Christ's crucifixion takes place at three o'clock. The statue of Jesus is put on the cross and then it is taken down around four-thirty and placed in a glass coffin for the evening funeral procession.

In 1964 Good Friday fell on March twenty-seventh and on this particular year the procession started around five–thirty in the evening, as was customary. The procession left the church in company of practically the whole town, every one dressed in black. Many women wore black *madrileñas* (lace veils) to cover not only their heads but also their faces. The men wore black tuxedos or dark coloured suits. The majority of women and young girls carried lighted candles, and men wearing purple robes served as the pallbearers. My impression of the procession was that it was very sad, but at the same time very beautiful. The streets were very dark since the town still had no electricity. After everyone had lit their candles and the procession had started to move, I had the impression that I was part of a small walking village. The beauty of this scene is impossible to describe. At the front of the procession, two lines of pallbearers carried a glass coffin containing the statue of Christ. People lined the sidewalks pushing out into the street, leaving only the middle of the street free for the funeral procession. After the last statue of the saints had passed, the people along the sidewalks fell in behind the procession. It was a custom for daughters to accompany their mothers and for sons to be with their fathers. I no longer had a mother to be with, but I still wanted to be with my cousins and did not want to be left at home.

Some of my cousins were planning to go for the complete funeral procession and service. I told them that I had to return no later than twelve-thirty because I was afraid that one of my aunts, in particular Aunt Chus, would discover that I was not at home and she would surely tell my father. I knew Aunt Chus was going to be home by midnight or a little later. One of my cousins said she would accompany me to the house.

Before leaving, I locked the door to the room that I had been using as a bedroom, put pillows under the covers to simulate my body and jumped out the window leading to the courtyard. I left half of the window open and went to join the procession around six-thirty. *

I think it was about quarter to midnight when I decided that it was time to go back home. The procession was almost half way through its route and was no more then three blocks away from my grandmother's house. I asked one of my cousins to accompany me to the house, but she decided to stay with the rest of the group and I had to walk home by myself. I was not running, but walking very fast. Usually, in this small town at that time of night, one might see one or two people on the streets, but not on Good Friday. Most of the people were either in the procession or at home and the rest were waiting inside the church for the procession's return.

I was walking briskly, about a block away from my grandmother's house, when someone suddenly grabbed me from behind. I felt an arm wrapping tightly around my neck bending my head backwards. A frightening and threatening voice said, "Close your eyes, arrogant young lady. If you scream or cry, I will kill you."

I felt something poking into the middle of my back.

"I've a gun in your back," the man growled.

He rubbed the gun along the middle of my back up to my head and threatened, "I have other people with me and you can't escape. One move or one little noise and you're finished."

Everything happened so quickly. It was dark and I could not

---

* Windows in the old houses in Guatemala are usually made of wood. The two halves swing to the inside of the house and the two wooden panels have a latch in the middle.

see the faces of the other three men. They were wearing wide-brimmed country hats and their faces appeared only as shadows. They did not touch me.

Then one of them said, "Way to go, Jorge, we have to teach these college girls that they should not look down on us."

All I could do is look up at the night. It was clear and I could see a myriad of stars in the sky. I was able to move my eyes downward but I was still unable to recognize the faces of these men. I was frozen. I was shaking. I wanted to plead and ask him to let me go. I opened my mouth and was able only to feebly utter the word, "Please."

The man behind me immediately tightened his arm around my neck and told me, "Didn't I say to be quiet? If you cooperate, nothing will happen to you."

I heard another voice, maybe the same one I had heard before, saying, "Jorge, here is the horse."

With only the light provided by the moon and the stars I was able to make out that the horse was very tall and silver coloured. Although I heard one of the men pronouncing the name Jorge, I still was not associating any person with this name. Then the man behind me, the one gripping my neck, ordered, "Erasmo, give me the bandana!"

I knew who Erasmo was, for this is not a common name in Spanish, and in San Pedro Pinula there was only one person I knew who had that name—Jorge Cárcamo's older brother. Now everything fell into place. It was Jorge Cárcamo who was holding me, the creep who had been following and pestering me for the past two months. The gun was still pressed into my back. I was so terrified I could not scream. I thought that the man was going to shoot me right there.

The man released his hold on my body and I thought that this might be a chance to escape. However, he immediately threatened, "If you try to run, you will have six bullets in your body." I felt a cloth wrapping tightly around my eyes. I tried again to get a good look at the person called Erasmo before being blindfolded, but was unable to because his hat obscured his face.

The man behind me quickly lifted me up onto the horse and

ordered me to straddle it. He then grabbed my hands and placed
them onto the horn of the saddle He climbed onto the horse and
sat behind me, tightly wrapping his left arm around my waist and
placing his other arm around my body in order to grasp the reins.
He whistled loudly, almost in my ear. Then someone whipped the
horse on its rear. I felt my abductor's legs moving, spurring the
horse, and it took off in a gallop.

The streets of San Pedro Pinula were paved with cobblestones
and all I could hear was the steely sound of the horseshoes hitting
the pavement. I believe we passed the Municipal Building on the
north side of the plaza because I heard men talking. This place
was the usual hangout for men. My father used to say that men
went there to criticize women, to tell dirty jokes or scary tales and
to be away from their wives.

The corner where I was kidnapped–2004

I do not know how long we were riding, but I am sure that we
had already left the town when he whistled again and I immediately felt the horse slow down to a trot. All the while I had my
hands holding fast to the horn of the saddle. He took this opportunity to get his face close to my face; his lips came very close
to my ear and using a low tone of voice mixed with a sarcastic
mocking and humiliating laughter, he said,

"So... aren't you going to plead for mercy? Do you know what

I am going to do with you? Why don't you tell me how great you are now? This should teach you that men like me deserve respect and admiration. No woman has ever looked down on me and you won't be the first one to do it and get away with it. Do you know how many women in town would die for my attention and you dared to turn it down? Wouldn't you like to laugh at me now? Do you think that because you're a college girl you're worth more than a man? I'll teach you to look down on me!"

He kept spewing his awful words, non–stop. The strong smell of liquor mixed with cigarette on his breath was making me sick. When he sensed that I was on the verge of vomiting my situation worsened. He tightened his arm around my waist and snarled,

"Oh! Now you're trying to tell me that I make you sick. This role is going to be reversed as soon as I make you mine. Do you know why I'll become sick? Because I know all college girls like you spend their time fucking all the male students and I'm sure that by now you must have a very good collection of lovers. How many? Can you remember? Tell me! You're nothing but a slut…"

His horrible talk and denigrating comments just kept going on and on. He would stop for a few minutes and then start again with even more awful comments and accusations than the previous ones.

"…You're a disgrace to me. I haven't been able to get you off my mind since the day I first laid eyes on you. You made me look like a clown in front of my friends. I really don't like you. You're the most ugly girl I've ever seen. You whore, you fucking slut, I should spit in your face. The only reason I'm putting my reputation in jeopardy by taking you in the way I did is because I made a bet with my friends that you will be mine and nobody else's…"

I was wishing that he would stop this talk. I was beginning to think that he was not completely sane. But he did not stop; the nauseating and demented talk continued.

"…Part of the bet I made with my buddies was to find out if you're a virgin. If you're a virgin," he said, "I am going to lose a hundred Quetzals. If you are already a *mujer* (which simply means woman, but in Spanish colloquial speech is used to label a woman who is no longer a virgin), I will be quite a few hundred Quetzals richer because I am the only one who wagered that you already have your hole as big as a train tunnel."

I was now more terrified by his talk and threats than I was when he held the gun against my back at the beginning of my ordeal. I thought that he was going to kill me very soon.

As we rode I tried to recollect all the incidents that took place since I had arrived to San Pedro Pinula and the few encounters I had with this man, and I could not remember ever laughing at him. I remembered that there was an incident during the *féria* at the *sarabanda* dance when he had asked me to dance and I refused. I recalled the day when he had asked me to go to the movies with him and I politely told him that I was not able to because my father was very strict. This was the time that I informed him that I had a boyfriend in Chiquimula where I was going to school. I recalled the day when he was sitting by the arcade of Mr. Wong's store with his friends and when I passed by he said, "A young girl like you should not travel alone. Can I come with you to keep you company?"

I did not answer him for there was nothing to answer. This kind of talk is very common among men in Guatemala, especially when men see a girl by herself. In Spanish these remarks are called *piropos*. I always thought that *piropos* were nothing but stupid comments.

We continued on our way. I do not know how long we kept travelling. I remember passing through some places where I felt twigs or tree branches hitting my face or my head. I heard dogs barking far away. Twice I heard some people and a horse approaching us. He again reminded me not to make any sound. He grabbed my left hand and ordered me to take the horse's reins and to keep the right one on the horn of the saddle. Then he released his hand from my waist, "Remember, I will kill you in an instant if you make the slightest sound. There are people approaching and you had better not say anything."

The passers-by greeted us, "Good evening and God be with you."

My kidnapper replied, "Good evening and God be with you too." His tone of voice was not demented sounding and commanding. Instead, it sounded polite and gentleman–like. I was amazed how fast he could change his tone and demeanor.

Every time his face came close to mine I held my breath for as long as I could. I tried to keep my mind busy, thinking about God. I prayed to God for many things. I prayed to Him to soften this man's heart so that he would let me go. I prayed for someone to hunt for us, to find us, and then take me home. I prayed for the passers-by to be some people who would recognize me and do something to help me. I prayed to God to help me not to throw up, very afraid that this would get him very angry with me. I wanted to cry out, but I dared not. I felt tears welling up in my eyes. The bandana must have soaked up some of the tears because very little fluid was running down by my nose. I needed to sniffle and to blow my nose, but I was afraid to take my hands away from where he had placed them. Besides, I had nothing to wipe my nose with. I could not see, so helpless, so terrified.

Finally, he stopped talking and I was able to hear the crickets singing again, along with many other night creatures making their usual melodious sounds. I became keenly aware of all the sounds around me, such as the horse's steps hitting the ground with a muffled sound, which gave me the impression that the ground was covered with either grass or soft dirt. He whistled again. It was a different whistle each time. At this whistle the horse slowed down and started to walk. He leaned and placed his head close to mine, his lips close to my right ear. I felt the hot air coming from his nostrils. I smelt the alcohol on his breath. *Please don't open your mouth.* But he started vomiting up his putrid words again.

"You fucking little whore, you make me sick. I'm going to teach you a lesson you'll never forget. You're going to be sorry."

Then he calmed down a little and while pulling my right hand away from the horn of the saddle he said, "Relax, and give me your hand." He whistled again and it was a different whistle than the one before. The horse stopped.

In a fairly civilized tone he said, "Open your hand." I did as he ordered, putting up no resistance at all, for I did not want to upset him. His right hand held my right hand and he pulled it closer to his waist. I followed his commands so well that I even thought that my arm and hand were not part of my body. They felt as if they were nothing but pieces of cloth that he was able to move in whatever way he pleased. He placed my hand on an object on the right side of his waist saying, "This is my gun and it kills if I use it. Don't make me use it!"

He then maneuvered my hand down to his leg and he placed it close to somewhere below his knee, probably close to the top of his boot. He pressed my hand against his leg. Through his pants I could feel his boot. He rubbed my hand several times around this area asking me, "Do you feel something bumpy in there?"

I did not answer because he had told me many times not to talk. I was afraid to say "yes."

With a sterner voice he asked me again, "Answer me, yes or no, do you feel this little bump inside my boot?"

"Yes," I replied.

"Are you sure?" he demanded.

And again I responded, "Yes."

He continued talking in a low, slurred, menacing voice, "That's my dagger and it kills. I wouldn't like to use it, but I will if you make me. So, here is the deal. I'm getting off the horse because I feel sorry for this animal with two people on its back. If you try anything foolish, just remember; I am this horse's master and I just have to whistle and the horse will obey my command. I promise I won't harm you if you simply follow my orders. I'm going to remove the bandana from your eyes. So hold the reins with both hands now."

I did what I was told and he started to untie the bandana. He kept trying to untie it for a minute or two and he was not able to do it, then he ordered, "Don't move, I have to use my knife to cut it because the knot is too tight."

I think he used his dagger to cut it because I felt the movement of his right arm reaching for his leg and pulling up the leg of his pants. I stayed still and I felt when he cut the bandana from the place where the knot was tied.

"What the heck, it's wet, you've been crying! Why?" he exclaimed.

The horrible man jumped off the horse and walked closer to

the horse's head by my right side. He must have put away his dagger, but I did not see him do it. I was still holding the reins of the horse and now I could feel the tears pouring down my face and the mucus from my nose joining the tears from my eyes, mingling and sliding down from my lips to my neck and down to my clothes. I wanted to believe that this was no more than a horrible nightmare from which I was just about to wake up. He was still standing by the horse's head with his hat pushed back so it was now hanging on his back by a string. He struck a match and brought it closer to his face to light a cigarette. This was the first time I got a good look at his face.

"Do you want a cigarette?" he said, putting out the match. "Answer me; it's safe here. Nobody can hear you; there's nobody around for kilometers."

I did not answer, and then he said with a louder voice, "Do you want to smoke?" It sounded more like an order than a question.

"No," I finally replied, "but could you please give me the cloth you removed from my eyes, I need to wipe my nose."

He did not answer me. I watched him reach into his back pocket, pull out a handkerchief and give it to me. I wiped my eyes and blew my nose. I did not immediately give the handkerchief back to him because I did not know what I was allowed to do and what I wasn't.

"So..." I asked with a shaking and timid voice, "May I keep it and use it again?"

The criminal did not answer and I assumed his silence meant that I could keep it. He came close to the saddle and opened a pocket. He retrieved a flashlight and pointed it to the path. Then he grabbed the horse by its bit and started to turn it around. For a moment I thought that he was going to take me back home. However, that was not the case.

"Hold onto the horn of the saddle or the reins because I'm leading the horse to a nearby creek; he must be thirsty."

The creek was not that far from where we were standing. Without the bandana around my eyes and with light only provided by the moon and stars I could see trees, which looked like black, painted and animated silhouettes, moving in the night breeze. By following the beam of his flashlight I was able to trace the narrow path, which was no more than one meter wide. This path was the only area that had no plant growth. As we approached the creek the path became rocky and I could again hear the sharp sound of the horse's hoofs. The creek was very noisy. It sounded as if it were carrying rocks instead of water. He kept walking ahead of me, pulling the horse. I could see his shirt and it appeared to be white. His pants were a little darker than the shirt, but I could not figure out the colour. When we arrived at a river-bank he gave the horse one of his whistles and it stopped. He removed his hand from the horse's bit and ordered me to let up on the horse's reins. When he rubbed his hand along the horse's mane, it bent down and started to drink. After the horse had drunk some water, it snorted. And then something very strange happened—the criminal made a startled jump and pulled his gun, looking from side to side very quickly as if he were being followed or afraid of being attacked. This would be the first time, but not the last, that I would observe this odd behavior.

I was very thirsty and I also felt as if I needed to relieve my bladder, but I dared not say anything. Maybe I did not need to pass my water. Perhaps this sensation was only pain I was feeling for the first time around my pelvic area, a result of it having been pressed hard against the wooden part of the saddle near the horn.

He approached the horse by the area of the saddle, more or less where he had been sitting before. I was afraid to turn my head and see what he was doing. I knew he was looking for something because the light from the flashlight kept moving in different directions. He now came almost in front of me. I heard a noise that sounded like a wine bottle being opened and he thrust a canteen between my two hands.

"Here, drink some water!"

When he offered me water I was suddenly not thirsty any more. I was determined not to drink his water; I was not going to take anything from this monster. What I wanted to do was to throw the canteen far away, but I knew that would not be a wise move.

He snatched the canteen out of my hands and said, "I guess you're not thirsty. Well I am." He drank from it and when he stopped he said, "I am leaving some for you because we still have a long ride from here and eventually you will be thirsty. Now, it is time to continue."

He made the horse do a quarter turn, took my hands and placed them along the correct length of the reins and we started to walk toward the path we had left a few minutes before. He was no longer using the flashlight, but he still kept walking ahead of the horse. The horse followed him without being pulled or commanded. We did not go back to the path. Instead, he led the horse close to a huge tree and tied it to the trunk.

Then he turned to me and said, "We're going to have a rest. You're getting off the horse…let me help you." He came close to me and tried to grab my waist in order to help me. I was getting a terrible feeling that something very serious was about to happen, or worse, that my life was about to come to an end. I thought that if I were going to die, the least I could do was try to fight back. At this point I was no longer afraid of his gun or his dagger; all I wanted was to end my agony as fast as possible.

"I can do it myself." I said brusquely and jumped off the horse. This was not the smartest thing to do, for as nervous, tense and afraid as I was, I fell off the horse to the ground.

He came to my aid and reached down to pick me up, but I pushed him away. "Leave me alone. If you really want to help me, let me go. Take me back home." I was angry and I used as a commanding voice as I could muster.

With a very calm and oily voice he asked me, "Did you say you want to go back home?"

"Yes, I do, please let me go." I said with much indignation. "Take me back to my grandmother's house… please."

"If you want to go, go! There is the road," he said with his hand waving me toward the road in a mockingly dismissive manner. "Go, move, start walking!"

"If I go, won't you shoot me, won't you go after me and shoot me or stab me?"

"No, I won't. I promise." He replied with a straight face.

I thought he was serious and that he really was going to let me go and I asked him, "Could you tell me what way I should take? It's so dark here."

At this point, he burst out laughing and came close to me, putting his arms around my body, saying, "Are you nuts? Do you really think that I would let you go? I've been waiting for this moment for sometime and I'm not wasting this opportunity. I promised you that I wouldn't harm you if you cooperate. I'm in love with you. I've only done this because I love you, and all I want is your love."

He released my body, took off his belt, which was holding the gun, and threw it on the ground. He then took the dagger out of his boot and threw it close to the gun. "Now, I have no weapons, do you believe me that I don't wish to harm you? It all depends on you."

When he said, "It all depends on you," his tone of voice became dark and threatening again. He started to hug me, kiss me and feel me all over my whole body. I froze. I knew what his intention was but I could not react. My feet were rooted to the ground. I was paralyzed, incapable of running, even if I had known the way out of this area.

☙

It is very difficult to describe what I had to endure during the next hour or two—who knows how long. All I know is that I had to tell myself that only my cooperation could possibly save my life. There were moments when I thought that I should fight back, thinking that this would force him to kill me and end my torture. I was picturing a quick death by a bullet: *How would it feel in my body?* I also was imagining a death from his dagger, with stab wounds all over my body. I was able to see the blood pouring out of the wounds: *Would this be a more painful and slower death?* I was even imagining that he might take me back to the river and drown me: *Oh God, that would be a horrible death.* With these thoughts I was able to block some of the things he kept saying to me, for his words were getting very ugly again. My mother used to say, "Looks can kill as well as a weapon." I can add to this:

"Words can also kill as well as a weapon." The verbal brutality this monster beat me up with at this time was more painful than any bullet or knife could have been. He attacked my soul, my mind and my honour; his words were so painful that to this day I still find them too difficult to write them down in detail.

"Okay, it's time to get down to business," he said. "Cooperate with me; show me your love; nothing is going to happen to you."

I realized that I had two choices: to pretend to give him the love he wanted or to face what he called his "best friends"—his gun or his dagger. At first I begged and then I cried; I even knelt down, asking him to take me back home. In my despair of wanting to be let go I even answered his questions with the answers I thought he wanted to hear.

"Do you think that I am a handsome man?"

I said, "Yes."

"Do you like me?

"Yes."

"Do you love me?"

"Yes,"

"DO YOU LOVE ME?" He asked again, this time screaming.

"Yes," I answered wearily.

However, as soon as I said yes he took my chin in his hand and pulled my face very close to his and hissed, "I should spit in your face for being a liar, you fucking bitch, you stupid whore. How can you tell me that you love me when you always brag about that faggot of a boyfriend you have in Chiquimula?"

"DO YOU LOVE ME?" He yelled at me with an even louder voice.

"No," I feebly replied.

This answer was even worse than the previous one.

"Oh, that's too bad because even if you don't love me you are going to be mine and nobody else's, ha, ha, ha! Do you think that my kidnapping you was just a game? Do you think that I forgot how many times I asked you out and you contemptuously told me no? Do you have any idea what that means to a man like me...to Jorge Cárcamo?" He was thrashing his arms in the air and pointing his finger toward his chest. "Are you aware that I can have any woman I want? Don't you know that women come to me and you are the first one I chased? And you dared to treat me like a worthless piece of shit. Boy, are you ever going to learn your lesson now, you fucking whore!"

He paused, possibly to see my reaction to his words. With the feeble moonlight I could see a sneer outlined on his face. He then continued his verbal attack.

"Do you love me?"

"No," I whimpered.

"Do you want to be mine?"

Again, I answered weakly, "No."

"You really have no other choice, do you, you stupid, fucking bitch? I just hope that you're a virgin because if you are not, there'll be serious consequences for you, bitch. I must tell you that by now the police are probably looking for me. I'm not afraid of going to jail. If you're a virgin, it'll be worth going to jail" He lit up another cigarette and offered me one.

"Why do you talk about jail," I questioned, "when all you have to do is take me to a place near by the town where I can find my own way to get home?" In the most sincere tone I could muster at that moment I continued, "I promise you, I will never say anything to anyone."

He threw the cigarette onto the ground and stepped on it furiously. He came close to me again and said, "You don't think very much of me, do you, you stupid whore? You really think that I'm so stupid that I'm going to believe you? And you're so dumb that you think that after this I would let you go free, just like that. I thought that college girls were smarter than that. Let's get things straight right now. You're here to stay with me until I no longer want you. Then, I'll be the one to take you home when I please. Do you understand?"

I still had the handkerchief in my hand and used it to wipe my tears and my nose. I was very exhausted and felt that my legs were not able to support my weight. I was weak, dizzy, thirsty, fearful and nauseated. I thought that at any second I would drop unconscious to the ground. I needed to sit down and lowered myself to the ground.

The horrible monster sat down close to me and said, "That's better. You are getting ready to lie down for me. Now, the next step is to start getting undressed while I go over there to take a piss."

He collected his gun and dagger from the ground and walked maybe four meters away from me. When he was nearing the tree where he was going to urinate he said, "Stay where you are. If you try to do anything crazy you'll force me to use my gun, which is something I wouldn't like to do."

He went to the tree where the horse was tied and urinated. He then came up to where I was still sitting and placed carefully his weapons back onto the ground

"Didn't I tell you to get undressed, *puta maldita!* I am going to fuck you in a way that you'll even regret the day you were born!" The monster was screaming and shaking his fist at me again.

After telling me this he quickly picked up his gun and muttered in a low, sick voice, "I guess I'm going to have to use a different approach with this little cheap bitch."

While giving the gun a few taps with his hand, he came closer to me, and in a low and threatening voice said, "Don't make me use this gun. Be nice to me, at least this one time. Do as I tell you. Believe me, nothing bad is going to happen to you."

I was so numb, scared and tired. A curtain descended, there was nothing but blackness; I became a half–alive body with no soul. I knew that this was the end of something in my life. If I was thinking about anything while he was raping me, it was about what was coming next. *Is he going to kill me? How is he going to kill me? How can I escape?* I was trying to think about anything except about what was actually happening.

After he had raped me he got up and said, "I guess that faggot of a boyfriend you had was not man enough to get you before me. Now it is time to start putting him in the past because you will never go back to him. Now you are mine, yes, mine, do you understand me—MINE!"

Dirty, naked and shivering, I lay on the ground, only capable of softly crying, soft sobs, tears flowing down my cheeks, trying to convince myself that all of this was only a nightmare.

ৎ

It is not quite clear what happened or what I was thinking for some time after that. I can only remember that I had to get dressed; I had to become decent; I was so cold. I got back into my black and white outfit. It was a two-piece outfit that I had made myself. The material was black with very small white flowers. The pants were pedal pushers or capri pants as they are now called and were fitted to my body to the middle of my calf. The pants had a slit on the side of each leg, a very firm waistband with loops and a white sash threading through the loops. The top, which was sewn from the same material, also fitted to my body and extended three inches below the waistline. It featured a sport neckline, white buttons along the front and short sleeves. The front of the top had two slits, each starting at the end of a dart.

After having dressed I sat down on the ground again. I bent my head on my knees and wrapped my arms around my head. I stayed in this position for a few minutes thinking about what his next step might possibly be. For the first time I felt no fear. I just felt angry, very angry. This was an anger that I had never experienced before and would never experience again. I felt as if this monster had just perforated my body with all six bullets of his gun. By this time I knew there were six bullets because the idiot monster had repeated it so many times. I felt so lost and helpless. I was feeling responsible for my own disgrace. I felt guilty but more than anything else I felt filthy. I was filthy and I smelt filthy. The stench of liquor from his breath was all over my body. I was in a lot of pain and felt cold, very cold, making me shiver. My teeth started to chatter. When I think back about to that exact moment, I believe that if he had killed me right then I would have gladly died. At that moment I even lost my faith in God and I started to question the kind of God who would allow something like this to happen to anyone:

Where was God when I was praying while riding the horse? If God really exists, why hasn't he come to my rescue?

I needed to pass my water and I got up again. As I was looking around for a place to go in the bushes I glanced at the despicable criminal. He was seated just a few feet away from me with his head down, resting it on his hands that were lying on his knees. I am sure that I heard the horrible monster sniffling.

He knew I was watching him, for he turned his head and said in a soft voice, "Don't get the idea that I am like this because I regret what I did. I'm just thinking that I will go to jail and you will be out of my sight. Yes, by now the police are probably after me, but they're going to have a hell of a time trying to get me. You may think that I'm an animal but just remember that it was not my intention to do this. I really liked you and I wanted you to give me an opportunity to love you. But your disdain and your haughtiness drove me to do this. You stepped on my pride, you mocked me, you deceived me, you called me illiterate, you treated me like a dog. You left me no choice but to teach you a lesson. You caused all of this."

"Wh–what?" I stuttered.

With my question he started screaming and shaking his fist and I saw that his face was completely contorted. "YOU'VE BROUGHT ME TO DISGRACE…EVERYTHING IS YOUR ENTIRE FAULT…YOU LEFT ME NO CHOICE!"

Then in a softer tone he continued, "Although you've brought me to disgrace, I want you to know that since I took your virginity away and I will respond like a man by honouring your name."

All that I could do was look at the miserable insect in disbelief and with total disgust.

The Monster

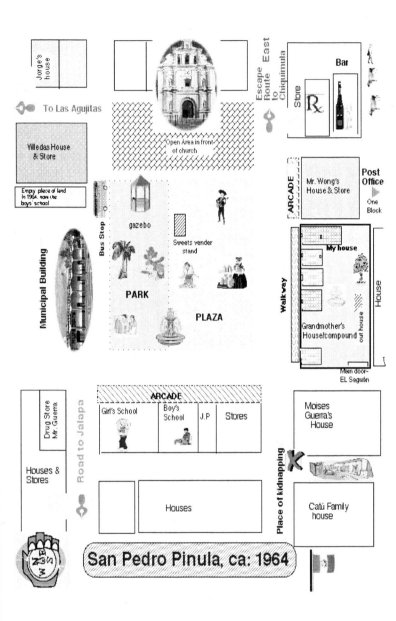

San Pedro Pinula, ca: 1964

San Pedro Pinula—Central Plaza area

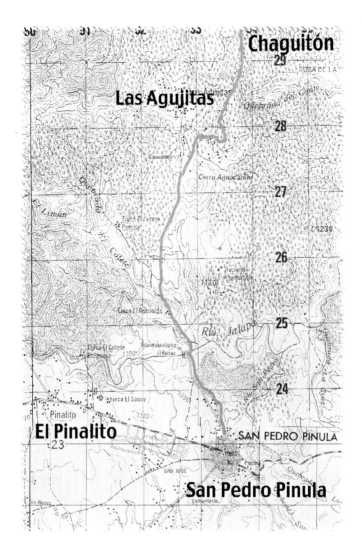

Map Showing Kidnap route

The route went north to Las Agujitas and then to the Cárcamo family farm in El Chagüiton. Each square equals one kilometer.

Chapter 7
The Ordeal Continues

I cannot believe that the inscrutable universe turns on an axis of suffering;
Surely the strange beauty of the world must somewhere rest on pure joy.
–Louise Bogan–

The monster continued talking his nonsense about his love and honour. I was not hearing him, for his voice was just another night sound like those from the insects and animals and his words had about as much meaning to me. He droned on and on, but I was blocking out everything by withdrawing into my thinking, trying to remember the things I might have done to him to deserve all of this.

I did recall that during the two months I was staying in San Pedro Pinula I had said several insulting things to him, the worst being that I had implied that he was a dog, and that happened only after I got fed up with his not taking a no for an answer. He drove me crazy following me everywhere. There was no place that I could go with my friends or my cousins where he would not appear. The worst part was, whenever he was with his friends and I passed by he made remarks about my body, my person, my looks, my way of dressing, my hair. He left no part of me without making some comment with his *piropos*.* Some *piropos* are in good

---

* *Piropos* are supposed to be flattering, public compliments about a women's good looks. They are part of Spanish culture. In North America they probably would be considered sexual harassment.

taste and make a woman feel nice. However, his *piropos* were lust-ful and sleazy and spoken with the intention of embarrassing and annoying me in front of his friends. One day I was riding my bi-cycle and he said, "I wish I were that bicycle so I could be be-tween your legs." I sped off as fast as I could peddle. I was so ashamed and embarrassed.

One day I went to the post office to send a telegram to Canche, asking him to go to the post office in Ipala so we could talk to each other by two-way radio. San Pedro Pinula and many other towns in Guatemala had no telephone service at that time, only two-way radio communication. Some other towns had tele-phone service only at the post office. So, when a person wanted to talk by radio or telephone with a person in another town he went to the post office to send a telegram stating the day and the time he was going to be at the post office waiting. At the agreed upon time, both people went to their respective post offices in their respective towns to complete the communication.

When I arrived at the post office the pest was there. It ap-peared that he knew that I would be there and I suspected that the post office workers, who were his friends, had told him that I would be there. During the complete time I was writing the tele-gram his mouth never stopped moving, to the point I could not concentrate on what I wanted to write.

"Why does a pretty girl like you have to spend money on someone who hasn't bothered to come to visit you?" he said, while leaning on the counter close to me. "Don't you think that he may have forgotten about you already? Why are you wasting your time when you can have me and I'm here?"

I did not even look at him. When I finished writing and was leaving the post office, he came very close to me and said, "I would love to receive a telegram from you. When are you sending me one?"

Without even looking at him, I answered him in a disdainful manner, "I'll send you one when you learn how to read and write."

On another occasion I was going to the *Agua Tibia* swimming pool with my swimming suit on my shoulder. I was going to pick up one of my cousins and my friend. The pest was there at his usual place, under the arcade in front of Mr. Wong's store. When he saw me he said, "I would love to be the water where you swim so I can rub your body. What is a young girl like you doing, going swimming without a lifeguard? Would you like to take me with you?"

I turned around and responded, "I wish I could, but I have no muzzle."

This answer was insulting and not part of my usual character, but I had kept quiet for so long, suffering from my humiliation, and I could no longer stand this harassment without answering him back.

One day, while I was with my friends in the park, a boy came to me and told me that Jorge was boasting in the bar that he was going to "tame that filly" and that he was going "to make me his." I laughed at that, thinking that was just stupid men's talk. How was he going to tame me when I did not even speak to him? How was he going to make me his when I had a boyfriend? How could these stupid barroom statements lead any one to think that he had plans to kidnap me?

I was suddenly yanked back into the horrible present when the monster yelled, "Don't you hear me?"

"Huh," I uttered.

"I'll repeat one more time. Obey me and don't try to leave me and I promise not to harm you."

"Yeah, sure," I mumbled. I was still unable to digest anything that he was saying, but I knew one thing for sure; I could not wait any longer to relieve my bladder.

"Excuse me…I need to tell you that I'm not trying to escape, I'm just going to walk behind those bushes over there to pee."

"Just do it where you are, there're a lot of snakes in this area," he growled.

I knew this was true, but I just could not pee right there in front of him. I kept quiet and stood without moving.

He got up, extended his arm and said, "Here, take the flashlight."

I took it from him and walked away. I knew he was watching how far I would go. I did not go very far and I did not relieve my bladder either. I only had the sensation of having it full. Perhaps the pain from the rape made me feel like I had to pee. I started walking back to where he was standing.

What is going to happen to me? What is he going to do to me now?

I gave him back the flashlight. He stood up again and said, "We have to keep going." He came close to me and made a movement as to grab me by my waist and I shuttered.

"Relax, I'm just going to put you on the horse."

"I can do it myself, thank you," I angrily replied.

I was shivering and my teeth were chattering from the cold. The monster went to get the blanket that was rolled up on the rump of the horse. *Don't take it,* I thought to myself, but I was too cold to reject it. I tried to mount the horse by myself, but I was unable, too shaky, too weak, and too nervous. He then lifted me up without my asking.

Before we started off the horse stepped on a loose rock, causing it to roll, making a sudden and loud noise. Immediately, the criminal grabbed his gun, crouched down, and started to look around suspiciously in the same strange way he had done when we were by the river.

I grabbed the horse's reins. The monster whistled and the horse started to walk with the monster walking behind the horse. I assumed the horse knew the route—it had to—and this was not a surprise to me, for my grandmother's horses also knew the route from her house in San Pedro Pinula all the way to her farm.

I kept riding the horse and the monster continued walking behind, keeping his taunting and filthy mouth shut for once. Finally, there was some silence. I wanted to concentrate on something nice in order not to think about what had just happened. But, unfortunately, my thoughts always came back to when he first grabbed me from behind. I kept trying to think about what I could have done to have prevented this horrible experience; but the more I thought about this, the guiltier I felt. I was now blaming myself for everything.

We passed several large pieces of land with cattle. This prompted him to make a comment or two, "This land belongs to Mr. so and so. He's very rich."

I could not see any houses nearby, which is also very common on Guatemala's farms. Many times cattle are kept very far away from the farmhouse and sometimes there was no farmhouse because the farmer and his family lived in the town and travel every day to the farm.

Several times he tried to start a conversation with me by asking trivial questions such as, "Is Chiquimula as big as Jalapa?"

I did not answer.

"Is your boyfriend in Chiquimula a nice looking man?"

I did not answer this time either.

"How many boyfriends did you have?

His banal questions did not lead to a conversation. I had no intention of getting into some sort of small friendly talk with him. He kept quiet for a few moments and then he started singing a Mexican song that I had never heard before, something amazing since in my house we listened to Mexican music every morning and evening on the radio. The song was entitled *El Rey* (The king).

He stopped singing to ask me another question, "Do you like the song?"

Silence

"Do you like my voice?"

No answer

"People tell me they like my voice. My friends always ask me to sing and I know quite a few songs. Do you know any Mexican songs?

Silence

Suddenly, he sharply ordered, "Stop the horse!"

El Rey (The King)

*I know that I am out
But the day when I die
I know you are going to cry for me
Cry and cry, cry and cry.*

*You will say you didn't love me
But you are going to be very sad
And that is how you are going to live.*

(Please refer to page 177 to see the words of the complete song)

I pulled the reins and the horse stopped. I was surprised he did not use one of his whistles to make the horse do what he wanted. I became more nervous because I thought he was going to ask me to get off the horse and start raping me again, or possibly kill me. He came close to the horse almost touching my left leg close to my knee with his face. He kissed and rubbed my calf with his chin and he asked me, "Do you want to get off the horse?"

His touch made me shiver and I screamed, "No, no, I'm okay just as I am!!"

He immediately started again with his annoying and badgering comments. "Aha! I thought you were deaf and mute," he mocked. "I was mistaken. Let's try this once more." And going back to his threatening manner. Balling his fist and shaking his arm, he snarled, "Did you like the song I was singing? Answer me, bitch."

"Yes, it was very nice," I finally answered with faked humility.

⌒

We continued our ride for a little longer in silence, a silence he had to break. "Do you remember when I came to visit your grandmother's house?"

I did not want to answer him. I did not want to talk to him at all, but something inside me told me that it was better to cooperate with him as much as possible for my own survival.

"Yes, I remember.

"Your grandmother really liked me, didn't she?"

"I don't know," I answered matter-of-factly. "I didn't ask her."

"I was nice to you, wasn't I?" He kept probing, trying to goad me into an angry response.

"Yes, you were," I replied politely.

"Remember when I came to your Uncle Herminio's house and your cousins called you?"

"Yes, I do."

"Did you think that I came to see you?"

(silence)

"Answer me! Did you think that I had come to see you?"

I replied unconvincingly, "No."

"Liar, liar!" He yelled. "You knew that I'd come to see you. That's why both times you practically threw me out of your uncle's house and your grandmother's house. The only time you were nice to me was when I talked to you in El Pinalito, when you were sitting on the water tank in front of your aunt's house."

I did not want to say anything else. I knew he was only using this conversation as an excuse to start tormenting me again, to work up his anger and to turn himself into the victim.

I was trying to recollect the incidents he had just mentioned. It was unbelievable that he was bringing up things that I had taken no notice of at the time. At the time my mind was on my boyfriend in Chiquimula and on my problems with my father in regard to my schooling. I paid no attention to this annoying country boy, this pest, who was always following me around, this idiot who kept saying stupid things. But when he mentioned specific events, the details would then come to mind.

I recalled that on one day I was walking toward Uncle Herminio's house, the place where I got together with my cousins every night. On my way there I stopped to talk to my aunt, and I met my cousin Vilma. She whispered in my ear that Jorge was visiting her house. Uncle Herminio's house was part of my grandmother's compound and it was the last house facing west, close to the *portón* and the *zaguán* (the receiving area).

When Vilma told me that Jorge was visiting the house I said in a very indifferent manner, "So…"

"He wants to speak with you and he's waiting."

I decided that I would not go to Uncle Herminio's house as I had previously planned and continued talking to Aunt Angelita under the pomegranate tree in the courtyard. She was holding a kerosene lamp to provide some light. My cousin came to me again and whispered once more in my ear, "You'd better come and talk to him. He said he came to see you and he won't leave until he sees you."

I went to my uncle's house and there he was, just like an invited guest, sitting with all my cousins. Lidia and her boyfriend Pedro were there along with Vilma's boyfriend, Lalo (a nickname for Eduardo), Cousin Olga, and Cousins Raul and Edgar, who were a little younger than me, and their mother, Doña Flora.

When I entered my uncle's house I greeted everyone and immediately asked the pest, "Are you the one who wishes to speak with me?" He stood up and extended his hand to shake mine, but I did not extend my hand to him. His insolent action to come and see me at my family's home without my inviting him angered me to the extent that I was ready to call the dogs on him. I was now so frustrated by his constant pestering and following me that I was unable to cope. I did not know how to politely give him a message that he would understand, but I thought I could handle the situation.

"Please, come outside with me so we can talk privately," I invited him, using a fake sweet voice. He jumped at the idea and we walked out through the front door and stood by the sidewalk.

He started to say something like, "I want…"

I interrupted him, "You're a stubborn idiot! Don't you understand that I don't want to see you, talk to you, or look at you? Leave me alone. You're not welcome in this house. Leave right now and don't ever come back."

"I just want to be your friend," he murmured.

"But I don't. You're worse than a burr on the pants, and if you have any brains you should understand that I have a boyfriend, and even if I didn't have one, I don't like you."

I was not able to see the reaction on his face. It was very dark and there was no lantern where we were standing. He put his hands in his pockets and started talking slowly and almost biting his words he told me, "I came here because your cousins invited me and for a so–called college girl, you have no manners."

He then briskly walked away and I entered the house using the *portón*. I was furious with my cousins. I was not sure if they had really invited him or if he had invited himself. I had a feeling that they were trying to set me up with him. At other times I suspected that one of my cousins was in love with him herself and was using me as bait in order to get him into the house.

When I entered from the back door of the house, all of the girls ran to ask me, "What happened, what happened? What did he tell you? Are you friends now?"

"I just gave him a big hug and a big kiss and I smelled that he had bad breath," I replied.

I do not know why I said this. I do not know if my cousins believed me or if they noticed how furious I really was. All I know is that they quietly retreated to my uncle's house while I went to my father's house to sleep. After arriving at the house, I threw myself on the bed and started to cry from anger.

⌁

As we were proceeding to where he was taking me I continued to think about what was going to happen to me now and how I was going to survive. But the monster kept interrupting my thoughts, giving me instructions. He was determined not to leave me in peace.

"We are approaching the place where we're going to live," he murmured.

I was not sure what he meant by that and I dared not ask.

"This place is my mother's and family's farm *(majada),*" he rattled on. "There's a man here with his wife and children. They take care of the *majada* (ma–h<u>a</u>–tha) while my family is in town during the dry season. I am warning you right now," he said, shaking his fist in my face again, "I don't want to catch you speaking with them. They're Indians and the man's wife does not speak Spanish. I am going to introduce you as my wife and you are to keep quiet. This man is a faithful and loyal worker and will tell me anything without hesitation. You therefore had better be careful what you tell him and what you talk about."

I did not respond and tried to return to my thoughts. Suddenly, I heard dogs barking. I now became conscious of the total darkness around me. I felt shivers going up and down my spinal column and I broke out in a cold sweat of terror:

Am I approaching my final destination? Where is this place? What is going to happen to me? Is this the place where I am to die?

The whole scene was dark, ominous and forbidding. The dogs kept barking, louder and louder. The horse started to climb a small hill and suddenly I saw the silhouette of a house in the moonlight and the flicker of two feint lights, which I assumed were either kerosene lamps or burning *ocote.*[*] As we approached the house an Indian man came running up to meet us saying, "Good evening, *señor* Jorge." The man did not talk to me.

"Juan, I would like to introduce to you my wife."

The Indian man took off his hat and bowed down from the waist, "Welcome, *señora.*"

I did not return the courtesy with a response. I just wanted to scream and tell the man that I was not the criminal's wife and that he had abducted and raped me, but I knew better and swallowed my words before they left my mouth. This addition of a fawning and obsequious servant to the already frightening and lugubrious atmosphere only added to my anxieties about what the criminal was planning for me in this place.

The Indian man tied up the horse on one of the posts of the house. The criminal then approached the horse with his arms raised up, signaling that it was time for me to dismount and that he was going to help me. He was on my left side, along with the servant-farmhand, who was now holding a torch up high to provide some light. A nearby *candil* (kawn–d<u>ee</u>l) provided the rest of the light.[*] I ignored his offer of help, swung my leg over the saddle and jumped off the horse on the right side.

The criminal came around the front of the horse, grabbed my arm and whispered hoarsely in my ear through clinched teeth, "I'm warning you, bitch, don't you dare try to humiliate me in front of my servants, ever again. Do you understand?"

"Juan," he commanded, still grasping tightly onto my arm "prepare something to eat. I haven't eaten anything all day!" He then looked at me with a sideways glance and added in a sarcastic tone, "Maybe my wife would like to eat something too."

---

[*]*Ocote* (o–<u>ko</u>–tay) is an Indian word for resinous pine sticks which are burned as torches to light houses in places without electricity.

[*]A *candil* is a kerosene lamp without a glass, similar to a smudge pot.

Juan's wife was inside but she heard the command and went to the kitchen to start a fire. Juan then started to update his master about the situation on the farm and asked about the criminal's mother, sisters and brothers. I was too preoccupied figuring out what was going to happen to me to pay attention to their conversation. Juan brought me a cup of *pinol*, a hot drink made from corn, rice, sugar and cinnamon.

I observed the farmhand and his wife while they were talking. Juan's wife was wearing a typical Indian skirt and had a poncho draped over her shoulders. She was shorter than her husband, probably by four centimeters. Her hair was long and braided with a bow at the end of each braid. Juan was about thirty-five years old and his wife maybe three or four years younger. He was stocky and dark, no more than one hundred and sixty-two cm tall. His hair was very dark and straight. He was wearing a pair of white pants and a white shirt. White cuffs peeked out from underneath the woolen poncho that he wore over his shoulders. Juan's wife wore no shoes, but Juan had on sandals. The soles of his sandals were made from old tire treads and were attached to his feet with leather straps. Indian people make and wear this type of sandal all over Guatemala.

In no time, Juan's wife had fixed eggs and black beans with tortillas, cream and cheese. The criminal started to eat as if he had not eaten for months. There was an old and weathered enameled tin plate in front of me, but I was not hungry. I knew, however, that I should be hungry. I still had a nauseous feeling in my stomach from the ordeal and I thought I would not be able to swallow any food or hold it down, even if I had been able to swallow it.

I tried not to cry, fearing that Juan might notice and that might trigger some questions to the monster. Once in a while I wiped tears from my cheeks without making it obvious that I was crying. The dining table where we were sitting was outside, under the roof of the arcade. I felt very cold and I arose from my chair to get the blanket that I had left on the horse. The criminal jumped out of his chair with the same brisk action he displayed when he took the horse to drink water at the river. He put his hand on his gun, prepared to pull it out of the holster.

"Where are you going?" he asked, placing himself in front of me.

"To get the blanket, I'm cold" I replied quickly.

"Stay where you are," he barked.

He started to walk toward the horse but Juan had already run and had taken the blanket off the horse's back. Upon returning Juan said softly, "It is cold here in the nighttime and you must wear a sweater or a poncho; this blanket is thick and warm."

I could not concentrate on anything for very long, but I tried my best to focus on the conversation between Juan and the criminal. I heard that the criminal's white horse was not his but his friend's. I also learned that his family did not know anything about me or about what was happening.

After the criminal had eaten, the servant's wife came to pick up everything and said, "Good night."

Her husband also said, "Good night." He then added, "It will be daylight very soon. I hope you both can sleep."

Juan and his wife left, passing by the little kitchen hut. I watched them, *ocote* torch in Juan's hand, disappearing down the hill.

Now we were alone again. The monster took the kerosene lamp and asked me to follow him inside the house. Although it was dark, the feeble light from the lantern allowed me to get a lay of the house. In the interior there were two dividing walls, making two big rooms. I found out later that one room was a bedroom for the females in the family and the other one was for the males. There was a wide space between the two bedrooms, which could have been used as a living room. However, people on farms do not worry about having living rooms. This family probably used the space to store tools or some grains during the harvest. The outside walls of the house were made of wooden planks about thirty centimeters in height and maybe three and a half meters long. The planks were not cut straight, which left spaces between each one of them. In some areas these spaces were as wide as three centimeters and in some other areas the

wood touched perfectly, one plank against the other. I could see
the outside through the small spaces and could also feel the wind
coming in. I would guess that the house was approximately one
hundred and twelve square meters (1200 sq. ft.). It had an arcade
or overhang on the outside where the eating area was located.

A second kitchen, smaller to the other one, abutted the east
side of the house. Near one of the corners of the house there was
a post to tie up the horses. The criminal tied up the horse on this
corner post. The house also had another type of hitch, a small
post lying on top of two small forked posts about a meter high. I
was familiar with this scene because my grandmother's farm also
had similar posts and hitches.

The monster led me into one of the rooms, "This is the males'
bedroom." He pointed at one bed, "This is my bed. The other
two are for my brothers." He took my hand and placed it on the
handle of the kerosene lamp and said, "Hold it, please."

He does know the word please after all. I almost forgot about the
pain and the ordeal I had been going through and I was on the
verge of laughing and making a sarcastic remark, but fear prevented me from doing that. I knew very well that the only way to
save my life was to keep quiet and act humbly. His present avow-
als of love and dedication did not fool me; I knew that my life
was very much in danger. His words said one thing, but by looking at his menacingly piercing eyes and by observing his constant
touching the butt of his revolver whenever I moved I could tell
where I stood.

The monster went out and came back a few seconds later with
a chair. He then asked; or rather, ordered me to sit down while he
started to prepare the bed by first shaking the blankets and the
pillows. This is a common practice in farmhouses, especially
when the house has not been used for a while, which was the
situation in this case. The house probably had not been used
from the time everyone had left for the town at the end of the
rainy season, around the end of November or the middle of December. He had to shake the blankets and check that there were
no spiders, scorpions, or worse, snakes. When he had finished
with the bed, he proceeded to remove his belt and the gun, plac-

ing them on the next bed, which was situated no more than a meter and half away.

As the monster was laying his belt with the holster on the bed, he glared at me and sternly warned me, "Don't you ever touch this gun. Remember, a lot of problems will be avoided if you don't contradict me or do things you are not supposed to. Do you need to go to the bathroom?"

I only moved my head to indicate no.

"You'll have to get used to the idea of going with me everywhere you want to go. If you have no desire to go to the bathroom right now, you must wake me up when you have to go."

He tried to remove the blanket I had over my shoulders. The blanket was caught under my rear and between my backside and the chair.

"Would you please get up so that I can pull out the blanket?" He said this in a somewhat exasperated tone. When I got up, he yanked the blanket and placed it on top of all the other blankets on the bed saying, "Just in case you feel cold."

He placed the flashlight on a small shelf on the wall and took the kerosene lamp from my hands, "Okay, it's bedtime." He then started mumbling in a somewhat distracted manner, "You refused to eat, but if you get hungry later on just wake me up. It won't be a good idea for you to get out of bed for anything without waking me up."

I only nodded my head to tell him that I understood.

For a moment, I got the impression that he was softening in his attitude toward me and I thought that I could ask him if I might sleep in the next bed. It seemed as if he had read my mind.

"I know what you are thinking, but you must not forget that now you are my *mujer,* (my woman) and you must sleep with me."

As he said this he placed the kerosene lamp on the chair I had previously been sitting on. I got into bed, fully dressed in my filthy clothes over my dirty body. I thought my clothes would keep me safe from him. That did not work. He asked me to get out of bed and undress, which I did very cooperatively. He made comments about my body and I closed my eyes. I was too ashamed to look at him, to see him looking at my naked body.

My eyes were closed and I could not see him, but I could feel his eyes running up and down my body. He was making admiring comments with words that were out of character with his rude and low class personality. His words of admiration and sweetness shocked me in view of the horrible things he had been telling me before and after he had raped me.

He was making remarks about every part of my body and my hair. In order not to hear his words, I tried to concentrate on the barking of the dogs, but that did not help. I tried to think about my father, my mother, my schooling; this did not help either. Finally, with a shivering voice filled with anger and humiliation I told him that I was very cold. He asked me to get back into bed. Then I opened my eyes and I saw him going to the bed where he had left his dagger, belt and gun. He placed his weapons on the chair together with the kerosene lamp. He climbed into bed and blew out the lamp. It was horribly dark. During the rest of the night, or whatever was left of it, he raped me again and again until early morning. Finally, he went to sleep.

I lay there without sleeping and without moving. I was afraid to move and wake him up. I felt exhausted and I wanted to close my eyes and sleep—to sleep and to dream that all of this was nothing more than a nightmare. Every time I was about to fall asleep I immediately woke up. My biggest fear was to move, to wake him up or to make him so angry that he would start raping me again, or maybe even kill me.

While I lay on the bed looking toward the roof I once more started to think about all the incidents or encounters I had with him. In my desperation and suffering I wanted to find out what I had done to deserve this. I still could not accept that this could have happened to an innocent schoolgirl from a well-known and respected family in the community. But now I was starting to realize that I was never going to understand anything and this was becoming a useless exercise. So, I tried to think about something more positive and I forced myself to think about the wonderful times I had had with Canche and our conversations about our future together. But then a most horrible thought flashed across my mind:

What will Canche say when he finds out what has happened to me? Will he still like me and love me as he said he did before? What about marrying me? I don't want to think about this. Let's try something else.

I then tried to conjure up memories of Livingston and to mentally picture the beautiful sea where I used to go and swim. I thought about my classmates, Doña Rome's boarding house, and the park with its gazebo where we went to listen to the band music every Thursday and Sunday. *Yes, I can really hear, I can hear the band's music.* Memories of the wonderful times I enjoyed at Marta Estela's hacienda came to mind. Finally, I fell asleep.

The sleep could not have been for very long. The rooster started to crow and I do not think that the dogs ever stopped barking the whole night. Through the cracks of the wooden slabs I could see the night disappearing and a new day was arriving very quickly. In the feeble morning light I was able to see that the roof of the house was covered with corrugated metal sheets, at least the part of the roof that I was examining. My eyes were glued to the roof, trying to drill a hole through it—to magically escape. I was in a trance-like state, unable to think clearly about anything. I do not remember how long I lay on the bed just staring at the roof, counting the grooves in the metal.

The sun quickly became brighter and everything inside the bedroom was now clearly visible. By moving my eyes up and down and side to side I was able to see the roof and the door. I was terrified to turn my head or move my body. Eventually, I would have to get the courage to wake the monster up. All of my normal feelings were gone. I had been in the same position for a long time and my legs and arms were asleep.

Do I dare wake him up or do I wait for him to wake up by himself? Do I have to go to the bathroom? Am I hungry? I have to move.

When I tried to get out of bed my body hurt all over. I barely managed to sit up. I do not know which pain was greater, the physical one or the one inside my soul. Anger was boiling inside me. The monster woke up and tried to help me out of bed. I pushed him away saying that I could do it myself. It appeared that he was trying to show me some kindness but I was not ready for that. When I reached for my clothes he snatched them away. He handed me a shirt, saying to me that my clothes were dirty. I put on the shirt because it was better to be clothed than naked, even if that meant wearing one of his shirts. This was the first time I actually saw the exact colour of the shirt; it was yellow. I believe it was the same shirt he had worn the night before. In the darkness it had looked to be white. For many years afterwards I detested the colour yellow.

I went to relieve my bladder and of course he went with me to guard me. When we came back inside he offered me his toothbrush, which I politely refused. He took a comb and started to comb my hair. I snatched the comb from his hands; I did not want him to do anything for me. He brought me breakfast prepared by the Indian lady, placed the food on the bed and went back to the eating area to get another chair. When he came back he took the food from the bed and placed it on this chair. I was hungry, very hungry, but I refused to eat. I do not know if this stubbornness was a result of bravery or of stupidity. I knew, however, that I was putting myself at risk. If he had wanted to make me eat or do whatever he pleased, all he had to do was to grab his gun and threatened me. I was not afraid that he would kill me here; there would be witnesses. Perhaps I was behaving in a resistant way because I no longer cared whether I lived or died. Just a few minutes before, I was frozen; lying in bed without moving for fear of disrupting his sleep, thereby causing him to start raping me again or worse, to become angry and kill me. Now I felt that I no longer cared about anything. I was not able to understand clearly my own feelings at this time.

In order to go to the place used as a bathroom we had to pass by the dining area, and when we did this, I put my head down from embarrassment. I could not see who was at the table, perhaps Juan, his wife and their children were there. When we passed by them I heard good mornings being said. I know I looked silly in the big shirt I was wearing. I had no bra or panties on. I grabbed the front of the shirt to wrap it around my body because I was afraid that the wind would lift it and they would see my private parts.

Upon returning from relieving my bladder, Juan's wife offered me a *guacal* (gua–kal) containing some water so that I could wash my hands. *Guacales* are round containers made by cutting big squashes in two halves. The squashes are dried and they become very sturdy. They are used for serving soup, for carrying water, for washing hands or for storing tortillas and other kinds of food. *Guacales* can also be made from the dried shell of a fairly large tree fruit called *Morro*.

The kitchen was a small hut with four posts, one on each corner. The roof was made of thatch (dried palm fronds). The kitchen had a high *poyo fuego*, a common type of stove or fire stand. This type of stove is found mainly on the farms of poor people who cannot afford a gas or kerosene stove. The stove counters are usually built from brick, short wooden poles, and dirt mixed with hay, but sometimes they are made from concrete blocks or rock. The stoves are about one meter high, two meters long, and about one meter wide. On top they have one or two raised rims, also fashioned from brick or mud mixed with hay. Some people simply place three big stones on the counter in order to sit a pot or pan above the firewood. The kitchen also had a *comal* (ko–mal), which was used to cook tortillas. A *comal* is made of clay and has a round surface of about sixty centimeters across and is about three centimeters thick. It sits on top of the raised circular rim of a clay oven. This type of clay oven has two openings, one for the firewood to go in and another hole on the back to ventilate the smoke. I noticed that there were some pots and pans hanging from the beams of the roof and of course, there was a big pile of firewood under the stove counter. I would not have had to see the kitchen to imagine how it looked. All kitchens on the farms look more or less the same.

Back in the bedroom the criminal told me several times that I should eat. I still refused. He picked up the food and took it back to the kitchen. Whenever he left the bedroom I sat on the bed looking at the gun on the chair. I wished that I had known how to shoot a gun so that I could have killed him when he returned to the room. I felt very angry with my father, who owned two guns, but who never took the time to teach me how to use them. Eventually, the monster took his belt and his gun and wrapped it around his waist. He sat on one of the chairs in front of me and forced me to look at him by putting his finger under my chin and pushing it upwards. Adopting a tender voice, he started to say things I had only heard before in the cinema. It was just as sickening to hear these words coming from the criminal's mouth as it was to hear the vile words he was spewing when he raped me.

"You probably don't believe that I love you," he cooed. "My love for you is so great that it made me kidnap you in order to have you by my side. Everything could be wonderful if you just learn to love me. I'm going to be away the whole day and I will return in the evening. Juan's wife or Juan himself will give you some food when you're hungry. I'm taking your clothes to wash them and I'm getting you some other clothes. I am crazy about you and I would give half of my life in exchange for your love. I want you to respond to me when I kiss you, when I hug you or when I make love to you." He took my hands and lifted them up to his neck and pleaded, "Please hug me, kiss me and love me. I want to kiss you, but I don't want to kiss a log. I want to kiss a woman who loves me."

I could not believe these words were coming out of his mouth:

How could he talk about his love for me when only a few hours ago he was calling me a "fucking bitch, a whore" and threatening to kill me? Is he nuts?

He kept talking and talking while I tried to block everything out by thinking about Livingston, the ocean, Chiquimula, Canche, my classmates; about anything except my present reality. I was incapable of showing any emotion. He released my arms and my hands just flopped down onto the bed. He took my face in his hands and kissed me. I sat there motionless, not responding at all.

Suddenly he stood up, "I see," he said, nodding his head. "I guess you don't want me to treat you with love and respect. In that case I am going to treat you as you deserve. Come with me."

He then abruptly grabbed my hand and forcefully pulled me to a room on the west side of the house. He quickly unbuttoned the shirt I was wearing and I thought he was going to rape me again. But that did not happen. He quickly left the room, taking the shirt with him and leaving me standing naked. I heard the door being secured after he had closed it. He was talking to Juan, giving him instructions and then I heard a horse leaving. I was not sure who had left, but I assumed it was the monster. Everything was now so unearthly quiet, with only the sounds of buzzing insects outside the room to stimulate the ear. I did not move for a while, silently surveying my new surroundings.

The room was built with very straight round poles, maybe pine, about ten centimeters in diameter. The poles were placed closed together, but light was still able to filter in from outside. One wall was a common wall with the house and the three other walls were made from these poles. The room had one window, which was missing the screen. In place of a screen, there was only a cheesecloth preventing insects from flying in. There was a shelf built on the wall. On the compacted–dirt floor I noticed some large metal tubs, which I knew were for milk. Neatly folded large pieces of one hundred percent cotton material and sections of cheesecloth were under one of the tubs. Ropes were hanging down from the ceiling, which looked exactly like the ones in the cheese room at my grandmother's farm. The ropes were there to hang the sacks of fresh bag cream, *Mantequilla de costal* (mawn–tay– kee–ya day kos–tal). Although everything in the room was extremely clean, the smell of cheese was everywhere and had impregnated everything. This scene was as bizarre and unreal as all of the other events surrounding my kidnapping—I was alone, completely naked, a prisoner, in a smelly cheese room for a cell.

Chapter 8
Prisoner & "Wife"

The only courage that matters is the kind that gets you from one minute to the next.
–Mignon McLaughlin–

My first day confined in the cheese room was not that bad. I was a prisoner, that is true, but at least I did not have to see the criminal's face and have him near me—touching me, raping me. The large pieces of cotton cloth and cheesecloth I found in the cheese room were big enough to wrap around my body to make a type of toga. I suspected that the criminal did not imagine that I would use the cheese strainers to cover myself. He probably did not even know they were there because the making of the cheese was usually the women's job on the farm. I am sure that he would have removed the cloths if he had known about them.

Juan must have been told that I was naked because whenever he came to check on me, to ask if I needed to go to the bathroom or to see if I were hungry or thirsty, he did not come close to the door. When he approached the room he first called out to me in a loud voice, "*Señora.*" He was probably standing in the hallway between the two bedrooms whenever he talked to me. His wife was the one to enter the cheese room with some food. The first meal consisted of beans, fried eggs, fresh cream, cheese, tortillas and coffee mixed with milk—very good, but I would soon learn this was not to be my daily fare. I tried to talk to Juan's wife when she brought me the food, but she did not understand very much Spanish. Indian women in the country often did not learn Spanish because they barely came in contact with the *Ladino* people.

The men learned and spoke Spanish in order to deal with any needed business outside of their immediate family or their village.

When I told Juan that I needed to go to the bathroom he sent his wife and she came carrying the same shirt that the criminal had taken away from me when he had first put me in the room. María appeared astonished when she saw me with the toga wrapped around my body. I signaled to her not to say anything by putting my finger to my lips. I never knew if she understood me or not, but I do not think that she ever said anything to her husband or to my kidnapper about my new attire. When I tried to explain to her that I wanted to go outside to the bushes, she still did not let me out the door until I put on the shirt. Her gestures told me that it was better to give the impression that this shirt was the only thing I had to wear. I did not mind María accompanying me to the bathroom. She was very respectful and although she kept an eye on me, she also allowed me my privacy—as much privacy as the vegetation allowed. To do one's business in this remote area one had to be inventive, for there was no toilet paper. I had to use whatever I found available to wipe myself—sometimes very broad leaves; but the usual instrument was a dried corncob (it works very well, by the way).

On the first day of my stay in the cheese room the criminal disappeared for the better part of the day and returned very late in the afternoon without the white horse. I did not see his gun either. In fact, he had not talked about or threatened me with his weapons since our arrival to the farm. I was curious to know where he had left the horse and gun, but I was still too afraid to ask anything.

I cannot remember how many days he kept me prisoner in the cheese room while he was away from the farmhouse. Some days he locked me up around nine in the morning, on other days he departed an hour or so later, depending on the time he awoke and finished his breakfast. He returned to the house early in the evening, sometime between four thirty and five thirty in the afternoon. I did not have a watch and could only guess the time of his arrival by the amount of sunlight still available. When evening approached I had to make sure I was awake, for as soon as I heard the criminal's voice, I had to quickly unwrap myself from my toga, neatly fold the cloths, and tuck them away under the big milk can where I had found them.

After the first couple of days I did not mind being in the cheese room at all, the silence gave me piece of mind and I was able to think, sleep, and pray. Although everything in the room was properly washed and cleaned, the strong smell of cheese sometimes gave me a headache. Many times I sniffed at my arms and legs and they too smelled like cheese. I tried to console myself, to cope, and to keep my sanity by comparing the different situations and trying to find some positives in each one. When I compared my discomfort in the cheese room to the horrors of the kidnapping, the raping and everything else that had subsequently happened to me, the cheese room was heaven. It was very humiliating having to go to the bathroom in the company of Juan's wife, but when I compared that to having to go to the bathroom escorted by the monster it was not so bad after all.

I was usually very tired from the previous night's raping and slept sitting on the dirt floor or curled up inside a milk container. Some of the milk containers, which resembled large metal washtubs, were big enough for me to crawl into and I was able to sleep curled up in a fetal position. I also used one of them as a chair by turning it upside down. The room received the afternoon sun, keeping it warm enough for me. Once or twice I felt very cold when the criminal did not return until approximately six thirty or later, after sunset. April is usually a warm month in San Pedro Pinula, but in the highlands it always becomes cool in the evening.

When I was not sleeping, the only thing to do was to think and pray. Many times I thought that I was losing my mind. I caught myself counting the poles around the walls of the room and then not being able to remember how many I had counted, forcing me to start counting again. I was in a constant state of exhaustion and terror-induced panic. There was no way to sleep during the night because of the monster's constant desire for sex and his constant inane and taunting talk. I just lay in the bed all night awake, thinking about anything except what had just happened or was going to happen again soon. Every night the ritual of degradation continued, always in the same manner. By now I knew the routine without having to hear any of his commands. We ate, he sang, he shook the blankets, I got undressed, he raped me once or twice, he fell asleep. I sure did not sleep, from fear that the criminal might kill me in my sleep. I did not talk to him unless it was to answer something he had asked me. Many times I rehearsed how to ask him a question in order to get the answer I was looking for and, at the same time, not to arouse his suspicions or his unpredictable and volatile anger in the process. At night I lay still on the bed, eyes wide open, trying to penetrate the darkness in the room—concentrating—trying to see the roof in the dark—trying to penetrate the darkness surrounding me in the room, to pierce the darkness that had now enveloped my life.

After a few days into my cheese room captivity Juan and his wife allowed me to eat at the table outside. It was obvious that they were fearful of being caught, for whenever they allowed me to do this or whenever María took me to the bushes to allow me more privacy Juan kept watch on the road. He was very vigilant to any noise all day. One time while we were eating outside on the table he warned me, "If Don Jorge appears, tell him that you were sick and that is the reason I let you out." On another occasion, when María was bringing me food, I asked her if she could tell me how I could escape. I tried to bribe her by telling her that my family would reward her if she helped me. I think she understood because she said something like, *"Mi maride y mi hije."* this is very bad Spanish, but I understood what she was trying to tell me, "I have a husband and children."

The criminal returned one evening with my black outfit and panties. They were washed, perhaps by Juan's wife. He also brought some other clothes, saying that they belonged to his sister. I wore these clothes every time he released me from the cheese room, but I still had to remain naked in the room—so he thought. The criminal's sister's clothes fit me perfectly. I presume the clothes had been left on the farm, stored there for the next rainy season when his family would return from town. I was also thinking that perhaps he went to town and had borrowed them from his sister. He never told me where he went during this period of my captivity.

Every evening, after arriving at the farm, he would eventually come to open the cheese room to give me my *freedom*. He usually would be singing his theme song, *El Rey* (The King, please refer to page 177). Now he was singing it with all of its ugly verses. He sang several other songs, but I assumed that this one was his favourite. One day he appeared with a guitar and now, after he had taken me out of the cheese room and we had eaten supper, he would get the guitar and start singing the revolting song, again and again. I think he knew or suspected how much the words bothered me, especially the words *and my word is the law*. At that point in the song he always sang louder while looking at me with a look of satisfaction. I even detected a smirk on his face when he sang that line.

I had not properly showered or bathed since I had been kidnapped. I stank like a farm animal from my own sweat and from the smell of the cheese, but mostly from the semen that had dried on and inside my body. I could not imagine how on earth the monster found me attractive enough to continually want to rape me or even be close to me. My body was sticky all over.

Finally, I got the courage to ask Juan if there was a place where I could go to take a bath or shower. I knew that Juan, his wife and children had baths. They looked clean and they did not smell cheesy as I did. Juan told me that there was a spring about a half-kilometer away. I asked him if his wife would take me there. He told me that this was not a good idea, for if "Don Jorge" returned while his wife and I were gone that would mean big trouble for him. I believed that he would have liked to help me, but more than anything else he had to protect his job and his family.

He said, "*Señora*, I have a family, I have children, and with this job I support them." I think that these few short sentences made up the longest conversation I had with him. The next day María came to take me out of the cheese room and she led me to the bushes near the house to go to the bathroom. When she brought me back she gave me a piece of cloth and a container with water. She did not talk to me; she just gave me the cloth and demonstrated with her hands on her body how I was to use the water and cloth. It felt very good to wash for the very first time.

These little wipe–offs were totally insufficient. I felt as if my skin were crawling with insects. I needed to take a bath; I had to feel clean. I was now at the point where I would do anything he demanded of me in order to get clean and I was going to have to give in a little.

"Jorge, is there a place around here where I can take a bath or wash myself? Could you please show me or take me there?"

Right away he started hurling his usual cruel and humiliating taunts at me. "Oh, after all you do know how to talk; all these days I thought you were mute. You never answer me when I asked you if you're hungry or if you're cold. You don't answer me when I ask you if you love me. All the time I feel like I am talking to myself because you don't make the most minimum sound to say anything."

"Jorge, please tell me, where can I wash myself? Would you please show me where to go or take me there?" I pleaded.

"Sure," he replied, "why don't we act nice to each other? I will take you to the spring where we get our drinking water and you can take your bath in there or wash up. I have soap, a towel and whatever else you need for your bath. In exchange, you give me a sweet kiss, hug me without my having to order you to do it, and you are to tell me that you love me."

I will die before I do that! I thought.

I remained quiet and when he saw that I was not responding he continued, "I'm waiting, let's make this deal. You hug me, kiss me and tell me you love me and I promise I will then take you to the spring. You take your bath in private and I come back to pick you up. You could also get the freedom to go to the bathroom by yourself in the daytime or nighttime. I also will give you clothes to wear when you have to stay in the cheese room."

I felt stupid to even think that this offer could be quite appealing, but it was. Just not having to suffer the humiliation of going about my bathroom activities in the presence of someone meant a great deal to me. On one hand, I was disgusted with his offer, but on the other hand, I was quite happy and surprised that he came up with this deal.

The criminal sensed my hesitation and added, "I know you don't trust me, but you have my word and I will keep my promise. There is only one thing I'm going to ask you, and this you must remember, don't you ever try to run away from me."

Since I was not clear about his expectations I asked, "So let me understand this. Do I have to do this each time I want to take a bath and every time I need to go to the bathroom?"

"Now you're really making me angry," he growled. "Do you think that I would settle for that? Are you acting stupid or trying to make me look like a stupid man? Do you really mean to tell me that I would request your kisses and hugs only when you need something from me? No, my dear college girl, what I want is for you to love me and to show me that you love me. I want your heart to be mine, not just your body."

I could see the veins in his neck were starting to expand. Danger. I noticed, however, that he was not wearing his gun and I had not seen it for a few days, so I felt somewhat safe—although I was sure he still had the dagger hidden inside his boot.

"But I don't even know how to kiss." I said in a hardly audible and demure voice.

"Here you go again," he yelled. He was now clinching his teeth, grinding them louder than ever and he had closed his eyes again. "Do you really think that I believe that crap? Are you telling me with a straight face that you never kissed that fag boyfriend you had in Chiquimula?"

His fists were balled so tightly his hands were turning white. Then he opened his eyes and still keeping his teeth tightly clenched, he snarled, "Don't even answer because I won't believe you. I'm sure he hugged you and kissed you and touched you all over and I'm sure you did the same thing to him. There's only one thing that I'm positive about and that is that you never had sex with him because I was the one who deflowered you—about the rest who knows?"

His whole body was vibrating and the veins on his neck looked like they were going to explode. He was grinding his teeth, his lips were so tense they barely opened when he talked, and the tone of his voice was as threatening, if not more, than it was on the night he first raped me. I knew that I was not going in the right direction and putting myself in real danger. A long silence followed; I could see he was trying to collect himself.

"Don't you understand," he continued, his body still shaking, "that I fell in love with you from the moment I saw you? Don't you understand that I am crazy about you? Don't you know that by kidnapping you I risked my life and I will probably end up in jail? Well, I didn't do this only on a whim. I did it because I love you as nobody could ever love you and all I want is to have you for the rest of my life. All I am asking is for you to love me a little. If you had given me the opportunity to take you out and to court you, I would have never done what I did. You left me no choice and right now you are making things difficult for yourself again, and for me too, which is going to leave me no choice but to treat you in the way you are asking me to treat you once more."

I was very tempted to ask him how he could make these crazy and lying statements about having fallen in love with me when he had told me the first rape that I was nothing but a slut, a whore, ugly, and dirt, and that he had bet his friends that I was not a virgin. I sensed, however, that the situation was too dangerous and decided that it was best to keep quiet.

After a few more minutes of reflection I decided to comply. After all, I would be getting some benefits too, at least that is how I saw it at the time, and what he was asking me to do was no more degrading than what I had already suffered. Finally, I said to him in a business–like fashion, "Okay, I accept."

"That's better, now you're smartening up," the monster replied.

The deal worked very well, I thought. He got what he had requested and I got what he had promised. There were times when I would go to the bushes and linger there as long as I could, admiring the scenery and inhaling as much fresh air as I could hold in my lungs. At other times, I took a few minutes to look far away in the horizon, trying to spot another house, a path; trying to figure out how to get out of there. Sometimes he would come and look for me or simply call me and ask me to come back immediately. He was still putting me in the cheese room, but now the door was not secured. I still could not get out of the room anytime I wanted. I had orders from the criminal that the only times I was allowed to leave the room was to eat or go to the bathroom. If I wanted to take a bath, I still had to wait until he came back in the evening or ask him to take me to the spring before he left in the morning. I was very curious where he went everyday, but I did not feel that it was the right time to ask. I was learning how to bide my time.

One day, when I was in the cheese room, one of the monster's brothers came to the house. The two were arguing. I could not hear everything because they were talking outside, in or around the eating area. The only thing I knew was that I was the focus of the conversation. It seemed that his mother had sent one of her sons to talk to the monster and tell him that he had to take me back to my family. I heard something like, "She comes from a family you shouldn't have messed around with." I plainly heard the monster asking his brother, "Do you know if the police are looking for me?"

"We don't know yet. Just remember that if they start looking for you and for her, they know exactly where our farm is and this will be the first place they will check."

I heard the two also mentioning farmland in an area called Las Agujitas (A-goo-hee-tas). His brother did not stay very long and before he left he said, "You have to go to town and talk to our mother as soon as possible."

That evening the monster stayed up late preparing for a trip. I had no idea where he was going until he said to me, "Tomorrow I'm going to San Pedro Pinula. I'll be back very late, after dark. You won't have to go into the cheese room. I've a little trust in you now and I want you to respect that trust. You'll have to learn how to do some things around here. What I want you to do when I'm gone is to stay with María. She will teach you how to make tortillas and cook beans."

That was the last day I spent in the cheese room.

⚜

The next morning the monster warned me once more, "I'm going to trust you that you'll not run away. Remember, if you do, I will find you anywhere you go and if I kidnapped you once, I'll do it again, even if that puts my life in jeopardy. Oh yes, there's one more thing: if anyone ever comes to the house, let Juan handle the situation. You are to come inside and stay inside. Is that clear?"

"Yes, I understand," I said, nodding submissively.

"Is there anything you would like for me to bring you?" he added.

"I just need a toothbrush," I replied, "and a deodorant, and some sanitary pads." I knew that my period was way overdue and I was not prepared. I felt very, very uncomfortable and embarrassed talking to him about feminine hygiene products. What I really wanted to ask him was to take me back to the town with him and then let me go to my family, but I sensed that that was not a wise request and decided not to go that route. However, I felt brave enough to ask him, "Jorge, where do you go every morning after you leave me in the cheese room?"

"Would you believe me if I were to tell you that I go into hiding, just in case the police are looking for me?"

I said, "Yes."

"Would you believe me if I tell you that I go to work the land where I will be growing my corn and beans this year?"

Again I nodded and said, "Yes".

"Well, that is exactly what I do even if you don't believe it."

I noticed that before he left he spoke privately, and for quite a while, with Juan. I could only guess that he was probably giving him instructions about how to watch me.

Then he came to me saying, "I will be coming back late. I want you to prepare dinner and wait for me so that we can eat together. You are to watch María in order to learn where to get the grains from the granary. Be a good wife!"

I was astonished that he looked at me as his wife. I thought of myself simply as his prisoner. I had realized that for the love of my own skin, compliance was working best.

When he finally left, he was not riding a horse and I could see that he had no gun; at least, I did not see him with the belt around his waist. He took his machete, something all farmers carry with them in this region. This machete was so important to him that he honed it every day. I heard the noise of the metal against the sharpening stone when I was in the cheese room.

I still felt that the monster was planning to kill me very soon and my mind was working very fast trying to put things together: *Is he really going to town? I wonder if he left the gun in the house?*

I knew how to make tortillas and how to cook other dishes. What I did not realize was that, with María I had to learn how to crack and mill the cooked corn on the grinding stone *(piedra de moler)*. A typical grinding stone consists of two pieces. The big piece is about thirty centimeters wide and forty-five centimeters long and has three triangular legs about twelve centimeters long. The top part is carved to create a slight hollow area where the corn is placed. The other component is also made out of stone and resembles a very fat cucumber, about twenty-five centimeters in circumference. Most people do not use the *piedra de moler* for grinding or milling corn. Usually, the cooked corn is first proc-essed through a mill to make the dough and then the *piedra de moler* is used to smooth out the milled corn dough *(masa)* to make tortillas. However, people who have no mill have to use this tool to first crack the corn and then to grind it several times until it turns into dough. Milling the corn this way is a very difficult and an intensely laborious procedure and it was obvious that Juan and María were very poor and had to mill their corn the hard way.

In the morning I spent my time preparing the dough for the tortillas. By the time I finished I had blisters on the palms of my hands. María taught me how to cook the corn, but she did not converse with me. She made signs, pointed to things, and took my hands to show me how to work the dough. We started the process by first using quicklime and water, bringing the mixture to a boil and putting in the corn. We let it boil until the corn became soft. Then we rinsed the corn to remove all the quicklime and it was ready to be made into dough. I had an idea how to do it, but I had never done it before by myself, for my parents always bought the tortillas already made. It takes too much time for working people to make them at home and my mother was always very busy with her sewing. María also braided my hair, which I am sure was to prevent it from falling into the dough or into the rest of the food.

Indian women with the piedra de moler.

There was not much to cook, only beans and corn to make tortillas. When I finished, I asked Juan if I could go to the spring. His head movement told me no. I went inside the house. I turned the house upside down trying to find the gun; but unfortunately, I never found it. I walked around the house several times, looking down the hill to see if I could see a road for escape, but the only road I saw was the little path leading to the spring. I was wondering if this was the path to San Pedro Pinula. I could not go and explore further because Juan was always on the alert, watching me.

I hated fulfilling the duties as a "wife", as the monster called me. But I knew that if I did not comply with his wishes he would find ways to make my life even more miserable and painful.

The monster came back when it was still light outside. He had been drinking heavily and stank.

"I got your deodorant and a toothbrush," he stated tersely.

"And the sanitary pads?" I asked.

"I forgot them," he said, with a shrug of indifference.

"How was your trip?" I inquired politely, trying to set the mood before he could get angry about my nosy questions.

"I heard in town that people have the idea that you eloped with me and the police are not looking for me," he said, with a self–satisfied look on his face. "We're going to stay here for only two or three more weeks. I have hired some people to build a house on a piece of land my father had left for the boys, in an area called Las Agujitas."

This information seemed to tie in with the pieces of conversation I overheard between the monster and his brother a few days earlier.

❧

I had been in captivity for over a month and the days passed without much change. I no longer had a guard when going to the bathroom in the bushes or going to the spring to take my bath. The criminal never allowed me to go to the spring by myself. When we went to the spring he always brought the machete and this made me nervous. When he saw how uncomfortable I was he explained that he had to take the machete in case we encountered snakes. This was true, because I saw him kill a coral snake and a rattlesnake with it.

The criminal demonstrated that he was starting to trust me more in several ways. First, I no longer had to go to the cheese room and second, he now allowed me to sit in front or back of the house, looking toward the mountains and the trees. This freedom came with a price—I now had to do the cooking every-day. He added more chores to my list: sweeping the house, making the bed, and washing the clothes. He was also calling me "his woman (*mujer*)" and I realized that I was now fulfilling the duties of a wife. When he went with me to wash the clothes he ordered me to prepare a basket to take with us and then we would eat by the spring as if we were two young lovers honeymooning in the woods. Eventually, he allowed me to go fetch water and wash the clothes all by myself—at least I thought I was by myself.

I still could not see any other paths and I was thinking that this path to the spring had to be the same one we had taken when we first arrived at the farmhouse. In order to go there I had to walk about a half of a kilometer, northwest. I then turned right onto a narrower trail and walked a little farther to where the spring was located. It was beautiful and peaceful there. It was so quiet I could even hear the sound of the bubbles of water breaking through the sandy bottom of the shallow pond if there was no wind or birds singing. Beautiful tall trees providing cool shade surrounded the little pond. Below the spring, where the little stream grew to a larger size, there were two big thick flagstones on top of other bigger rocks. These flat stones were there to be used for the washing of clothes. Many times, when I was washing the clothes the monster wandered around, but I could hear that he was not far away; he was usually whistling his favourite songs, such as *El Rey, Tu y Las Nubes*. He also forced sex on me quite often at that place.

While the clothes were drying on top of the bushes I sat in peace and was able to do some deep thinking without any interruptions and without his constant questioning. However, quite often this peace was destroyed when the monster suddenly appeared from nowhere and caught me thinking or crying. When this happened I knew that I was going to be in for a hard time; it was time for him to conduct a trial. The ritual would always unfold in the same repetitive manner. He started by first describing how jealous he was in a way that really made me shake with fear. Then his physical appearance dramatically changed. He balled his fists and started grinding his teeth, he closed his eyes, his forehead started to sweat as if he had been under the sun, his nostrils expanded, and his breathing sounded more like the puffing sound of a bull than normal human breathing.

"What are you thinking?" He would bellow. "Are you thinking about your faggot boyfriend again?"

These were usually the first questions and if I said no or if I remained silent, he would then go into insane accusations: "You're planning to do something; I know it, you fucking schemer, you sleazy whore. You're planning to run away. You're planning to kill me when I'm sleeping!"

He was often right on both counts and that scared me because I thought that I was doing or saying things that were making me too transparent.

"You were crying about that faggot boyfriend of yours. I know it," he screamed." What does he have that I don't for you to love him so much?"

That was a good question and I could have given him a huge list, but I knew that it was best to stay quiet. He usually calmed down quickly when I remained calm and did not answer him.

As soon as the monster started letting me go to the spring by myself I began to nurture the idea of running away. I knew I had to do it sooner or later. I could not imagine spending the rest of my life with this crazy man. But I also knew that I had to do it right because if he caught me he would probably kill me. In addition, if I were not careful, I could get lost in the hills, be bitten by snakes, or be attacked by wild animals.

A few times when he allowed me go by myself to wash the clothes I walked back to the main path while the clothes were drying on the bushes. Instead of turning left toward the house, I turned right and started to wander off to see where this path would lead. I always came back after walking no more than a few hundred meters. I had to be very careful because many times he came to meet me at the spring and sometimes he surprised me by coming to meet me half way from the house.

One day I went to the spring, left the clothes drying on top of the bushes, and decided to go and explore a little farther. I suspected that one particular path might lead to San Pedro Pinula. I walked close to half a kilometer or a little more. I was not planning to run away, not at that precise moment; but I certainly was trying to get familiar with the area and maybe even find someone who could help me or at least tell me if this path was the way to the town.

I was just about to turn back when I heard his voice calling me and ordering me to return. I do not know how on earth I thought that I could outrun him. I became so nervous and so fearful that I was not able to think straight. I took off and ran. When he caught up with me he grabbed my neck with both hands. I thought he was going to strangle me to death.

I begged him, "Jorge, please forgive me. I promise I will never do it again."

I noticed that he had no gun and that was a big relief. He kept his hands tightly around my neck and screamed, "Where were you going?"

"I was just exploring," I stuttered, shaking with fear.

He threw me on the ground, grabbed my hair and dragged me over the ground and rocks. I thought that this was going to be the end of my life. He dragged me about by the hair for at least a hundred meters but it felt like a kilometer. Then suddenly he stopped.

I could not move. When I finally tried to sit up and was having much difficulty, he helped me. He then calmly sat down in front of me. I had a lot of scratches on my face, elbows and calves. I was wearing one of his sister's dresses and the back of it was totally torn and some parts of my back were bleeding. The most excruciating pain was on the back of my head. It felt as if my scalp was coming off together with the hair. I started to shake and cry and I asked him innumerable times for forgiveness.

"Jorge," I pleaded, "I was not planning to run away. I just got scared when I heard your angry voice yelling at me."

I had not seen him this angry before and I was terrified. His nostrils were flaring as if they were not able to take in enough air. I could hear the grinding of his teeth. His eyes kept roaming all over my body, but this time not with the usual lust. I knew he was examining my wounds and probably wishing to strangle me. He was holding me by the upper parts of my arms, and I could feel the pressure he was applying to them.

"Do you think you can walk?"

The first thought that came to my mind was to tell him that I could not walk. I thought he would have to leave me there and go for help.

"I don't think so," I whimpered. I knew I could walk, but I thought this was my only opportunity to save my life or at least not be beaten up more severely. I did not know what he was going to do with me once we were back in the house and I had to stall. I knew that it was going to take him at least twenty-five minutes to get me back to the house and that would be enough time for me to think of something. My classmates always praised me for how good of an actress I was and I thought: *Why not use my acting abilities to save my life?*

"No, I'm in a lot of pain. I don't think I can make it," I whined.

"That's fine. I'll have to carry you then," he quickly replied.

How can I let this monster carry me in his arms when only a few minutes ago he had almost killed me? I'd better keep acting now or he'll kill me for sure.

So, I pretended to be unable to walk and he carried me in his arms all the way to the house. He was strong and very muscular, and even though I was not very heavy, he had to make several stops before we reached the house. I think my weight at that time was about forty-seven and a half kilos (one hundred and five pounds).

He left me in the house and went back to the spring to collect the clothes. That night I did not eat and pretended to be sicker than I actually was. He left me alone in the bed and took his brother's bed instead. I was in so much pain that I woke up several times during the night. The monster had left two kerosene lamps burning and I noticed that he was not sleeping, just sitting on the bed, watching me, glowering at me, guarding me.

Chapter 9
To The Hell of Las Agujitas

Violence is the last refuge of the incompetent.
–Isaac Asimov–

I stayed in bed for two days, pretending that I was not able to move. My acting was working and I asked the criminal to take me to town to see a doctor.

"That's too dangerous for me and besides, I believe that you may try to trick me. However, if you don't feel better in two more days I will take you to see a *curandera* (Indian medicine woman) because the time for us to move to Las Agujitas is near and you need to be well enough to ride a horse."

For another four days I stayed in bed, getting up only when I needed to go to the washroom and sitting up only long enough to eat. I was sore, scratched and bruised. Some of the scratches were swollen, but I knew that I could walk around if I had wanted to. Juan prepared some kind of potion made from boiled leaves. The criminal applied it to my open wounds.

I was healing very rapidly, but I was wishing not to get well because the monster was now leaving me alone and the respite from his stupid talk was welcome. He was sleeping in one of the other beds and there was no raping, and this was even more welcome. I was wishing I could be sick all the time.

While I was in bed the criminal stayed in the house guarding me and singing. At least this time he did not sing *El Rey*. Now he sang *ad nauseam* a different song, *Tu y Las Nubes* (You and the Clouds. Please refer to page 179 for the words). I knew this song because my father and mother used to sing it too. The criminal's complete demeanor would change whenever he sang this song. He came to where I was resting and stroked my head, using his fingers to comb my long hair. He looked very sad. I even think I saw tears in his eyes at times. He kissed me and softly said, "I love you so much and you can't imagine how sorry I am for what I did. I promise you I won't do it again. Please, don't abandon me. I suffer so much when you pay no attention to me. I've never loved anyone before and no one has ever loved me. I've had many women in my life, but you are the only one I've had who was a virgin. I need you and I want you to love me. You made me feel so insignificant when you paid no attention to me, but I never felt defeated. I want to win your heart."

I did not respond, but he went on and on with this sickening talk. "Whenever you hear this song, *Tu Y Las Nubes* you are to think about me. This song is dedicated to you because that is how I saw you at the beginning...very unreachable. My friends laughed at me when I told them that I liked you and that I was in love with you. They mocked me saying, 'You're in love with the impossible because she doesn't even look at you.'"

I could not tell whether this talk was a manipulative ploy, crazy imaginings, or sincere feelings. Slowly, however, this talk was having an effect—I was starting to feel sorry for him. I even started to feel guilty for thinking about escaping. This was probably the first time I had him in front of me for a long period of time, where I was able to pay attention to his facial features and I found him to be a handsome man. I was even thinking that I could fall in love with him.

If only I had not been so mean to him, he would not have had to kidnap me. If I had not run away from him when he called me, maybe he would not have beaten me up.

Once, I went to him, hugged him, spontaneously kissed him and thanked him for taking care of me. I remember how surprised, happy, and satisfied he looked. Tears welled up in his eyes and he kept saying, "Please don't ever leave, for if you leave me

I'll die, you're all I have."

Thank God, immediately after one of these episodes, I became sick and disgusted with myself. I actually thought that I was going insane. These fluctuations of feelings would continue for some time.

The monster was now singing a new song, *La Que Se Fue* (The One Who Left, (please see page 210 for the words). I knew this song too, because I had listened to it every morning on the Mexican music radio program. I was thinking that he definitely was living in some type of mental fantasyland. In this song, a woman rejects her suitor, causing him horrible suffering. In the way he sang the song it seemed as if he were giving me a clear message—I was that woman.

❦

When I became well enough to resume my regular chores the criminal told me to get ready because he was taking me with him on a trip.

"Where are we going?" I asked him.

"To the fields," he replied. "After what you did I need to keep a close watch on you."

I knew that I had done the right thing to pretend to be sicker and more hurt than I actually was—I had escaped with my life. But I also knew that, in the future, it was going to be more difficult for me to explore possible ways to escape.

We left early in the morning and I think we took the same path as the one to the spring. I really did not pay that much attention to where we were going. I was walking a short distance behind him and once in a while he turned his head to check that I was still following him. The two dogs were with us too. I liked these dogs because their barking was the only sign of life I heard every morning while lying awake in bed, waiting for daybreak, waiting to get out of bed, waiting to get away from the monster.

What if he is planning to kill me in the fields, leave me there? Nobody will ever know what happened to me.

Suddenly, the monster yelled my name and when I raised my head to see what was the problem, I saw him striding back toward me. He looked angry and I thought that I was in for it, but he was only trying to be emphatic.

"Do you really want to know where that road leads?" he questioned, pointing to the path. "If you're thinking that it leads to town, you're right. Do you know how far you are from the town? It's about three and a half hours by foot. I know exactly how many times you wandered on that road and how far you went before turning back. I know exactly each one of your moves because I always follow you. I may look stupid to you, but I'm brighter than what you think. I know exactly what you've been planning since the very first day. I'm telling you this for your own good. Don't you ever try to escape because that will be impossible? I'll follow you to the end of the world and bring you back. You'll never be able to get away from me." His words were intermixed with a horribly malicious and sarcastic laughter.

While he was talking I felt dizzy and wanted to throw up. I was sweating—a very cold sweat—and I must have looked sick because he helped me sit on the ground. I had barely made it to the ground when I vomited. He poured some water from his canteen onto the red handkerchief he had tucked in his pocket and wiped my face and forehead. I did not know what was wrong with me; was it a result of his beating me, was it result of my not having eaten enough when I was convalescing in bed? He offered me water and I drank a little.

He kept talking; he would not shut up, which made me even sicker, almost making me throw up the water I had just drunk. "Do you know that we are going to Las Agujitas?" He asserted, ignoring my plight. "That place is a lot closer to San Pedro Pinula than this one. Las Agujitas to Pinula is probably only one hour by foot. Today, I want you to see the land I'll be cultivating, I want you to know right now that I'll be watching you every minute once we move there and you will be coming with me to the field every day. I won't leave you alone in Las Agujitas. It will be better if you don't try any silly stuff.

We came to a huge piece of land; he pointed to it, angrily saying, "See that land? That's my share of the family land where I should be growing my corn and beans. Unfortunately, we cannot stay on this farm because I had a big argument with my mother about you. After my brother's visit I went to talk with her. She tried to convince me that I should take you back to your father before the police come after me. She has no business getting in the middle of my life and I probably was a little too rough with her. So, she told me that in two week's time she did not want to find me in her house."

He kept jabbering on about different things, but I felt so ill I was unable to pay attention. "Jorge, can we please go back to the house? I am not feeling very well at all."

He looked at me and said, "You're very pale. Do you want some more water?"

I sipped some more water and immediately threw up again. He then took me back to the house. I was not able to hold any food in my stomach that evening or the next day. I was shivering. Suddenly, I realized that my period had not come. I was also hoping that my period was just late, as had happened many times in the past. For three days I was not able to hold any food down, not even water. The monster sat down with me one evening and tried to force me to eat. Juan's wife brought me a herbal remedy to drink. It tasted awful and I threw up once again.

The monster became annoyed and told me, "Why don't you drink this stuff? You're not even trying to get well."

I felt very weak and all I wanted to do was sleep. After another two days the monster appeared to be worried. He kept asking me which part in my stomach hurt and he even brought food to my bed, which I never ate. The smell of his cigarette really bothered me and the smell of food turned my stomach upside down. I was suspecting what the problem was. In my heart though I was hoping that it was simply indigestion, or maybe some kind of flu, or food poisoning, or perhaps amoebiosis. I had been vomiting for a week when I asked the criminal to take me to a doctor. I knew that San Pedro did not have a doctor and he would have to take me all the way to Jalapa and perhaps someone who knows me would see me. Unfortunately, he said that going to Jalapa was not a good idea for him and he would take me to see a local *curandera* (an Indian medicine lady) instead.

I kept throwing up every time I ate or drank something. We were only one week away from moving into the shack in Las Agujitas when he took me to see this woman. The monster brought a horse for me to ride and he walked alongside. It took us about an hour to get to a little shack made of *carrizo*. *Carrizo* is a thick reed, something like bamboo, but thinner. The shack had a thatch roof (palm fronds); there was a single door and no windows. I saw a very skinny dog by the door and of course, there were the usual chickens and some other types of animals.

The Indian lady spoke very broken Spanish, but she spoke a lot better than Juan's wife. The monster explained to her all of my symptoms. She looked at me and took me inside an area divided by a rope with two blankets hanging from the rope. In this way she divided her bedroom from the kitchen and the eating area. She had a cot for a bed and there were some pictures of saints hanging from the forked beams of the shack. The monster did not go in, but I am sure he was able to hear everything.

She took my hands and held them, putting her fingers on my wrists and then she asked me, "Are you going to the bathroom a lot?

"No."

"Have you had your first period already?"

"Yes, I had my first period when I was eleven years old," I answered.

"When is your next period?" she asked.

"I can't remember exactly... but I think it is late."

"Show me your breasts; I want to see the nipples." Pointing at the aureole around my one nipple, she said, "You have all the signs of being pregnant."

I had been suspecting this myself, but I was hoping that it was only one more time when my period was late. My periods had never been regular.

The *curandera* went outside to invite the monster in. She did not have to tell him anything—he had heard it all. He entered the house, knelt down to my level and laid his head against my stomach.

"A child, MY child! I am the happiest and luckiest man in the whole world. I'm going to be a father, I'm going to have something that really belongs to me and I'm having it with the woman of my dreams."

I had never witnessed such happiness from a man about to become a father. It was as if he had won a million Quetzals. He was ecstatic. I thought that his joy was too exaggerated, almost unreal, as if there was something supernatural in his fathering a child. For days he talked about nothing else except this baby, HIS baby. He told me it had to be a boy and he was going to name him Jorge Arturo, after himself. Several times he got upset with me because I could not eat without throwing up and he said he was very concerned for the well–being of his child; there was never any mention of my well–being.

Three days before moving the criminal took me with him to Las Agujitas to see the land and arrange for a shack to be built. The poles and the palm leaves for the roof were lying on the ground. The monster had arranged with some local Indian men to build the shack *(covacha)*.

It was almost two months from the night the criminal had kidnapped me when we packed up and left for Las Agujitas. He loaded up our meager belongings—a few dishes and clothes on the horse and that meant we both had to walk. The long walk was arduous for me and we had to stop several times. The criminal did show kindness in this way in view of my pregnancy. When we arrived the shack was ready for moving in.

I had now resigned myself to what I thought was going to be my life's destiny. I viewed myself as the woman (*mujer* in Spanish can mean both woman and wife) of this man and the future mother of his child. I no longer expected the police to come after him or my father to try to find me. I no longer thought about why my father had not come looking for me. I was no longer considering an escape since the criminal was treating me in a more civilized manner. I was carrying his child and this was protecting me. I did not want to disturb anything.

Las Agujitas was not a village, it was more like a small settlement consisting of a few small houses, and there was no house or shack near ours. The road to town, more like a rough path, was only ten meters from the shack and there was a barbed wire fence along the path bordering this piece of land. An average of ten to fifteen people passed by the house everyday, either going to San Pedro Pinula or returning from there. During the weekends the foot traffic was a little busier and on market days, much busier. There was a shallow and narrow stream about fifteen meters away from the shack. From this stream we carried our water for drinking, cooking, washing cloths and taking our baths. He eventually told me that this was the stream where the horse drank water on the night he kidnapped me. He showed me the place where he raped me, but he phrased it this way, "This is where I made you mine." No wonder there was something familiar about this little river. I could not recognize anything else around the area. He gave me strict instructions not to talk to anyone. Many times people crossed the fence to ask for water since we lived so close to the path. I poured the water and the criminal brought it to them. Sometimes he would engage in a conversation with the passersby, but I was never allowed to talk to them.

We did not have very much food, only tortillas and beans. Many times we did not even have beans and ate nothing but plain tortillas with salt. The criminal's mother came to visit us once. She walked up to the barbed wire fence, not stepping into the shack. Since the criminal had ordered me to stay inside I did not talk to her. I noticed that she brought quite a few bags, which I presumed contained food. The two of them were speaking quite loudly and I saw that when she tried to hand him the bags he rejected them. He then turned around and came into the shack very upset, cursing his mother. I did not dare ask what the problem was, but eventually he told me, "My mother and I argued about you. She told me again that I should take you back to your family. She brought food and when she said, 'I brought you this food just because of that girl; otherwise, I would not have brought you anything.' I told her, 'Keep it, you need it more than us.'"

We went to Las Agujitas a few days before his mother and the rest of his family went to their farm, the one we had just left. He explained to me that his family did not stay on the farm full time. They came to town every weekend and that Juan and María took care of the farm during the weekend. The monster had built the shack on a big piece of land that had belonged to his late father. The shack was about four by five meters and its walls were made of wooden poles, which were not very straight and one could see through the spaces to the outside. It had only one door and no windows. The roof was covered with palm fronds, just like all the other shacks around that area. Inside the shack there was a cot with a mattress, which he had brought from his mother's farmhouse, and a stand built of wood to place the *piedra de moler* (grinding stone). The criminal built a one–foot high fire stand *(poyo fuego)* where I cooked the tortillas and beans, but we had no table or chairs. The wind whistled and blew into the shack from every direction. It was very cool in the evening, so we had to leave the fire burning the whole night, necessitating us to collect firewood every day.

In order to supplement our meager food he took me with him when he went to kill birds. He spotted their nests during the day and when night came he pointed the flashlight beam straight at their nests. The birds would come out when they saw the light and when he turned off the flashlight the birds fell to their death onto the ground.

The criminal started his farming at Las Agujitas by burning a big piece of land for planting corn and beans. He told me that he was no longer going to use the already cultivated land on his mother's farm. I assumed that was because of the arguments with his mother.

During our stay in Las Agujitas the criminal made two trips to his mother's farm, each time very late in the afternoon, leaving me alone in the shack. Those were two very frightful evenings for me. On his second trip it was already getting dark when he left. I went inside the shack and as I was entering I saw a snake slithering away. I did not see where the snake had gone and I was afraid it was still in the shack and might strike at me, so I decided to stay outside, sitting on a rock until the criminal returned home.

I never had paid too much attention to the night wildlife in this place, even during the long nights when I was lying awake in bed for hours. However, I was now sitting outside in the dark, alone and with no weapon to defend myself. The sounds of the night creatures seemed louder than usual: the clicking of the crickets, the hooting of the owls, and the chattering of the cicadas. I thought I even heard wolves. There were instances when I thought that someone might sneak up on me: to kidnap, assault, rape, or kill me. I saw shadows of various animals, real or imaginary. I visualized being devoured by an unknown strange animal. I was thinking that it would have been nice to have the criminal right there with me or to have one of the dogs from the farm to keep me company. It was horrible. I cried and I prayed to God that the criminal would return soon. I do not know how long I was out there. Then I heard some whistling, I heard him whistling one of his favourite songs. Although he was still far away, too far to see him in the dark, I could see the glow of his cigarette and in my desperation I ran toward the little light to meet him.

"I'm so glad you're here!" I cried, reaching up to hug him. "I saw a snake in the house and I've been waiting outside all this time for you. I'm so scared."

"This will never happen again," he said with a consoling voice. "I no longer intend going back to the farm, but if I have to go you must come with me. I will no longer leave you here without any protection."

The criminal asked me to stay outside and he entered the shack with the machete in his hand. Using his flashlight, he searched the roof, every corner and the spaces between the poles of the shack, but he found no snake. He started the fire, lit a kerosene lamp, and asked me to come inside. We sat down in front of the fire watching the sparking firewood burn and he told me, "I'm so happy you came to meet me and give me a hug. I hope that you'll do this all the time, not just when you need me."

This was one of the few times that I spontaneously displayed any affection to the monster.

While sitting on the floor looking at the fire I was thinking:

Why didn't he return by horse from his mother's farm? Did he really go there? Maybe he was hiding somewhere watching me and making the noises I was hearing?

I had to ask him, "Jorge, why didn't you get a horse to ride from your mother's farm? You've told me how dangerous it is to walk at night because of the snakes."

"Because I don't want to use anything that belongs to her. She keeps putting her nose into my life and I don't tolerate that. That's also the reason I'm not planning to work my land at the farm. I'll do my farming in this area even though it will be harder work. This land has not been used for farming and it needs a lot of preparation."

Although I was very curious, I did not ask what the fights with his mother were about. Just by looking at his eyes, I knew how upset he was and I thought it was in my best interest just to listen to him and not ask any more questions.

He then asked me a question, one that did not make sense to me, "If my mother, or any of my family, come here and ask you to go with them to town, would you?"

I knew this was a tricky question that would require an even trickier answer.

"What do you think; should I?" I answered.

"Definitely not. I don't even want you to talk with them at all. That's why we may never go and visit them in San Pedro Pinula or at the farm. Is that clear?"

"Yes, it is. I'm now with you and I would never do anything to contradict you."

When I said this, he turned his head and looked at me as if he were trying to penetrate into my deepest secrets.

"I really liked the way you greeted me tonight. I knew it then and now I know it…you are totally mine. I have you and now my child is coming. I don't need my family, especially my mother who thinks that she knows everything. Now that I have you my life is complete."

∽

The days passed without much change in my life. The monster

continued referring to me as his woman, teaching me some things about farm life, things that I had not learned at my grandmother's farm. His attitude toward me had certainly changed, for I appeared to have changed from what he called a haughty girl into a very humble and subordinate girl, a girl who now accepted her destiny. But how wrong he was. I was just becoming more cautious. I was still thinking about escaping and I was still trying to figure out where he kept his weapons. I had not seen his gun around his waist or lying around the shack since moving to Las Agujitas. I had no idea what had happened to it. I had not observed him putting his dagger in his boot or taking it out. I was not sure if he discarded it or hid it somewhere. However, he always kept his machete with him, and he used it whenever we went around the land. He had to use it to chop down small dried branches of trees for firewood or to cut down weeds in order to open a path for us to walk, or to kill snakes.

My morning sickness was becoming worse. I was still preparing and drinking the potion the Indian lady had given me, but it did not help; it made me even sicker. One of the smells I hated the most during this early period of my pregnancy was that of cigarette. Out of consideration for me, he stopped smoking close to me and I was very grateful to him for doing that. He continued to talk incessantly about the baby. I was starting to hate the child growing in my womb, a child conceived in violence and hate. I daydreamed about being married and pregnant with Canche's baby, a child that would have been conceived in love. These innocent fantasies of a fifteen-year-old girl were protection against the harsh reality of the situation, but at the time I felt that these fantasies were no more unreal than the violence and squalor I was actually experiencing.

The monster's nervous reactions to unusual noises had not gone away. He still reacted as if someone were after him or as if he were afraid of someone suddenly appearing from behind to attack him. If someone stopped by the shack to talk, he always stood with his back to a wall. By now I had become so accustomed to these reactions that if one day passed by without my witnessing this weird behavior, I would have thought that something was not right.

One day around noon the monster asked me to go and check the land he had prepared for cultivating grains. "We need to keep an eye on the birds and scare them away so they don't eat the seeds."

We had made a scarecrow and asked me to place it in the middle of the field. He told me, "I've already dug out the hole and all you have to do is place the pole in the hole and then push dirt around it."

I was a little afraid to go because the path was lonely, although the field was not very far away, perhaps a twenty-minute walk. I did not want to go, but there was little choice except to do what he had told me to do.

"While you're there I'll go and get more firewood and bring some water," he added.

When I was placing the scarecrow in the middle of the field I thought I heard a noise like steps crunching dead leaves on the ground. I stopped what I was doing, in case I was the one making the noise myself. I tried to look around without moving my head, shifting my eyes from one corner to the next. Then I noticed something moving. I screamed as loud as I could. A person appeared from behind a tree and was walking straight toward me. It was the monster.

"You scared me!" I yelled in panic.

"I just wanted to see if you would try to do anything you are not supposed to. You have to remember that after you tried to escape from the farm I lost my trust in you. I want to trust you and that trust is coming back little by little. Unfortunately, I have to use these tactics to test you."

༄

In Las Agujitas I wished many times that I had the isolation of the cheese room on his mother's farm. In that room I was able to cry, think, and even talk to myself without being questioned or watched. Although the monster was treating me somewhat better in a physical way, probably out of respect for his child, life with him remained the same with the mental torture. In fact, the mental persecution was on the rise. I had to be on guard that he did not catch me deep in thought, not even for a second. Whenever he saw me thinking he started a constant barrage of questions and accusations revolving around the same topic.

"Do you still love that college faggot boy?" he probed. "Do you still think about him? If he loves you so much why doesn't he come and try to find you? I feel so sorry for you."

I do not think that he was capable of conceiving that when I became quiet I was thinking about my family, my mother, Aunt Teresa, my sisters or my classmates. He thought that I had nothing else to think about but Canche. Of course, there were times when I was thinking of Canche, but my thoughts were mostly about my broken future, my unfinished schooling, my ruined life, my turning into another farm girl just like my cousins, most of whom never even went to school beyond grade two.

The monster constantly repeated how much he loved me and how much he would suffer without me. I was sure he was convinced that I was now in love with him. Perhaps I was doing things or saying things that made him think that. He was no longer saying, "If I don't have you I will suffer." His words now were more or less around the terms, "If you stop loving me, I will die."

My confusion of feelings toward this man, which had started at his mother's farm, continued at Las Agujitas:

What is the use of trying to hold on to the past? All is lost. After all, he is taking care of me.

But immediately my thinking would switch:

How could I have thought that I had fallen in love with a man who did what he has done to me? How can I feel sorry for him?

And then I would flip back to the previous thoughts:

No one else cares for me except this man. Where is my father, where is the rest of my family who are living only a few kilometers away from this horrible place? Why doesn't someone come looking for me?

I was so alone, so isolated, and so dependent on this horrible man. However, the main reason I was so confused was that I really did not have time to myself to properly think things out. I could only think about how to survive the mental torture, the death threats, the lack of food, the lack of sleep—from day to day, from hour to hour, from minute to minute.

Don't say anything to make him angry or suspicious. Be submissive, don't look sad or pensive, get the firewood, cook the food, keep looking down so he can't see the eyes—the tears.

He never left my side, sometimes sitting and watching me for hours with his evil, hypnotic stare.

◦◦

If I could find any positive aspect about living in this shack it was that I felt that I was closer to civilization. I saw people passing by, walking on the trail that led to town. Once in a while someone would pass by and ask questions. Of course, the monster never allowed me to speak to these people; he answered all of their questions himself. Many times people would approach the shack to ask for a drink of water or fire to heat up their coffee. When this happened, they looked at me and I am sure they made comments about me in their own Indian language, which was *Pocomán* in this region. I was happy that people were seeing me and I thought that maybe someone would say they had seen me in this place when they returned to San Pedro. I was able to hear dogs barking and occasionally see them with their masters. Several times in the early morning I heard the clucking of chickens that were being carried on the backs of the people who were taking them to be sold in the town during market day. When I saw the venders returning from the town in the late afternoon I checked the position of the sun. Calculating the remaining daylight, I knew that this place could not be more than an hour away from town. The Indian people of the region, after having sold their vegetables, pigs and chickens in the town, shopped in the town's stores to buy the things they needed. No later than four o'clock they would start heading back to their homes in the many small villages that surround San Pedro Pinula. Of course, this routine varied depending on how far the village was from the town, but more or less by four o'clock in the afternoon on Sunday and Thursday market days they were heading home.

◦◦

The rainy season had already started and the first few times it rained the water went through the shack, washing away the dirt floor. I thought that we were going to be washed away along with the dirt. The criminal and I sat on the bed and watched the water run through the shack. While we were sitting on the bed I compared my present situation to the future I had dreamed about before this nightmare had begun, a future of graduating from college, of becoming a teacher and of marrying the man I loved. Here I was, living in a flooded shack with a demented criminal.

One evening, while we were sitting on the cot to escape the water, the criminal looked very dejected and started talking about his disillusionments: "I don't belong in this shack. You don't belong here either. I hate my mother for putting me through this. All the wealth my father had left to the family was also for me and she condemned me to live like a beggar. You and I should be on the farm with the rest of the family and not be suffering in this slum. You're weak. You need to eat better food and here we are, eating nothing but tortillas and salt. I want you to know that this won't last forever. We're getting out of here. When everything is settled and when I feel that I can freely move around I'll find work and not return to this slum or to anywhere close to my family."

This was the first time he had talked about his feelings and plans. I knew by the way he was talking that he was not planning to let me go, which was my only concern. I had suspected this, but now I was sure about his plans for me. His statements about his mother causing his dismal life were very revealing, although at that time I did not fully comprehend their significance. I was sick, malnourished, pregnant, in a robotic state and could only think about how to survive. I was incapable of analyzing anything too deeply. Much later, however, I was able to reflect on this and to see that the criminal took no responsibility for his own actions: I made him kidnap me because I ignored him. I forced him to rape me because I did not freely give him my love. I made him keep me prisoner because I was untrustworthy. I made him beat me and almost kill me because I attempted to find a way home. His family was to blame for all of his prior failures and for his present poverty. I was not just in the hands of a dangerous and not-too-bright criminal; but worse, I was the prisoner of an extremely angry, frustrated and dangerous mentally disturbed man.

On a very warm day in early June, around four o'clock in the afternoon, the criminal and I were fixing our tortillas when we heard firm steps coming toward the shack. The steps became louder and louder as they approached closer and closer. Suddenly, my twelve-year old brother, Jesus Carmelino, was standing in front of us, and behind him were three police officers.

Then everything happened very quickly. My brother pointed his finger at me and said, "Yes, that girl is my sister…that is Gabriela."

The police officers drew their guns and ordered the criminal to put up his hands. He raised his arms and two of the officers got closer to him, ordering him to put his arms straight out in front and they then placed handcuffs around his wrists. One officer was still pointing his gun at the criminal as if he were ready to shoot at any time.

Strangely, instead of thinking about why the police were there or saying anything to them I began to examine their uniforms as if I had never seen them before. The uniforms comprised dark blue pants and sky blue shirts with long sleeves. The pants had a vertical stripe on each side in lighter blue colour, the same as the shirt. The national crest was  sown on one of the sleeves. The crest consisted of a quetzal (a tropical bird and the national symbol) perched on a rolled–up document with the date of Guatemalan independence inscribed on it. The document was lying on top of two rifles, crossed to form an X and two swords, again forming an X. Two laurel wreaths framed the whole ensemble. The officers wore dark blue police hats with a broad band and the national crest in black was positioned on the band.

I felt that I was not part of this scene, but rather, I was outside of the action, watching everything from a distance—like watching the cinema: *There's no use saying anything; no one can hear me anyway.* Nothing appeared to be real—only a dream. At the time, I felt that this scene was just as improbable as my kidnapping and rape. I was now totally anesthetized to my absurd and brutal reality.

Once the criminal had been handcuffed the police pushed him out the door. They ordered me to follow them and this snapped me out of my trance. We started walking toward San Pedro Pinula. The criminal and I were instructed not to talk to each other at all.

"Is my father waiting for me in San Pedro?" I asked.

"We are not here to provide you with any information, we are here to capture both of you," one policeman said in a very officious tone.

"Why am I being arrested?" I persisted.

"These are the orders we have."

I never asked any more questions during the rest of the trip.

The walk was difficult. I could barely keep up with them and many times the criminal politely asked the police officers to slow down for my sake. My brother was walking beside one of the police officers, the criminal was in the middle of the other two officers, and I was walking alone behind them. Whenever the criminal turned his head to check on me the officers immediately told him to keep going. The criminal tried to be very chummy with them and although the officers kept up their official decorum, it appeared to me that they were buddies with him.

While we were walking I was imagining all kinds of scenarios that were going to take place once we had reached San Pedro Pinula and the most constant image was the one of seeing my father coming to meet me and telling me how happy he was that I was alive. I pictured Aunt Teco coming to greet me, perhaps with some of my cousins. I was even imagining my father and my mother coming together to meet me.

We arrived in San Pedro Pinula just as the sun had begun to set. The police took us to the Municipal Building and told my brother to go home. To my surprise, there was only a jail cell waiting for me—no father, no Aunt Teco and no family members.

Where is my father? I turned my head in every direction. There was nobody in the Municipal Building except officials. I tried to tell the police that this situation did not look right to me, but they were not willing to hear me.

One of the police officers guided me close to a jail cell all the while talking, "Here is where you will be staying tonight. If you need to use the washroom just call any of us and we'll let you out. Tomorrow morning someone is going to wake you up very early and will show you how to clean the washrooms." I hesitated, still looking around for someone who could help me. "Get in," the officer insisted. The door clanked behind me.

I could not comprehend the reasons the police had to lock me up in a cell as if I were an assassin or some other kind of serious criminal. My cell was pitch black and there was no electric lighting. This surprised me because I had seen the Municipal Building illuminated by electricity before, electricity provided by a generator. There was no chair, no bed, no blanket and no food. I was not hungry anyway. Food was not a need for me at this moment since I was still throwing up anything I ate.

Why isn't Papá here waiting for me? Where is he? He has to be in town because my brother is here. Why doesn't he come to see me and get me out of here?

I cried and this was the first night I had cried for a long time. I cried more than I did on the night the monster kidnapped and raped me. I was so scared. It was so dark. Eventually, I had no more tears in my eyes. I became so tired from crying that I fell asleep, sitting down on the floor with my back against one of the walls. I was dead tired but I could not sleep. I was only thinking, trying to figure out what was going on.

In the darkness and isolation my imagination was running in every direction. The smell of urine pervaded the air. I could hear mice running across the floor and gnawing in the ceiling. I was imagining that there were scorpions and poisonous spiders up there too, falling on the floor and crawling toward me. I even had the sensation that these creatures were crawling up and down my back. I thought about the cheese room and how good and comfortable that room was compared to this one.

Does Aunt Teco know what has happened to me? What is she thinking? Does she still love me? Does she know where my mother is? Why hasn't she done something in my favour? Where is everybody? Why am I in jail? I'm only fifteen and I've done no crime.

It looked as if all the police officers had gone home. Maybe there were one or two left behind but I did not see them. For a while there was some light, provided by a gasoline lantern hanging from a tree to illuminate the patio. When the last police officer went off duty the lamp was turned off and I was left in total darkness. The church clock sounded, I started to count its rings—eleven. At eleven-thirty it rang once. After a while there were twelve dongs to announce midnight and then again one dong at twelve-thirty. At this point I must have fallen asleep. When I awoke I waited to hear the church clock ring. At last, I heard one dong and I thought that it was one o'clock in the morning. Then immediately I heard a second dong.

Well, it's now only two o'clock. I didn't sleep for very long.

The muffled street noises of people walking on the cobblestones and talking gave me some distraction, but these sounds were gradually dying away. A burst of laughter occasionally sliced through the silence, laughter from the group of men who customarily gathered late at night under the arcade of the Municipal Building to talk about work, crops and women. This noise also gradually diminished as the men left one by one. After a while, there was a complete tomb-like silence, interrupted only by the sounds of scurrying mice and the ringing of the church clock every half hour.

El Rey—The King

Yo se bien que estoy afuera,	I know that I am out,
Pero el dia que yo me muera,	But the day when I die,
Se que me vas allorar,	I know you'd cry for me,
Llorar y llorar, llorar y llorar.	Cry and cry, cry and cry.
Diras que no me quisiste,	You'd say you didn't love me,
Pero vas a estar muy triste,	But you are gong to be very sad,
Y así te vas a quedar.	That's how you will be left.
Con dinero y sin dinero,	With money or without money,
Yo hago siempre lo que quiero,	I do what ever pleases me,
Y mi palabra es la ley,	And my word is the law.
No tengo un trono ni reina,	I have no throne or queen,
Ni nadie que me coprenda,	And nobody to understand me,
Pero sigo siendo el rey,	But I continue being the king,
Una piedra en el camino,	A rock on my path,
Me enseno que mi destino,	Taught me that my destiny,
Era rodar y rodar,	Was to drift along, drift along,
Rodar y rodar, rodar y rodar.	Drift, and drift, and drift along.
Despues me dijo un arriero,	Later a muleteer told me,
De que no hay que llegar primero,	No need to get there first,
Pero hay que sabe llegar.	Only to know how to get there.
Con dinero y sin dinero,	With money and without money,
Yo hago siempre lo que quiero,	I do whatever pleases me,
Y mi palabra es la ley.	And my word is the law.

The criminal sang the last line of the chorus of this song, *and my word is the law*, over and over when he was in a particular nasty mood.

Tu y Las Nubes—You And The Clouds

Ando Volando Bajo,
Mi amor está por los suelos,
Y tu tan alto, tan alto,
Mirando mis desconsuelos,
Sabiendo que soy un hombre.
Que está muy lejos del cielo.

Ando Volando Bajo,
No mas porque no me quieres,
Y estoy clavado cotigo,
Teniendo tantos placeres,
Me gusta sequir tus pasos,
Teniendo tantas mujeres

(stanza)
Tu y las nubes me traen loco,
Yu y las nubes me nan a matar,
Yo pa' arriba volteo muy poco,
Tu pa' abajo no sabes mirar.

(verso Segundo)
Yo no nací para pobre,
Me gusta todo lo bueno,
Y tu tendrás que quererme,
O en la batalla me muero'
Pero esa boquita tuya,
Tendrá que decirte quiero.

I am flying very low,
My love is on the ground,
And you are so high, so high,
Looking at my dissolutions,
Knowing that I am a man,
Who is very far from the sky

I am flying very low,
Only because you don't love me,
And I am glued to you,
Despite having so many pleasures,
I like to follow your steps,
Despite having so many women.

(stanza)
You and the clouds drive me crazy,
You and the clouds are going to kill
me,
I barely set my eyes to look up,
And you don't even look down.

(second verse)
I was not born to be poor,
I like whatever is good,
And you will eventually love me,
Or I will die in the battle,
But that little mouth of yours,
Will have to say I love you.

It is easy to see that the criminal used this song's message in the stanza (*and you don't even look down*) to vindicate his crime against me.

.

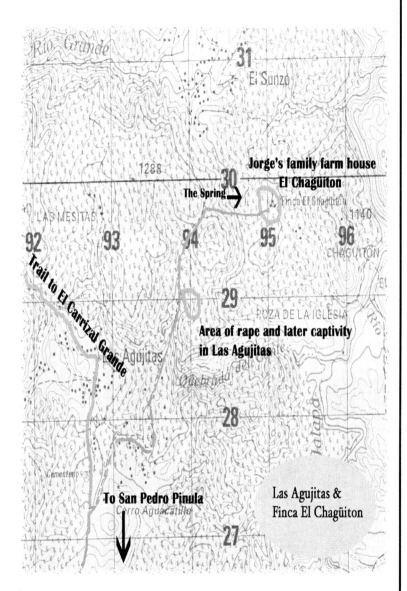

Map of region north of San Pedro Pinula where I was held captive. One square equals one square kilometer.

Los Chorros near San Pedro Pinula

This is place with natural pools of water and a falls, a favourite place to go to with my cousins and friends.

An Indian family in front of a typical covacha.

This shack is palatial compared to the monster's shack in Las Agujitas.

Part III

Abandonment
And
Desolation

Façade of the church in San Pedro Pinula with its bells.

Chapter 10
Trial and Error

Justice consists not in being neutral between right and wrong, but in finding out the right and upholding it, wherever found, against the wrong.
–Theodore Roosevelt–

The church bell rang six times and morning finally arrived. After an hour or so, a police officer came to open the door of the cell. He told me that I had to go and clean the ladies' washroom. He showed me where the supplies and tools were and told me to hurry. I saw the criminal already getting the supplies and tools from a different place and I gathered he was getting ready to clean the men's toilets. These toilets were more or less of an outhouse style. We call them *letrinas* in Spanish. They consist of a sewer like space approximately eighty centimeters deep with concrete or brick walls. A platform with a hole placed on top of the walls allows a person to sit. In order to clean these *letrinas* one has to get the broom inside the hole and start pushing the feces down the outlet, which connects to the sewer. The water reservoir needs to be opened so that the water can carry the feces down the sewer while the sweeping takes place. One has to sweep until the brick that lines the bottom of the well is visible. For a pregnant woman, this sort of job meant immediate sickness and throwing up, at least for me. The stench was unbearable and I had to leave the area in order to breathe purer air.

A police officer saw me and said, "Leave that! Your man is

going to do it." The criminal did do it and I was very grateful, thinking that it was a nice gesture.

Toward nine in the morning two police officers came to my cell and told me, "You have to come with us. Your father needs to speak with you and while you two are talking he is going to give you some breakfast."

As I was walking to the meeting room, my anger toward my father for having taken so long to intervene and for not stopping the police from putting me in jail was rising inside me. At the same time I was very happy that he had finally come and that this whole horrible experience was now soon to end. I was sure that he was going to take care of everything. I knew that in spite of all the arguments we had in the past he was my father and he was surely here to save me. Now the criminal was going to pay for what he had done to me. Now was the time for justice.

While I was waiting, I started to rehearse the words I was going to tell the monster when I confronted him accompanied by my father. I would finally be able to tell the monster my feelings without fear of being beaten or killed. I would have the opportunity of calling him all the names he so very well deserved. My father would then take me home, and the monster would have to stay in jail. I would then eventually return to college, and marry Canche. I had it all planned.

The policemen and I arrived at the room where my father was waiting. As soon as I spied him I longed to run and hug him; I wanted him to come toward me and hug me too. I was happy to see him, in spite of my anger. But I immediately noticed that it was not the most appropriate time to do that; his facial expression told me to stay away. He gave me no greeting. I could see that he was not looking at me with compassion, but more with reproach, disdain, anger and coldness. He approached the police officers and spoke with them very quietly. The officers left the room and my father closed the door. As soon as the door was closed he gazed at me intently and asked me a question—a question that hurt so much, a question that totally devastated me.

"Why did you do this to me?"

I did not know what to say. I did not even know what he

meant. I probably understood the question, but I did not want to admit that my father was accusing me of being at fault for my own disgrace.

Instead of answering his question, I asked him, "Papá, why did it take you so long to come for me. I…" He interrupted me before I could finish.

"I'm the one who asks the questions in here," he emphatically said.

I nodded submissively and said, "Yes, I understand."

"Do you know what you have done with my name, my honour, to my family's honour and to your complete future?"

I shook my head in a negative manner and replied softly, "I didn't know I had done anything wrong."

"Don't act stupid!" he retorted caustically. "I am talking about your running away and giving yourself to that good for nothing (*mequetrefe*). What did you see in him? I took you away from Chiquimula to prevent a disgrace and then you come here and do this to me."

My father kept talking and I just put my head down and listened. His words did not make any sense. He threw at me one accusation after another. He did not give me a chance to speak or to defend myself.

Finally, he paused a little and said, "I have come to take the last step in your favour and I need you to tell me what you want to do."

I did not know what choices I had. I did not even know if there were any choices. At this point I did not even know if I wished to have choices.

"What do you mean? All I want is for you to know that I did not run away with him and…"

He cut me off again, obviously not wanting to hear my side of the story.

"Do you expect me to believe that? Do you think that the judge will believe you? Do you think that people in this town will believe you? How do you expect me to believe what you just said if all this time since you arrived from Chiquimula you didn't do what you were supposed to? Didn't I tell you to go to Jalapa and register in the college? Instead, you chose to stay here in San Pedro Pinula. You went to the evening Good Friday procession without my permission and no one knew you had left the house. I know that you complained to some of your cousins about your dislike for this man's constant chasing you. But people also saw the two of you together in El Pinalito and according to what they say you looked very friendly with each other."

"Papá, I didn't register for school in Jalapa because I was hoping you would send me back to Chiquimula, and besides, I didn't want to stay with Aunt Chus. I..."

"I don't want to hear any of this." He interrupted again, staring angrily at me.

"...Papá, Don Licho was staying with her when he came to Jalapa to..."

"I said I don't want to hear this!" He insisted. "Don't you hear me?"

I was now being cut off before I could even open my mouth. He was not letting me finished one sentence. Finally, I had enough. I had learned that I could expect many things from my father, but not that he would blame me for my own suffering. I had no problem if he wished to punish me for going to the procession without his consent, or even if he said that he hated me for disobeying his orders. Blaming me, however, for what had happened to me at the hands of the monster was something I could not handle. I had a total feeling of abandonment, loneliness and wrath.

I exploded and started yelling at him. "I thought you cared about me! Now I'm sure that you only wanted custody of me in order to use me as a maid for my brothers and my sister and for yourself. You took me away from my mother against my will." I could not stop, for all of the anger that had been building up over the years was now boiling over. "I had to be the mother and maid in the house. How many times did I have to go to the bar at two o'clock in the morning to bring you home? You took me away from my school and scholarship. You did nothing when I told you about Don Licho and your own niece. I even feel like telling the whole town about what he did to my cousin."

As soon as I mentioned Don Licho's name my father became very angry, "You're defaming Felícito's character and that is a serious crime, punishable with jail."

At this point his threats had no effect on me. He was always threatening me with jail anyway, ever since I was a little girl. *Is jail any worse than my present hell? I've already been in jail.*

"You're nothing but a gambler and a cheap father. If you'd left me with my mother, none of this would have happened!" I was screaming again. But immediately, I realized that my anger was controlling me. I calmed and was able to say with a civilized voice, "I'm sorry for screaming, but everything I'm saying is the truth."

I was feeling so much hate; I hated the monster, I hated Don Licho, I hated my complete paternal side of the family, I even thought I hated my father. Most of all, I hated the fact that I had been born, especially that I had been born a female. I was now thinking that he and the criminal were acting in collusion to destroy me—that there was a conspiracy afoot.

My father was now very agitated, his arms were flailing in the air, "You're inventing everything to justify running away with that guy. You have stained the name of the family. I never believed your lies about Felícito. You're right, I should have left you with your mother."

I knew that he said this not out of concern for me, but rather, from the point of view that my mother had no means of financial support and that would have caused me to suffer and possibly starve to death—saving him this present embarrassment to society of having a daughter who had lost her virginity.

We continued hurling awful and terrible insults back and forth until we both were exhausted. Suddenly, my father changed his tone and said with a serious voice, "What do you want? Do you want to come with me, or do you prefer to marry this man? If you wish to live with me, I will have to discuss this with your brothers and see if they agree."

My brothers? What on earth do they have to do with this? Why does he have to consult with them?

"You must realize," he continued, "if you come with me, your chances of finding a husband after losing your purity is going to be very difficult. As you can tell I'm assuming that you were a virgin and Jorge was the first man in your life. A man doesn't want to marry a woman who has lost her virginity. If you were a virgin, he has to marry you. If he refuses to marry you, he'll go to jail for the three years that remain until you become an adult. If you refuse to marry him, he'll go free. However, you've been with him for more than two months and if he declares in court that you were not a virgin, there's no way to prove the contrary, for too much time has already passed. And if he says that, there is no law to make him marry you in order for you to at least regain your honour, your reputation, and my name."

"And what happens to me if I refuse to marry him and choose to go with you?" I said calmly, looking at him with narrow and suspicious eyes.

"Here is what I've decided." He now was speaking with a voice of a lawyer in a negotiation session. "If you come with me, you will not go back to school. You will stay home and do the house chores for a monthly salary. From that money you will have to buy the things you need for your personal use."

It became apparent that my fate with my father was not going to be any better than the one I possibly would have with the criminal, maybe even worse—with the difference that my father would not threaten me with a gun. But I realized immediately that this was silly thinking and I tried to see some positives in going to live with him. One of them was that I would be near Aunt Teco who would surely help me in any way that she could. She had always been a good support to me. She always had time for me, to talk about my pain and my problems whenever I approached her. She also knew how to influence my father in many ways, especially around the area of his stinginess. There was no doubt that going with my father was my best option, even if that meant that I would never go back to school or find a man to marry because I had lost my precious virginity.

After a pause I finally replied, "Papá, I want to come with you, but I have to tell you that I'm already pregnant."

There was dead silence in the room. He just stared and stared at me. He then started to talk to me in a very severe manner. "Well, that changes the whole situation." He hitched his chair closer to the table and started tapping the table to emphasize his words. "It is bad enough that you have lost your virginity but it is even worse to bring a child out of wedlock. Can you imagine yourself raising a child without a father? People will always criticize you and it will be impossible for you to ever find a husband who would accept you with a child. Look at your cousin Hilda. When she had become pregnant and abandoned by her boyfriend, her father kicked her out of the house, abandoned her, left her to fend for herself to save the honour of the family and to stop the gossip. I can tell you many other stories similar to this, if you want."

I sat there stunned. I had hardly slept the night before in jail and was almost in a trance. For once, I could not say anything.

Virgin, virgin, virgin; honour, honour, honour—that's all he can talk about. What about me? Why doesn't he ask about my torture, my beatings, the rape, my ruined health? Can't he even see how awful I look?

"…This is the time to save our family's name and your honour," he lectured on in a monotone voice, "Jorge is an adult and you are a minor. According to the law he has to marry you or go to jail for kidnapping and sexual violation of a virgin. He would have to stay in jail until you turn eighteen…"

What? The monster would only get three years in jail for all that he's done to me? What is my crime that nobody, not even my own father, wants me? I am the victim here. I have been a good girl all my life.

"…Remember, if he refuses to marry you," my father droned on, "he will go to jail for three years. If you refuse to marry him, he will be set free and you will be left with a child and with a remote chance to marry someone else because you are not a virgin. Besides, if you don't marry him, people will assume that you had lost your virginity before all of this happened and that he's the one who's refusing to marry you because of this."

The message could not have been clearer. I felt as if the sky had collapsed and flattened me like a tortilla. The anger toward everybody in my family welled up again, toward my brothers for being so lucky to remain with my father, toward my mother who had disappeared just when I needed her the most and especially toward my father. But my greatest anger was toward the monster who had made a total hell out of my life. Now I knew how a person could want to seek revenge on another.

My father started to talk again but now his voice sounded very far away; I had become as numb as I was on that first night during and after the rape. I could not hear words any more. His voice was just noise in the room—a hum, a buzz.

He changed his tone again and looking straight into my eyes, he said, "You can still come with me if that is what you want, I just don't know how you are going to support yourself and your child. I will still pay you five Quetzals a month for doing all the chores in the house. You will be the maid in the house and not expect anything else. I can't offer you more."

With these words I knew my thinking was right. My father was only making the appearance to be giving me alternatives. In reality, he was leaving me with no options. I was now picturing myself as a maid in his house forever, never to marry, no chance to continue my education, branded a whore, belittled constantly by my brothers, shunned by the community and my extended family, and this child looked upon as a bastard by the community. Could living with the monster be any worse than this? Probably not. The future he had painted was correct. This is what I had been taught all my life—a girl had to be virgin to get a husband and that I had to marry my abductor.

It was clear that my father was doing his best to convince me to marry this monster for the sake of his and his family's honour. I felt abandoned, disillusioned, sad and angry. Anger was directing my thinking now, not rational thinking—anger at the lack of justice and anger with my father.

"Papá, you're right," I blurted out, "the best thing for me is that I marry Jorge—this is what you want and this is now what I want. I can see that it is of no use to continue this talk."

Having said this, I got up quickly out of my chair, spun around, and marched out of the room without looking back. The two officers who had brought me to the room were waiting to take me back to my cell. Another police officer later brought me the breakfast I was to have eaten with my father.

That very same afternoon we went to the court hearing. Now I knew what I had to do when in court. I had to erase the stain I had placed on my family's name by losing my virginity. I had to make sure that the outcome of the hearing would be marriage to my abductor. I do not remember many of the questions that were asked; nor can I recall my exact answers. I knew that for a marriage to take place I had to answer that I had run away with the monster. My father coached me very well on this point before the court hearing.

In the hearing room I was under so much stress that the Justice of the Peace had to ask every question several times before I realized that he was talking to me. The only questions I clearly remember were those revolving around the theme of virginity and sex. That was what the hearing was about anyway; it was not about my being kidnapped, raped and held prisoner. Everything seemed to be pre-arranged. I just had to give the right answers. It was all so sickening.

"Did you bleed when he penetrated you?"

I said, "No."

"Did you go with him with your own will?"

"Yes."

"Was Jorge Cárcamo the first man you ever had sex with?"

Again I answered, "Yes."

The Justice of the Peace then asked, "Do you wish to marry him?"

"Yes," I said in a hardly audible voice.

During the complete court appearance I was continually crying, even during my testimony. The Justice of the Peace made a comment, "For a girl who is getting married to the man whom she loves you don't look very happy." He ordered that we had to marry within the next two days.

After the hearing, the criminal and I were released from custody and we walked silently to his mother's house. The house was empty, a tomb—my tomb. It was the middle of the week and probably everyone was at the farm. This was good, for I had no desire to see or speak to anyone. I was now completely drained, emotionally dead, having no energy to do anything.

⌘

The next day we went to my grandmother's house to get my belongings. Again we did not meet or talk to anybody. It was farming time for my grandmother and uncles too.

We returned to his mother's house and I started to look through everything, trying to find something to wear. He was watching all my activities, as usual. Suddenly he pulled out a dress from a suitcase and held it up, "I want you to wear this dress for the wedding; it shows your curves very well."

How does he know that?

"I should have spat in your face when you refused to dance with me that day."

Then it hit me—this was the dress I was wearing at the *sarabanda* dance during the *Candelaria* Feast on the second of February, a dress I had made myself. It was blue, fitted tightly to my body. It was cocktail length and had a slit on each side. The upper part had short sleeves and a low cut in the back. I was amazed to see that the dress fit me as it had before, perhaps even a little looser. I was pregnant but I had lost so much weight since my abduction.

The wedding took place in the afternoon on the tenth of June and I wore the dress he had selected. The criminal took me to the Municipal Building and we were married in front of three city hall employees who served as witnesses. A stand-in for the Justice of the Peace performed the ceremony. No one from either family was present. My father had left San Pedro for Livingston right after my appearance at the hearing the day before. He did not even say goodbye to me. There were no congratulations from anybody following the ceremony and no reception. And this was fine with me.

My criminal husband and I walked to his mother's house to

live as husband and wife. How sickening and disgusting this walk was.

Now you're legally MINE!" He boasted, shaking his fist in the air. "You're mine, you're mine! Your faggot boyfriend in Chiquimula never had a chance against me, ha, ha, ha!" He kept spouting these taunting remarks all the way to his mother's house.

I remained silent, only thinking about how I was now going to survive. I knew that I was on my own, abandoned by my parents and family, and if I were to save myself I would have to do it myself. Now I knew on what ground I was standing. I also knew that the monster only looked at me as a prize he had won. I was in more danger than ever, now that he was secure in the knowledge that I had no family support. I was thinking that he would eventually tire of me and in one of his fits of anger do something really horrible—maybe even kill me.

Although I was left with no choice but to marry this monster, I still had fight in me and was determined not to give him the satisfaction of thinking he had succeeded in winning me as his "wife", as he called me. I was more determined than ever to survive this hell. This was war. I was now convinced that only one of us was going to come out of this alive and that was going to be me. The desire to avenge my ruined life was taking root.

I have to destroy this monster. Nobody else can do it. I will destroy him with my own hands. He is going suffer as I have suffered. I just have to think of a plan.

Municipal Building: jail, and marriage hall

Stay close to your friends; stay even closer to your enemies.
–Lao–Tzu–

Chapter 11
The Loving Wife

It is by its promise of a sense of power that evil often attracts the weak.
–Eric Hoffer–

After the wedding we spent a few days at his mother's house. The empty house afforded the monster time and space to establish our married routine. For the most part life resumed as it was before our arrests with the exception that the monster now felt free to move around. He went to celebrate his marriage and his future fatherhood by getting drunk every evening with his buddies. I was not allowed to go out into the town by myself or to talk to any of my relatives and friends. I stayed awake every evening waiting for the drunken lout to come home. When he returned in the evening I became very amorous, trying to convince him that I was now madly in love with him. I had no real plan yet, but in order to allay any suspicion that I was up to something, I knew that I first had to make him believe that I was truly and madly in love with him.

During the long hours by myself I had time to do a lot of thinking. The same thoughts would spin around in my brain until my head felt like it would explode. The most common thoughts were nothing but simple conjectures consisting of *what ifs*. What if I had not gone to the procession? What if I had just gone to Jalapa as my father wanted? What if I had not been pregnant, would my father have taken me with him? What if I had not become angry with my father before the court session, would he have been more conciliatory with me; would he have asked me about what had happened and would he have believed me? What if the monster had tried to kidnap me without the help of his friends and his gun? I imagined how brave I would have been: *I would have escaped for sure.* I blamed myself for not fighting hard enough, for not screaming and for not trying to get away. Why did I not pay attention to my aunt in El Pinalito when she pointed out to me that the man buying cigarettes was looking at me in a strange way? I also was now blaming myself for having put myself at risk with my haughtiness toward the monster. This was his way of talking, of course. This was his propaganda; but unfortunately, I was now half-believing it myself.

The criminal's mother's house was large, but not as big as my grandmother's. The living room was at the front and its dimensions were about five by five square meters (270 sq. ft). It had no ceiling and the big wooden beams were exposed. There was a wooden dividing wall with a door separating the living room from his mother and sisters' bedrooms. The house had a floor covered with faded square bricks. The living room had a second door leading to an L-shaped arcade that faced the patio. A huge hammock was hanging from the arcade's beams.

On the north side of the arcade, facing south, there were two bedrooms. I stayed with my *dear husband* in one of the bedrooms and I assumed this had been his bedroom before the kidnapping. The other bedroom was for his brothers, Erasmo and Álvaro. I do not know where Erasmo slept because I never saw him or heard him going to sleep in his bedroom. There were two beds in our bedroom. The second bed was eventually removed and a night table was placed in front of the bed against the opposite wall of the room. I asked the criminal who had been sleeping in the other bed. He said it belonged to his brother David. This was the first time I heard him mention his younger brother. I learned later that David was usually staying with his oldest sister and that was the reason he was not around.

In the corner, where the two sides of the L–shaped arcade met, three stairs connected to a meter–wide sidewalk that led to the kitchen. The kitchen was quite large, having a big table accommodating at least sixteen people very comfortably. The only other piece of furniture was a wooden china cabinet with screen doors. The cooking area of the kitchen had a big clay and hay (*adobe*) counter (*poyo fuego*) for cooking. As in all Guatemalan kitchens, there was the *piedra de moler* to refine the dough for tortillas. Behind the kitchen there was another room where the saddles and other equipment for the horses were stored. The granary was also in there. I would not have had to enter that room to know what was in there, for almost every house in San Pedro Pinula had that kind of storage room.

The house was surrounded by a three meter high wall made of adobe pierced by a big door, the *portón*, which served as the main entrance when people were coming in or going out on their horses. There was nothing planted in the courtyard and it smelled of cow manure. Although I did not see cows, I am sure that the yard was used to milk cows during the dry season. At the time we arrived at the house the cows would have already been moved to the farm because the rainy season had commenced. The yard was very big and on the southwest side there was a simple hut without walls, roofed with clay tiles (*tejas*). In this hut the family washed the dishes and clothes and collected water for their daily use. The outhouse was situated beside this hut. Hitches to tie the horses were located in front of the arcade.

On the first weekend after the wedding the monster's family returned to the house from the farm and the monster and his brother Erasmo immediately had an argument concerning me. I heard Erasmo telling him, "You don't deserve that girl."

The criminal responded, "Are you saying that because you want her for yourself? Is that what you want? Are you trying to conquer her when I'm out of the house?"

This could have turned very ugly, but their mother came to break up the fight. After the argument with his brother the criminal turned on me and in a very accusatory tone he started his now all too familiar interrogation process:

"Do you think that my brother Erasmo is a handsome man? Is he nicer looking than me? Has he tried to make a pass to you when I am not here? You would probably like to see if he has a bigger prick than mine. Tell me, bitch, what were you two talking about? It was about me, right?"

"No," I answered, "we were only talking about food and the kitchen."

"I don't believe you. You college sluts always lie!"

He did not order me not to speak to Erasmo but I knew that this verbal outburst was his way of telling me that I was not to talk to him at any time. This also led me to believe that he probably did not want me to communicate with anybody in his family unless it was in his presence and with his permission.

All of the criminal's brothers and sisters had more or less the same facial features: very light skin, and very straight teeth making for a nice smile. The criminal, David and their sister Vilma were the only ones with darker hair. Vilma looked more like the mother. The rest of the brothers and sisters had reddish–blonde hair and one sister, Carlota, even had freckles. They all had wavy and abundant hair. All of the Cárcamo brothers were very muscular and about one hundred and seventy centimeters tall (five feet five to six). Álvaro was much thinner, but he still had a muscular build, probably due to the hard labour on the farm. They were all handsome people. I think that the prettiest of all the girls was Vilma. She had beautiful, wavy and long black hair that hung below her waist.

Vilma did not come to visit her mother at the house when I was there. I later learned from Vilma's husband, Cesar Sandoval, that Mrs. Cárcamo did not approve of their relationship and that put a distance between Vilma and her family. The criminal was very close to his sister Vilma. He took me to visit her and encouraged me to befriend her. The criminal was also a good friend with her husband. At that time I could not have realized how important their friendship would be in deciding the denouement of my ordeal.

When the monster was out getting drunk I stayed in the bedroom, only going out to the kitchen to eat something, keeping quiet and avoiding everyone, just waiting for his return. When the monster was away I felt very uncomfortable being in his mother's house. I barely talked to her, to his sisters or to his brothers when they were living in the house on the weekend. Anyway, I was under strict orders to remain in our bedroom, as he called the torture chamber. I did not see or hear the criminal talking to his mother, not even once. I spoke to her the few times when I saw her in the kitchen. She barely returned the complement to talk to me. It felt as if everyone had strict orders not to communicate with me in any way or form.

One thing I noticed and surprised me was that the monster was now comfortable staying at his mother's house with me. In Las Agujitas, before the wedding, he said that he did not want to have anything to do with his mother or to have anything that belonged to her. What had changed and why? Since I was only to know what the monster himself voluntarily told me, this remained a mystery.

Many times I had the urge to approach Erasmo to ask him if he was one of the people in the group who had helped kidnap me. I felt that he knew that I wanted to ask him something. On one occasion he came to ask me if I knew where his brother had gone. Erasmo had to know that his brother would not inform me of his daily activities. I thought that he just wanted to find an excuse to start a conversation. He told me not to be afraid or shy to go to the kitchen and eat whatever I wished because I needed to take care of the baby and myself. The rest of the conversation was related to my school in Chiquimula and some other unimportant things. Curiously, I perceived that he was looking at me with pity, or that he wanted to tell me something. Unfortunately, we were not able to talk very long because the criminal came home earlier than usual that evening.

⊷

The criminal's brothers and sisters left for the farm very early on Monday and we stayed until Tuesday and then we departed for Las Agujitas, returning the following Friday evening. When we were back in the shack in Las Agujitas the criminal was perfecting his techniques of mental torture. His accusations against me were the same as before, but the intensity and harshness of the questioning was now totally unbearable. He was becoming increasingly bolder and crueler now that we were married. He threw at me that he was sure that Canche and I had come close to having sex, or that we indeed had sex. He kept insisting that I confess to things that had never happened. He described in detail other sexual acts that he thought Canche and I had performed together—what a sick and vulgar imagination he had. When he talked like this my stomach would start to heave and I felt like throwing up.

There were so many things I wanted to tell the idiot. Mostly things related to how brainless he was. It was so difficult to contain myself and to bite my tongue. When I felt like vomiting I did everything to suppress this feeling, for whenever he saw a disgusted look on my face he threatened me, "You're lucky you're carrying my child, otherwise things would be different."

Does he really mean this? This was important information, for I now knew that this thing, this growth in my womb, was very important to him. I was now actually happy I was pregnant; my pregnancy was saving me from who knows what kind of beatings. But every time I thought about the fetus itself I hated it. I then would immediately get a guilty feeling and I prayed, "Oh God, please forgive me for loathing this innocent thing inside me."

During the long nights of interrogation I learned to look firmly at the monster while my mind flew off somewhere else. I had to focus my thoughts on something unrelated; otherwise, I would have gone crazy. When he was interrogating me I had to shake myself into the real world and ask him, "What did you say?" My mind had flown somewhere else for peace and safety. That was the way I blocked his words from destroying my spirit;

that was the way I prevented my brain from being poisoned by his venom; that was the way I mentally survived. I became very good at this—an expert.

~⋑

One day the monster decided to search through all of my belongings. When he was pawing through the suitcases he came across a package of letters tied up with a pink ribbon. Canche had written these letters to me during the two months of school holidays of 1962–1963. I also had one or two letters dated 1961. Among my memorabilia was a diary with some photographs placed between the pages. These photos were of Canche and me with our school friends at the Independence Day parade where I marched as a majorette. The diary did not have much written in it, as it was a one–year diary for the year 1964. I wrote about passing my exams, seeing Canche in Chiquimula, the moments we were together and about my sadness of having to leave Chiquimula. Unfortunately, I had written some lines about the day I had gone to the post office in San Pedro Pinula and seeing the pest there waiting for me. The notes in the diary about him were not very flattering. I referred to him as *an illiterate farmer who followed me everywhere.*

Another box contained the special school memory book from 1963. At the end of the school year each student buys a nice book and asks his or her friends to write down their names and addresses along with a short poem or a funny anecdote—something that will bring memories back later when one reads it. We call it a *Libro de Recuerdos.* My book had the names of all my classmates and friends, male friends included. In the book some of my male friends made remarks about *my beautiful body.* One of them even wrote a poem referring to me as a *kind, intelligent person with a body of a mermaid.* Other male friends expressed their feelings through poems or written notes. My book was filled with these little notes and poems and it became very good ammunition for the criminal.

He waved the book in front of my face and said, "I bet you fucked every one of these guys who wrote in this book. You were nothing but a whore. I wish I had found this before I married you. If I had known the kind of trash you were I would have preferred to go to jail for kidnapping you instead of giving you the honour to be my wife and to carry the name Cárcamo."

As if it were an honour to be called Mrs. Cárcamo!

I did not dare say this to his face, for he was again making that horrible grinding noise with his teeth and his breathing had begun to accelerate faster and faster; his nostrils were expanding, wider and wider. I was expecting the worst from him at any minute. As usual, he was able to control himself when I kept quiet.

These letters were now his weapons of choice against me when it was interrogation time in the evening. He read and reread the letters several times a day and every time the teeth grinding would start, then the angry threats, and finally the names: liar, slut, bitch, whore. There was nothing bad or erotic in the letters; they only contained the innocent confessions of love from a young boy to a girl.

His favourite exercise now was to read each one of the letters aloud, making fun of the ways Canche expressed his feelings for me. Then he would stop reading, look at me, and start the interrogation: "Did you answer his letters in the same way? Did you tell him that you loved him? Show me how you kissed him. Show me how you hugged him. Did you open your legs for him? Did he touch your tits?"

His questions came so fast I really did not have time to answer him or to do a demonstration for him, even if I had wanted to. His warped brain was working overtime. There was nothing to answer anyway, for he would have called me a liar no matter what I had said. I thought that the cheese room was bad, the kidnapping horrible, the rape horrendous, but I was now thinking that this constant verbal torture was the worst ordeal. It was really taking a toll on me. I felt that I was losing my mind, my strength and my resolve to survive.

I begged him more than once, "Kill me and end this once and for all."

"If you weren't carrying my child, I would have done that a long time ago! You'd better believe that, bitch!"

The criminal found a ring in one of the boxes, the ring that

Canche had given to me in the church after our last walk in Chiquimula. Canche told me that his mother had given it to him and that he was now giving it to me as symbol of his pledge that he will marry me.

The criminal examined the ring very closely and with a suspicious and threatening voice he asked me, "What's the complete name of your faggot lover in Chiquimula?"

"José Esteban Villeda Sagastume" I calmly answered.

"Who's this fucking E.S. on the ring?" he bellowed.

"Those are the initials of his mother's name."

"What's her name?"

"Elvira Sagastume."

"I don't believe you. These initials belong to another secret lover you've kept hidden from me."

Although he had read in my diary where I had written about the ring he continued to terrorize me for days about this. Eventually, he became tired of this particular game and the questioning about the ring stopped. I do not know what he did with the ring. He probably sold it or exchanged it for alcohol. At any rate, the ring disappeared forever and he never mentioned it again.

One day the sadistic criminal came across a letter in which Canche had written: *Whenever you hear the song,* Buscando Una Estrella (Looking Upon a Star), *please think about me.*[*]

I guess the criminal had never heard his popular song. After all, the songs that he sang and whistled were the particular Mexican rancheros he liked, the ones that portray nothing but machismo attitudes. He tried to force me to sing the song, but I was not able to. I knew the music and the words; I just was not able to make the lyrics come out of my mouth. I tried to hum part of the music and it sounded more like a shaking sound from the throat of a person with a bad cold than anything else. Finally, after many attempts, I was able to hum the tune in a somewhat recognizable fashion. He looked at me with his cold and insane looking eyes and said, "From now on, if I ever hear you whis-

---

[*] This was originally an American 1960 hit song sung by Gary Miles.

tling, humming or singing that stupid song again, you'll be very, very sorry."

However, I kept singing the song to myself. I was as defiant as ever and determined that he was not going to completely get his way; he was not going to control my mind.

One evening the monster held the letters up in front of me and snarled, "So, based on what these letters say, you will throw yourself into the arms of that fag boyfriend of yours if you ever see him again. I bet that if he were living here in Pinula, you would have already run to him and slept with him. These letters reveal to me that the love you're showing me is phony. I don't trust you; I don't trust college girls; you're all nothing but tramps and whores. You must be planning something against me. Your amorous ways don't convince me. I'm not stupid. Just remember, if you try to do something against me, you'd better do it right because if you don't, you're finished."

He threw the letters and my *Libro de recuerdos* into the fire. He then tore off the few pages where I had written in my 1964 diary and flung them into the fire. As the pages were burning he took my face into his hands, violently twisted my head around, forcing me to look at the fire.

"There!" He yelled. "Say goodbye to that garbage, and say goodbye to the sweet words of your lover in Chiquimula. All of that is nothing but stupid crap from all your other lovers and your trashy, prostitute girlfriends."

I gazed at the fire and I knew he was watching me to see if I were crying. I felt like crying from my pain, anger, and humiliation, but I was able to hold back my tears for my own protection.

My situation was becoming more and more precarious, for the monster was becoming more unstable and dangerous by the day. His talk was becoming more violent and incoherent, his actions more unpredictable. I was now sure that he did not kidnap me out of some twisted and sick notion of love; he just wanted to seek revenge on the girl who had embarrassed him in front of his friends. However, the immediate danger was that he was still suspicious that I was faking my love for him, that I had ulterior motives. He had no trouble telling me this. His paranoia was defeat-

ing my plan to have him lower his guard.
What kind of devil is he? How could he penetrate into my brain? Have I been giving him any signals?

❧

The warning he had given me right before he burned the letters, the one about my being *finished* if I were to try something against him, made me shiver, for I had been thinking about killing him every day since the wedding. Every time I was thinking about how to get out of my misery I always came to only one particular solution—there was no other way out for me but to kill him. Killing him was becoming an obsession, a thirst. I wanted to make the monster pay for all the harm he had done and was still doing to me. These thoughts of revenge scared me, but they were now persistent and they were interrupting my more pleasant and practical thinking. I wanted to end my pain and suffering once and for all and if I ended up in jail, it could not be any worse than what I was already suffering. I was not even thinking about Canche or my education anymore.

This thinking followed a pattern: first, I started with gentle thoughts, imagining ways of escaping when he was away from the house. Then my thoughts would turn to the monster's dying a somewhat natural death when he was out. I was hoping that his drinking might kill him. I pictured him drunk, falling from his horse and breaking his neck. At other times, I imagined him stepping on a poisonous snake, being bitten and subsequently dying a most horrible, painful death. Many times I imagined him getting into a fight and being killed by someone at the bar:

That would be a good thing to happen; then I wouldn't have to kill him.

I thought that maybe some black magic might do the job:

If I wish hard enough I might be able to make him disappear from this earth. I just have to think hard on this and he will just vanish into air.

But the thought that came to my mind most often was the one of my killing him. This idea was eating into my brain and dominating almost all of my waking thoughts: *I have to find the gun; I have to find the gun. Where does he hide the gun?* Sometimes I thought that the devil was giving me power. I saw Satan's face in front of me, talking to me. I started to wonder if I were still functioning properly or becoming insane.

Ah, yes, maybe I can find some loroco roots, boil them and poison him.

One of my classmates in elementary school once told me that the roots of the *loroco* plant, when boiled and drunk, would kill.* I hated the monster with every ounce of my energy and every time I thought about what he had done and was doing to me the desire to make him totally disappear from this world consumed me.

I also detested this thing, this tumour, growing inside me, this product from this horrible man. I had a nauseous feeling not only from the sickness of my pregnancy but also from the attachment the monster was showing toward *his* unborn child. Quite often he got close to me, professing his love, lowering himself to the floor to touch and rub my stomach. There was such joy in his eyes. With his hands on my belly he would tell me how happy he was about his becoming a father. I wanted to vomit and I surprised myself how well I was able to contain my anger and total revulsion.

For a long time his behaviour confused and overwhelmed me, but now his cruelty was only impelling my resolve to kill him. It was making me strong, or so I thought. At times my thoughts, feelings and desires frightened me. I felt guilty, very guilty and even became afraid of myself. I felt as if there were two powers inside me fighting against each other. One power was telling me that God would punish me for disobeying his commandment: THOU SHALL NOT KILL. When I prayed, a crucifix appeared in front of my eyes. I actually saw the image of Jesus on the cross talking to me, with his lips moving, telling me that what I was thinking was totally wrong. But there was another power in front of me, speaking to me, "Seek revenge! Kill him! You must—you must kill him! Don't let him get away with what he did to you! He

---

* *Loroco* is the Guatemalan word (probably of Mayan origin) for a leafy vegetable used to flavour typical dishes, especially rice. Its botanical name is *Fernaldia Pandurata* and it is native of El Salvador and Guatemala.

does not deserve to live!'"

I did not know how I was going to kill him and I knew that it would be difficult. I was only sure of my first step—I had to keep trying to earn his trust. I had to re–double my efforts to become the amorous and obedient wife. It did not matter to me what I would have to do, what indignities I would have to suffer or what price I would have to pay. I was going to earn his trust.

Over the next few days in Las Agujitas I became even more romantic and ardent in showing my love. I was giving him very deep, loving kisses and spontaneous hugs. Oh, how this made me sick. The criminal always told me how much he wanted me to love him. Well, I surprised myself by not finding it difficult to act this part, for all I had to do was to think about my suffering. I felt so weird, dirty and guilty—even evil; but, at the same time, I felt good. My plan, so I thought, was working; I was gaining power; I could feel the power growing in me.

On the first weekend of July we went to town. My stomach was just starting to show and the morning sickness had now disappeared. I still did not talk very much with his mother, brothers and sisters when we went to their house in San Pedro Pinula, only a few insignificant sentences.

His mother made a comment, "Your stomach is starting to show and you should be wearing maternity clothes."

Before I could answer his mother the criminal interjected, "I want everyone to see her stomach, to know that she is pregnant. She doesn't need maternity clothes." He was still acting as if he had done something superhuman by getting me pregnant.

On this particular weekend at his mother's house I had nothing else on my mind except to carry out my intentions. It appeared that he trusted me a little more and this would open up better opportunities to carry out a plan, once I had thought of one. He saw that I was not trying to run away, that I was more comfortable around his family, and that I was showing him how much I loved him. He was now telling me some things about his life and plans he had never told me before, although he was still tormenting me about Canche without compassion whenever he saw me in a pensive mood. When he came close to my stomach to hear his baby, I pretended to be very happy about being the mother of his child and I was sure that I was fooling him. He bragged to everybody about his future fatherhood while I was wishing and praying that this thing in my womb would die at birth.

My imagination was running rampant and it was impossible to think about anything else but exterminating him. I shook my head, trying to shake out the evil thoughts. I was feeling that I was not any better than he. My thinking about doing away with him was becoming less abstract.

First, kill him with his gun or dagger and then find a solution to this growth in my womb. Why should I waste any opportunity to destroy him since he has already destroyed me? Why should I feel guilty?

One Saturday morning at his mother's house I swore that I was going to eliminate the evil monster that very day. I had just endured a particularly horrible night of interrogation and mental torture. Now I was sure I had the will and courage to carry out my plan; I just had to find the way and the opportunity to do it. I had been trying to pay particular attention to the places where he kept his weapons, the machetes and the dagger, but I did not know where he kept his revolver. This gun had disappeared for a while and suddenly appeared as soon as we were at his mother's house. That was a mystery to me because I was watching almost every one of his actions and I cannot remember seeing him hiding or retrieving the gun.

Was the gun even his? Did he leave it at his mother's house before we moved to Las Agujitas? Where is the gun? Where does he hide it? I need it!

I was living in a constant state of confusion about many things when I was with the monster, a confusion that he probably had deliberately fashioned himself to keep me off-balance, and the mystery of the gun was one of these situations. During my captivity I could not find answers for many of his other strange ways and activities.

On the Sunday morning of this same weekend stay, after another complete night of mental torture, the monster noticed that my eyes were very swollen and he started questioning me, "I know you've been crying. Was it for your faggot boyfriend again? Do you think about him all the time? I feel so sorry for you, you poor thing. It doesn't matter if you love someone else, you're still mine and you'll always be mine, etc, etc."

He was not totally wrong about my crying but he was wrong about the cause. I had been crying because of the deep pain I was feeling when I thought about my destroyed future, my miserable life with him, and my disgusting pregnancy. I had been also crying about my father's lack of action for not having saved me from this horrible man. But I was particularly crying that night for myself; for faking love to the man who had destroyed my life; for having felt compassion at one time for the worthless criminal; for the rage inside me—a roaring rage running through my arteries, contaminating my whole body and changing me into a different person, a person I could no longer recognize—a person who wanted to kill.

After the monster had tormented me for a while about my crying he left the house early, right after breakfast. I was very tired from having had to stay up and be tortured all night; but as soon as the horrible creature had left, the re-occurring thoughts of sorrow and anger I had the night before raced back into my head. This time, however, they were mixed with resolve to finally do something against the criminal. I had the desire for revenge, a desire so strong it left me dry. I felt like I was in the middle of a hot desert without a drop of water to drink. Now I was concentrating only on one thought:

I HAVE TO KILL HIM. It's either I kill him or he will eventually kill me, if I don't become crazy first. He said that he would have already killed me if it weren't for my carrying his baby. There's no other solution. Now…it's just a matter of when and how. I have to find a way.

I do not know how many times I glanced at the wall where the machetes were hanging and each time I wanted to grab one of them. I was so weary and numb; I was so tired and confused.

I suddenly heard a voice, then another voice, and another. This made me alert. The voices were all saying the same thing, sometimes separately, sometimes in unison, "Don't be stupid.

Take advantage of the opportunity."

I looked up and saw that the voices were coming from the wall—all of the machetes on the wall were talking to me. My hands started to sweat, my heartbeat became faster and my breathing was shallow, sounding more like a puffing noise of a train locomotive than my normal breathing. I tried to substitute other thoughts but it was becoming more and more difficult. I turned my head to look somewhere else—at the roof, at the floor, but the machetes would not shut up.

"Here I am…kill him with me."

"No, no, don't listen to him, kill him with me."

I put my hands to my ears, but the voices went on and on.

"I'm the best, kill him with me…with me…with me!"

I was about to run to the wall to grab one of the machetes, if only to make it shut up, when the monster unexpectedly came home and ordered me to pack up and get ready to return to Las Agujitas. The voices stopped and so did my desperation to seek an immediate solution to my problems, but it did not break my resolve to do away with the monster.

I'm sure that there will be other opportunities.

A guarisama in its sheath.

Evil, when we are in its power is not felt as evil but as necessity, or even a duty.
–Simone Well–

La Que Se Fué—The One Who Left

Me canse de rogarla,	I got tired of begging her,
Me canse de decirle,	I got tired of telling her,
Que yo sin ella de pena muero,	Without her I'd die from suffering,
Ya no quiso escucharme,	She no longer wanted to hear me,
Si sus labios se abrieron,	And when her lips did speak,
Fue pa' decirme ya no te quiero.	To say , I don't love you anymore.
Yo sentí que mi vida,	I felt as if my life,
Se hundía en un abismo,	Was submerging in a abyss,
Profundo y negro,	Black and deep,
Como mi suerte,	Just like my luck.
Ella quiso quedase,	She wanted to stay,
Cuando vió mi tristeza,	When she saw my sadness,
Pero ya estaba escrito,	But it was already written down.
Que aquella noche,	That was the night,
Perdiera su amor,	When I would lose her love.
Me cance de rogarle,	I got tired of begging her,
Con mis manos sin fuerzas,	With my hands without strength,
Alce my copa y brinde por ella,	I raised my cup and toasted her
No podía despreciarme,	She could not reject me,
Era el último brindis,	It was the last toast,
De un bohemio por una reina.	From an inebriate to a queen.
Los mariachis callaron,	The Mariachis quieted,
De mis manos sin fuerzas,	From my hands with no strength,
Cayó mi copa sin darme cuenta.	the glass fell off without my noticing.

This song is a classic from the morose, and self-pity school of Mariachi music. Mariachi music, like country-western music in the United States and Canada, covers a wide area in its themes: love, domestic life, betrayal, historical events, gambling, prison, horses, farm life, and getting drunk. So, the monster's chosen songs or themes are not indicative of the total genre.

Esta Noche—This Evening

Esta noche me voy de parranda,
Para ver si me puedo quitar,
Una pena que traigo en el alma,
Que me agobia y que me hace llorar,
Si me encuentro por ahí con la
muerte,
A lo macho no le he de temer,
Si su amor lo perdí para siempre.

Que me importa la vida perder,
Ya traté de vivir sin mirarla,
Ya luché por no ser infeliz,
Y tan solo encontré dos caminos,
O lograrla o dejar de vivir,

Esta noche le doy serenata,
No me importa perder o ganar,
Esta noche le canto a la ingrata,
Dos canciones que la hagan llorar,

This night I am going on a binge,
To see if I can take away,
This sadness I have in my soul,
Which overwhelms me and
makes me cry,
If I find my death somewhere,
I am a man and I won't be afraid,
If I lost her love forever.

It doesn't matter if I lose my life,
I tried to live without looking at
her
I strived not to be unhappy,
But I only found two roads,
I've to win her or give up my life.

This night I will serenade her,
I don't mind if I lose or I win,
This night I will sing to the un-
grateful girl,
Two songs that'll make her cry,

In this song I am the "ungrateful girl" that the monster just cannot win. *This sadness I have in my soul, which overwhelms me and makes me cry,* was another sickening line that he sang over and over to make me feel guilty for not giving him my love.

Chapter 12
The Big Opportunity

When you embark on a journey of revenge, dig two graves.
–Confucius–

During our travels from Las Agujitas to San Pedro Pinula the monster sang the usual songs: *El Rey, La Que Se Fué* (The One Who Left) or *Tu y Las Nubes* (You And The Clouds) and now he was singing a new song: *Esta Noche* (This Evening. Page: 211). He sang it every time he was around me. He whistled it while looking at me in a very weird manner. When we were staying at his mother's house, he ran to the radio and turned the volume higher when the Mexican singer José Alfredo Jimenez was singing it and said to me, "I dedicate this song to you." The monster sang it while sober or drunk, while walking or riding the horse on our way back to Las Agujitas. He sang it in the kitchen, in the patio, in the bedroom, in the streets, in the living room, even when he was in the outhouse. The only time I did not hear it from his lips was when he was sleeping. This song is a waltz and it has a very pretty melody, but I was sick of it. Definitely he was telling me that I was *the ungrateful girl* in the song and that he was prepared to die before losing me. I was disappointed that the words of the song did not give me a clue as to whether my plan to make him think that I loved him was working, and that was now my main concern.

We arrived in San Pedro on the second weekend of July, one month after the wedding. On the first day of this weekend the monster came back to the house early in the evening. He was so drunk that he dropped himself on the bed like a dead animal. He called for me and asked me to take off his boots. This was a shock, for he had never asked me to do that before. When I pulled off one of the boots I became quite startled. There it was—THE DAGGER! I removed it from his boot and I put it on the bed. He half-opened his eyes, like a dozing cat. He was watching me. He fumbled around with his belt, trying to take off the holster, but was not able to do it. With a slurred voice he asked me to help him, another shock. I came close to him; his legs were spread out, hanging over the edge of the bed and I had to get between them in order to unbuckle the belt. I could not budge him because of his drunkenness. I finally was able to get him to lift his abdominal area with my help and I was able to re-move the belt. He kept opening his eyes and looking at me. I placed the belt with the holster and revolver near the dagger on the bed by his left arm. He closed his eyes again. His request for help to remove his gun and his boots not only shocked me but puzzled me as well, and I tried to get inside the meaning of it. I was thinking that maybe he was very drunk, more drunk than he had ever been before, or perhaps he was starting to trust me, or maybe he was trying to trap me; I was not sure.

I sat on the stool by the small table in front of the bed. I looked around the room. I looked at him with his arms spread open in the same position of Christ's arms on the cross. He looked so peaceful. I even thought he looked very handsome. He was wearing a red polo shirt with a creamy pair of pants. I looked at the ceiling and looked at the walls again. I gazed intently at the wall; the machetes were hanging from big thick nails. It was a collection of deadly machetes, all with beautifully crafted leather sheaths. His favourite, a type of long machete called a *guarisama* (there are many shapes and types of machetes and each has a particular name), was hanging on the wall too. I kept looking at these weapons around me; the machetes, the gun and the dagger, and the hunger for revenge took over all my thoughts again. The interior voices were screaming at me, telling me, "This is your chance, KILL HIM NOW! All of your suffering will be finished if you finish him off. Hurry, before he sobers up!"

There was a moment that I could not feel if I were awake or alive. It was as if I were living an awful nightmare and simultaneously experiencing a beautiful dream, a dream about to become reality. I forgot that there were other people in the house. All I knew was that I felt that the biggest moment of my life was about to happen. I felt as though I had become blind and deaf, but very powerful. My resolve and desire for revenge and justice was growing stronger by the second. I had to carry out the just sentence that no court in Guatemala would carry out. I had to rid the world of this evil, this monster, this evil monster. I could only see this monster and his gun on the bed, nothing else was visible. He looked totally out of this world and the gun was within my reach.

Suddenly, everything became blurry. I cannot remember walking toward the bed. I do not know how I was able to get close to the gun and take it out of the holster. I was shaking. I looked down. The revolver was in my hands. I had never held a gun before. It felt heavy and I had to hold it with both hands. The monster did not wake up. I had a feeling of power and triumph. Then, strangely, a feeling of calm, peace and wellbeing swept over me. I pointed the gun at him, right in his face, right between the eyes, and with shaking hands I pulled the trigger. There was a click, but nothing happened. *There has to be bullets in the gun.* I pulled the trigger again—another click; once more the gun did not go off. *Oh no, what's happening here?*

At that moment the horrible monster opened his eyes and looked at me with a look I had never seen before on his face—a look of surprise mixed with terror and hatred, a look that told me that this was the end; I was going to die. That look made me immediately come back to reality. My body was covered with cold sweat from my indescribable fear. He did not even appear drunk anymore. After that short contact with his eyes everything happened very fast. In no time he was standing close to me. He snatched the gun from my hands and threw it back on the bed. He put his face close to mine and abruptly pulled me close to his body. He was holding my wrists so tightly I felt no circulation in my fingers. I dared not say anything. I was terrified. He screamed,

"You fucking little bitch, you tried to kill me! You just dug your own grave. I knew you were a tramp and I'm so stupid to have let my guard down."

He released my left wrist, but kept holding onto my right one, tightening the grip and then forcing my hand down into a swan lock by bending it down from the wrist. He yelled at me, "Walk!" He forced me toward the wall where the machetes were hanging. He released my wrist and hand and I had to hold it with my other hand to ease the pain. He yanked the *guarisama* from its nail. He then pushed me with such a force that I went crashing face down onto the floor screaming.

I heard a man's voice coming from outside the room, "Leave the girl alone!"

The monster ran to the door and screamed back, "She tried to kill me, stay out of this!"

I got up from the floor and I saw him rushing towards me with the machete in his hand. I had no chance to plead for mercy. I saw what he was going to do and I turned my back to him, as if that were going to save me from the sharp edge of the machete. An image of my body cut into pieces with blood all over flashed across my eyes for a second. He hit me on my back with the flat part of the blade. He hit me with such force that I went flying face down onto the floor once more. He hit me again, and again. He hit my head, my back, my legs and my arms again and again. I must have lost consciousness because I cannot remember how long he kept hitting me.

When I finally came to, I had no idea how much time had passed. I did not know if I were alive or if I were living in the afterlife. I did not know how I got on the bed. I was just very surprised to have some feeling in my body. I wanted to check my body and find out how injured I was but the monster was with me, holding my hands as if nothing had happened. His face was now very calm. He asked me with a sweet, baby–like voice, like he were talking to a hurt child, "Why did you want to kill me? I didn't want to hurt you or hurt my child. Please forgive me." He was crying. He looked as if he actually had been crying for some time, for his eyes were as red as cherries. He repeated several times, "Please…forgive me."

I could not, and dared not speak. I was hurt and his pleading for forgiveness was making no sense to me.

I felt as if every bone in my body had been broken. The most excruciating pains were in my back and in my abdominal areas. These pains were different than the ones I was feeling on my injured neck, arms and legs. The pain kept me from sleeping. I did not know what day it was or how many hours had passed since he almost had killed me with the beatings. The house was quiet indicating that the rest of his family had gone back to the farm. Only the monster and I remained in the house. He would not leave my side. We did not speak very much. When I opened my eyes he asked, "Why, why?" I pretended to go back to sleep in order not to answer because the truth would have brought more danger into my life and a lie would have been ammunition for him to torment me again. Two or three more days passed and I was still feeling the back and abdominal pains. I did not know what was happening to me. I went to the washroom and I noticed that I was bleeding from my vagina. At first I thought I was bleeding from internal injuries. Then I thought I had not been pregnant at all and the blood was a result of a heavy period.

We eventually went back to Las Agujitas. I had not told the monster about the bleeding, but I knew he was going to find out as soon as he tried to force sex on me again—which is exactly what happened.

The bleeding got worse and worse and the monster did not take me to see a doctor. He asked me several questions about the bleeding and then left the shack. When he returned he looked very tired and sad. He shuffled over to where I was sitting and said, "I know what's wrong with you. I talked to the *curandera* and she thinks that you probably lost my baby."

He put his face on my stomach and was making sobbing sounds as if he were crying, saying, "*Maté mi hijo, maté mi hijo* (I killed my son, I killed my son)."

I felt no sense of loss for the aborted child and thought: *Oh well, he has no son now, ha, ha, ha—too bad for him.*

The monster took me to town and went to talk to his mother. His mother scolded him and argued with him, urging him to take me to the hospital in Jalapa, but the monster refused.

Erasmo joined into the conversation, "You won't escape jail if something serious happens to her."

Erasmo then came to me and told me, "You need medical attention. My mother told me that you lost the baby. You need to go to the hospital in Jalapa. If Jorge doesn't take you I will, even if I have to fight him. I can give you the money so you can go by yourself. However, I don't think you're strong enough to make the trip on your own."

This offer was a shock to me. How was it possible that this man, whom I believed was one of the men who had aided my kidnapper, would now be kind enough to look after my wellbeing? Now, my fear was that the criminal was going to start with his jealous and suspicious accusations against his brother. I was astonished when I heard him thanking Erasmo for his offer. Of course, he did not trust his brother to take me to Jalapa. He had to do that himself.

On our way from his mother's house to the bus stop he started to coach me, "If they ask you at the hospital what happened to you, you must tell them that you fell from a horse at the farm. If you tell them the truth, I will have to tell them that I did this to you because you tried to kill me with my own gun. I am not afraid of jail. Jails are made for real men like me. You will also go to jail and I think it is better that we keep all of this between the two of us. If I go to jail for beating you up, I will make sure you go to jail for trying to kill me."

I was so sick and weak that I did not think that I was going to make it alive to the hospital in Jalapa. I asked the criminal to send my father a telegram telling him that I had gone to the hospital. He said he would do it, once I was admitted.

At the emergency admission area the nurse asked me, "What is the problem?"

Before I could say anything the criminal interrupted, "She fell off a horse and maybe she's lost the baby."

"What is your name?" inquired the nurse.

"Gabriela Folgar," I replied.

"De Cácamo," the criminal had to remind me, with a note of pride in his voice and a smirk on his face.

After I had undressed, the nurses and the doctor questioned me about my injuries. I lied to them, telling them exactly what the criminal had instructed me to say.

Doctor Carías, a doctor whom I previously had known, examined me and said, "I am going to do a D & C. What you really need is an operation as soon as possible. You are too weak at the moment to have it. You have lost too much blood and are anemic. You will have to come back later for the operation. Even for the D & C* you need at least two blood transfusions." The doctor turned to talk to the criminal, "Mr. Cácamo, the blood bank has no more blood of your wife's type."

The criminal asked, "What type of blood does she have?"

"O Positive," answered the doctor.

"That's my type too; I can give blood," he announced proudly.

And he was not just posturing; he did donate blood for me. Maybe he did this out of compassion or maybe he thought that the hospital was not a convenient place for me to die, there would be too many questions. Dr. Carías performed the D & C and I stayed in the hospital for about seven more days.

On the day before I was discharged from the hospital Dr. Carías came to give me instructions: "You are to refrain from sex, get a lot of rest, and eat well. The nurse will explain what you will need to do for hygiene. There is so much damage to your uterus. I recommend that you guard against any pregnancy and come back, no later than three months, for an operation. Maybe then, you might be able to think about having children. If you become pregnant before the operation, you will not be able to ever carry a

---

* D & C is a procedure to scrape and collect the tissue (endometria) from inside the uterus. Dilatation (D) is a widening of the cervix to allow instruments into the uterus. *Curettage* (C) is the scraping of the contents of the uterus.

full–term pregnancy."

At first I did not say anything to the doctor. My eyes were tearing and he probably thought that this was because I was sad for having lost the baby. But no, it was not that at all, I was crying about what was awaiting me, my fate, after my discharge.

The doctor tried to console me, "Now I know it's very sad to lose a baby, but remember, you are only fifteen years old. You will have children after you get well and strong. It will take time. Don't become discouraged."

"Thank you for giving me hope," I replied affectedly, not wanting to be judged as a person with no heart. Actually, I was happy that this thing in my stomach had aborted.

I was still very shy to talk about sexual and reproductive matters, but I knew that my survival now depended on my being more open in this area and on being more forthright to the doctor about the monster's mentality.

"Doctor Carías, please tell my husband about your medical guidelines. He won't believe me, especially if I tell him that there will be no sex. My husband had sex with me even when I was bleeding from the miscarriage. We will probably be going back to Las Agujitas and he needs to have instructions to follow."

"Don't you have relatives in Jalapa and in San Pedro Pinula with whom you can stay?" the doctor asked.

"I can't stay in any of those towns,"

"Where do your parents live?" asked the doctor.

"They're separated and my father lives in Livingston," I answered.

"I have a good friend, an ex-teacher of mine, who works there. His name is Carmelino Folgar."

"Mr. Folgar is my father."

I saw a sudden look of perception in his face. "Of course, how could I have been so blind? I should have clued into it. You are Folgar de Cárcamo. I saw your father not long ago and he told me what had happened."

Dr. Carías did not go into details about what my father had told him and I did not ask. I was very aware that he was a former student and very good friend of my father, for when we lived in

San Pedro Pinula he was our family doctor and he never charged my parents any medical fees. The last time he had seen me was when I was a little girl.

"For your best recovery you must go to your father," he instructed.

"My father might not welcome me because we had a big argument before I got married."

"I understand, but I still suggest that you follow my advice and go to your father for at least three weeks," emphasized Dr. Carías. "I will send a telegram to him and your husband should send him one too."

The criminal finally agreed to the doctor's recommendations. I had to dictate the telegram to him since he told me that he had never written one before:

GABRIELA VERY ILL, LEAVING HOSPITAL TOMORROW. HEALTH DELICATE. DOCTOR ORDERED SHE STAYS WITH YOU. ARRIVE TOMORROW. I RETURN TO PINULA NEXT WEEK.

The criminal tried once more to convince me to stay at his mother's house. I did not trust him to stay away from me and I told him that we must follow the doctor's orders or I would die. In fact, I did not want to go to my father's house either. I knew the situation would not be good after the hurtful things we had told each other before the court proceedings. However, I concluded that it was probably better to be around my family in case my health deteriorated or in case the monster would try to do something foolish with me. I do not think that even when my appendix had burst and I almost died was I feeling as sick as I was feeling at this time.

Dr. Carías gave me the necessary medication free of charge, but we eventually would have to buy more and the criminal had no money. We left the hospital and boarded the first available bus for the long, arduous and painful trip to Livingston.

Chapter 13
Back to Livingston

It must have been the first or second week of August when we left Jalapa. We started very early in the morning in order to make the trip to Livingston in one day. The bus went from Jalapa to San Pedro Pinula, then to San Luis Jilotepeque, Ipala, Chiquimula, and Teculután. At Teculután we transferred to a different bus, the coach bus that travels down the main highway from Guatemala City to Puerto Barrios. After that, there was the hour and a half ferry ride to Livingston. We arrived in Puerto Barrios at ten minutes to six, just in time to catch the last boat to Livingston.

When we boarded the *Santa Marta* in Puerto Barrios to go to Livingston I had to endure the stares from the people who knew me so well. They looked at me with curiosity, but nobody came up to talk to me. I think that this was because I looked so ill or maybe because I was with a strange man. I could not hear their conversations, but seeing the curious looks on some of their faces, I had no trouble imagining what they were saying to each other about me.

The boat docked in Livingston at seven-thirty in the evening. When we arrived neither my father nor any of my brothers were on the pier, not even Aunt Teco. I assumed that my father did not tell her about our planned arrival. My father's house was only two or three blocks away from the pier, but the walk was excruciatingly painful, for it was a steep uphill climb.

People, mostly black people speaking Garífuna, were looking at me and whispering to each other. A few of the comments I heard and understood were:

"Doesn't she look awful?"

"I can hardly recognize her."

"She looks like a dead person."

"I wonder what happened to her?"

"Is that the man she married? He's nice looking."

"She doesn't even look up, she use to be so friendly."

I thought that I would never reach my father's house.

In contrast to the initial cool reception at the pier, my father had a nice dinner ready for us, although I noticed something unusual.

"Where are my brothers?" I inquired.

"They went out," he replied dryly, without lifting his head from his plate.

My father was no longer living on his farm in Campoamor. He was now living in the town, renting a house with only three small rooms—two bedrooms, a combined kitchen and dining room. The shower was outside, next to the outhouse. In the house he had assembled a extra twin bed in his bedroom right beside his bed. My two brothers slept in the other bedroom. My sister Eneida's crib was in my father's bedroom and it had to be dismantled it in order to make room to make room for a mattress for the criminal.

"Where is Eneida?" I asked.

"I've sent her to San Pedro to stay with one of my cousins," he replied.

I did not ask any more questions and went to bed. The monster and my father stayed up talking about what had happened to me. The liar told me the next day that he had told my father that I had fallen from a horse and I had lost the baby. He also told me that my father had asked him to travel to San Pedro Pinula the next day to pick up my sister Eneida.

I could not believe that my father would ask someone whom

he did not know to be responsible for my sister. It reminded me so much of his attitude toward me three years previously, when I was left stranded at the train station in Puerto Barrios. I wanted to say something, anything to warn my father; however, I was too sick and weak to have any input. When I questioned my father about his sending the criminal to get my sister his only reply was, "Since you're going to be home you can take care of her and I will have the opportunity to see her." Another non-answer.

When the criminal left to pick up my sister I thought about taking the opportunity to talk to my father, to ask him if I could stay in Livingston and never go back to San Pedro Pinula. I never brought up the subject, however, for I just had no energy to plead, explain and argue. When I reflect back on this period I think I was more fearful that my father might prevent me from speaking again, or perhaps, not believe me if he had permitted me to relate what had actually happened to me. I was thinking at that time that I must treasure the help I was getting and not say or do anything that might make him upset.

Livingston in 2005, The Main Street

I was able to eat much better at my father's house and this contributed greatly to my recovery. But what helped me the most was that the monster had to sleep away from me. My bed was just beside my father's bed and after Eneida had arrived I slept with her. I did not spend much time in bed convalescing after the first week, for I was soon doing the cooking and taking care of my sister. My father knew that I was not able to do too much and during the first two weeks of my stay he continued to pay the lady he had hired to do the laundry. He treated me with more kindness, openly expressing his fears that he thought that I might die. I saw his eyes watering whenever he looked at me. I also thought that I was going to die, but I was not afraid any more. At times I thought that death would bring an end to my physical pain, to my humiliation and to my disgrace. My body and spirit could not take much more suffering. There were occasions, especially when the pain was intense, when I felt that I was already dead. Thank God, these thoughts of death would quickly dissipate like confetti in the wind and my iron-like tenacity to survive would quickly return.

My medications were very expensive. The monster told me that my father gave him money to purchase them. He also said that my father had instructed him to never tell my brothers about these expenses.

Even though my father was treating me with some kindness, daily life was not pleasant at all. The biggest problem was the behaviour of my brothers. They were constantly putting me down and making fun of me. The worst culprit was my older brother Carlos. Several times he commented, "Something stinks in this house." He even told me that he could not wait for me to get well and "to get the hell out of our house." One particular nasty comment was, "That's nice, first you run away with your lover like a prostitute and then you both come here to live off my father. You've no shame. You're just like your mother."

I did not complain to my father because it would have been of no use. He told me that my brothers did not want me in the house and I knew that his boys were the princes in the house and they could do no wrong. Besides, Carlos was right. I was the one living off my father's charity because I was already married. Since I had no voice as a daughter in the house, I thought it best just to remain quiet.

How different the monster treated me in front of my father and brothers. Now he was   a loving husband, helping around the house, bringing me a chair, talking politely to me. How fast he could change the way he behaved. What an act. It made me sick.

There was no opportunity for my father and me to talk about my situation. When the monster went to San Pedro to pick up my sister I was too sick to talk. Later, when I felt better, the monster did not let me out of his sight, unless it was at bedtime or when he or I went to the bathroom. There were a few times when my father sent him out to buy vegetables or things we needed for the house, but I was still unable to talk to my father for my brothers and sister were always around. The monster's constant guarding and controlling me had to be tiring and only a mentally sick person or a person with a very warped brain would even attempt it.

Aunt Teco came to visit me often, but again she and I never had a little moment alone, for the monster always politely placed himself in the middle. He wanted to know everything we talked about. I remember one funny instance when Aunt Teco wanted to tell me something she did not want the monster to know. She spoke to me using a code language (*Jerigonza*), a corrupt form of Spanish used mainly by teenagers, something like Pig Latin in English. Using this language, she said, "This guy is worse than a burr," and we both burst out laughing.

"What did she just say?" He asked surlily.

"You're a handsome man," I replied, keeping a very straight face

"You're a liar, I don't believe you." Later, after Aunt Teco had left, he said, "If you speak in that stupid way once more I will never let you talk to your aunt again."

The monster also hated when I used a vocabulary he did not understand. I think he was embarrassed about his lack of education. I picked up on this quickly and I knew how far I could go in playing with his feelings of inferiority. "Oh, I'm sorry for using a word you don't know." I would say with barely disguised satisfaction. My little digs were the only revenge I had at this time.

I went out of the house very few times and only for very short and important trips. One day I went to buy groceries across the street. When I was coming back I passed in front of Don Milton's bar and restaurant. The monster must had been watching me walking toward my father's house and perhaps he saw or imagined one of Don Milton's customers come out to look at me when I walked by. Brandishing a knife, he went to warn Don Milton and everyone at the bar that he never wanted anyone to ever look at me again.

I just could not believe how crazy and dim-witted he really was. In Livingston he had no friends, no relatives, no one to support him or come to his defence. Don Milton was a very popular person with everybody in Livingston. If the criminal had made any attempt to hurt him or any of the people in the bar he would have been a dead man. He would not have been able to hide or escape—the only exit from Livingston was the ferry.

I could tell that the monster was not a happy person at my father's place, probably because he felt vulnerable—having no friends, surrounded by imaginary or real enemies and having no quick escape if things went bad for him. He kept asking how I was doing. I thought at that time that he was inquiring about my health simply to find out if I were ready for sex. I kept lying to him and telling him that I was still bleeding. Actually, the bleeding had stopped the day after the doctor had performed the D & C in Jalapa. The monster never had the opportunity to physically check me and find out that I was not telling him the truth.

I was feeling uncomfortable too, not just because of my brothers' remarks but also because of the strange way my father was acting. I had been observing the manner in which my father was bonding with the monster, never hesitating to ask him to pick up my sister Eneida in San Pedro Pinula, trusting him with his money by sending him to buy things, and taking time to sit down to have coffee with him. I had the feeling that my father wanted this marriage to work. This was becoming very unsettling for me, for it appeared that my father did not have a clue about what kind of man he had in his house, and what was even more unsettling, he showed no interest in finding out either—never once asking me anything about him. I was also beginning to realize that living with my father, while affording me time to physically recuperate, was not providing a solution to the BIG problem. I was still in the same situation as I was after the court hearing. If I were ever to get out of the mess for good, I would have to do it myself—but the next time to do it right.

ϖ

One morning the criminal woke up, abruptly sat up and announced, "I want out of here, we're leaving."

"Could you please give me a few more days with my father?" I implored.

"No, we're leaving tomorrow morning," he insisted.

My father did not intervene or interfere. "Jorge is your husband and you have to follow him," was his only reply when I told him of the monster's decision.

I understood my father's position. As a person who assiduously followed custom it would have been impossible for him to say anything else—I was duty–bound to follow my husband. No amount of compassion or concern for my health could be allowed to interfere.

The next morning we left the house at five o'clock. My father got up to say goodbye to us. I saw tears in his eyes and he looked quite sad. We boarded the boat and, as usual, as soon as the hawsers were loosened I became seasick. The boat was crowded and the monster pulled me close to him, wrapping his arm around me so tightly that I could hardly breathe. He was acting as if he had to demonstrate to these strangers that I only belonged to him.

As the boat was moving away from the pier, light was rapidly filling the sky, creating beautiful pastel colours. As the shoreline gradually receded from view, the houses became smaller and smaller until the tropical vegetation finally swallowed them up; and the protection that Livingston had afforded me was also now moving farther and farther away, to disappear once again from my life.

ϖ

On the long boat and bus trip back to San Pedro Pinula I was either seasick or carsick and I did not talk to the monster at all. This gave me time to think about many things.

I was grateful and surprised by the kindness my father showed me. There were so many things I would have liked to discuss with him, if only the opportunity had become available. The one huge and burning question was: "Papá why do you and other people think that I had run away with this man?" Judging from my brothers' cruel comments and by the way they treated me in the house, they also believed that I had run away with the criminal. Aunt Teco also made an allusion to something similar during a conversation with me, but I was not able to clarify anything with her with the monster always in the middle.

It was not easy to forget the conversation I had with my father the day after the monster and I were arrested in Las Agujitas. I tried very hard not to get angry when I recalled his blaming me for my own troubles that day. At that time I was unable to ask him the meaning of his questions or to analyze what he was saying due to my poor health, anger, confusion and lack of experience. However, while recovering in Livingston I had time to think deeply about my situation:

Did my father's family give him wrong information about my conduct in San Pedro Pinula? If people in San Pedro Pinula were telling him that I had run away with the criminal, how was it possible that my father, a very intelligent person and a person who knew me so well, could have believed such a thing? My father knew that I was dreaming of eventually marrying Canche. While we were in Livingston it would have been so simple for my father to ask me, "Gabriela, what actually happened, tell me the whole story? I want to hear the truth from you." I was not able to arrange a private moment away from the monster on my own. However, my father could have found a way to talk to me in private if he had wanted to. If he had really wanted to get to the truth, he had the means to do it.

Another confusing situation was that I felt that no one was being completely honest with me.

Was I betrayed in some way? Does anyone care? There has to be people, particularly in San Pedro Pinula, who know more about what happened to me than they are saying. Anyway, who cares?

I was lying to myself, however. I did care about the image my father had of me. I still loved him in spite of everything, and his feelings and thoughts about me still meant a lot. At one minute, I was blaming him for my disgrace, and then in the next minute, I was wanting to believe that he had tried to do everything possible in order to see that justice would have taken place in my situation—I wanted to believe this more than any thing else. I wanted to kill the feeling of dislike I was developing toward him—but his silence was making this difficult.

We had to change buses in Chiquimula. The bus stop was on the plaza right across the street from my former school. There was a forty-five minute wait and we sat on one of the park benches. Some students, boys from the boy's school and girls from my school, were mingling in the park. I kept my head down, for I did not want any of my past school mates and friends to recognize me. My biggest fear was that Canche would appear at any moment. How humiliating and painful this wait was for me; a girl who had been one of the most popular students, but who now looked liked a scarecrow; a girl who had to hide from the embarrassment of her disgrace; a girl who had to hide because she had a maniac for a husband.

The monster noticed my discomfort and humiliation and used it to mock and taunt me, "Don't you want to show me your school?" Looking at the schoolgirls in the park with their uniforms, he sneered, "Is that the way you dressed?" When a student waved at me he said, "Who was that girl? Was she your messenger to your faggot boyfriend?"

His words were interspersed with sardonic laughter and his face was contorted in hatred. I just buried my head in my lap.

"What's wrong? Why are you hiding your head? Why don't we go over there to the school? Come on! Take me on a tour! Come on, let's go. Are you ashamed of me, ha, ha, ha?"

Thank God Canche was not in the park, for the monster would have recognized him from the photos and who knows what might have ensued. The monster was able to make every waking minute of my life a living hell, even on a bus trip.

At last, the bus to San Pedro Pinula arrived. When we left, it was the first time I was happy to be leaving Chiquimula. Immediately, I ratcheted myself back into survival thinking. I was still very sick and I knew that the monster had no money for doctors and medicine. I did not know how I was going to get the operation that Dr. Carías said I needed. The monster probably would not even take me to the general hospital in Jalapa where I could get the operation free of charge. I could now see that he was rapidly tiring of me and had no interest in my health; I was of no use to him. I was no longer a spoil of conquest, but rather, a financial burden. Most importantly, I was now sexually useless. The monster probably was also worried that I was going to try to kill him again and this could not be pleasant thinking for my *dear husband*. And yet, he was still carting me around.

The thought occurred to me that he could have simply sent me to Livingston by myself after the D & C operation in Jalapa, and then forget about me. I would have been happy to be rid of him and my father or other friends and relatives would have had to take care of me. By marrying me, he was exonerated from any crime anyway. The more I thought about this, the more I was becoming worried about what was coming next.

Why does he keep me with him, torturing me? Surely, he can see how sick I am? What is he planning? Is he so twisted and evil that he enjoys witnessing my suffering, and now, my approaching death? I have to escape soon.

The façade of niceness and respect the horrible monster displayed in front of my father was finished. I was going back—back to the hell of Las Agujitas.

Part IV

New Beginnings:

Justice and Restoration

Chapter 14
Deliverance

"One man scorned and covered with scars still strove with his last ounce of courage to reach the unreachable stars, and the world will be better for this.
–Miguel de Cervantes–Don Quijote de la Mancha–

We arrived in San Pedro Pinula in the late afternoon. I was physically tired and weak from the trip, and emotionally exhausted from the monster's constant badgering during the trip. After entering his mother's house I only wanted to lie in bed and try to sleep, but this was not to be. The monster immediately forced sex on me. This was the first rape since the miscarriage and I noticed immediately that something was horribly wrong. His raping me was now so painful, so horribly painful. It was more painful than when he had first raped me. I was experiencing a type of pain I can now only compare with the pain of giving birth. I was so glad nobody else was in the house; I was screaming and crying the whole time he was in me.

The insensitive monster yelled at me, "Shut up! You're faking in order to prevent me from fucking you. You won't get away with this. This is one of your little tricks to keep me away from you, you stupid little bitch!"

"No, Jorge, I can't stand the pain, something is wrong. Please, please, leave me alone. I can't stand the pain. I feel like I'm going to die!"

But he would not stay away. He was like an animal trying to

make up for the sex he had been deprived of during my convalescence at my father's place. He raped me time and time again
that evening. The pain was so intense that many times I even
suspected that Doctor Carías had done something wrong inside
my vagina or to my uterus when I was in the hospital. Memories
of my Aunt Florinda and her screams from the pain of her cancer
raced across my mind and I thought that I also had the same type
of cancer that had killed her. I immediately started to bleed again
and I knew that this bleeding was not normal and was of serious
concern, but there was nothing I could do. Now I was sure that it
would not be very long before I would find death.

When I glanced at myself in the mirror the next morning I
looked awfully pale and sick. I took another look at myself, more
closely, and was shocked, for I was unable to see any of the very
good and attractive looks that I thought I once possessed. I was
not looking like a fifteen–year old girl, but more like a very sick
woman of perhaps forty years of age. I, who many times in my
conceited ways thought of myself to be very good looking and
possessing a beautiful body, saw myself now as being very ugly.
My ashen, ghastly-looking face made people stare and talk. I was
so thin that every bone in my face was outlined; my eyes were
sunken and lined with dark rings. My body now looked so old
and frail. I was not even standing with the erect carriage I once
had. It was frightening to see the deterioration that had taken
place to my health and appearance in only six months. The cruel
monster was now telling me, "It's too bad I threw away your
make-up." He had thrown away the little make-up I had weeks
before because he said he wanted me to have the "natural look of
a woman", as he put it. He was now probably seeing what I was
seeing—I looked like a cadaver. I guess the natural look was not
that appealing to him any more.

On the day after our arrival the monster left the house and
when he returned he told me that he had made plans with his
brother-in-law, Cesar Sandoval, to go to a small hamlet outside of

town to start up a business and that I was to go with them. Vilma, Cesar's wife, was going to stay behind in San Pedro to take care of their baby.

Approximately a week later, the three of us left for El Carrizal Grande. This village, as I remember, was more than three hours by foot from San Pedro Pinula and maybe two hours by horse. Cesar saw that I was in very bad shape and made sure that I would have a horse to ride. He and the monster walked all the way. Before the trip to El Carrizal Grande, Cesar tried to convince him to leave me with Vilma. He tried to make him see how weak I was. But the monster told him that I had to go with him wherever he went. I read in Cesar and Vilma's faces that they thought I probably would not survive the trip.

When we left his mother's house there still were no other people around. I did not talk to the monster or to Cesar while we were traveling and they did not talk to me either; they just talked to each other, making plans about the business they were opening. By listening to their conversations I learned that Cesar had already traveled to El Carrizal Grande and had taken some stock there for their business. Their conversations also told me that they were in a partnership and were going to open a store. I was slotted to do the cooking and cleaning for both of them. Cesar talked excitedly about there being no grocery store and no nurse or doctor in El Carrizal Grande. He had some training as a nursing assistant and he was planning to help people with injections. He also talked about getting some medications to sell. When doctors in Jalapa or San Pedro Pinula prescribed injections, their patients would have to stay in one of those towns or travel there for each injection until the treatment was completed. Cesar thought that with his nursing knowledge he could do injections for people and they would not have to travel.

The two had made an agreement that the monster would be the one to go to San Pedro Pinula to do the buying for the grocery store. The monster also had plans for me aside from the cleaning and cooking. I was to work writing and reading letters and documents for people who were illiterate. This is a common money making activity in the countryside. Illiterate people in need of having a document read or of having a letter written to a government office pay people who know how to read and write to do this. Naturally, these plans were made without including me in the discussion.

෴

Cesar was in his early thirties, very slim, a dark tone to his skin and had straight black hair. He was so slim that you could see his cheekbones outlined under the skin. He had a very nice profile with a straight nose, straight teeth and a winning smile. I would not call him a handsome man, but I immediately recognized that he had qualities I seldom found in many Guatemalan men until then: he was kind, knew how to read people and was very respectful of women. The monster had a great respect and admiration for him. It was incredible to me that this man, a person who, at least in my presence, would not listen to anyone or take advice from anybody, came to Cesar to consult with him and afterwards follow his ideas.

I was curious why Cesar had decided to go to such a remote location as El Carrizal Grande and I asked the monster. He told me that Cesar liked to drink and in order to straighten up this part of his life he thought that being far away from the town and from his friends would be the best course of action.

Even though I was riding the horse, the trip was still insufferably painful. We traveled north to Las Agujitas, close to where I was held captive a few months earlier. But before we reached the place where I was first raped and where we were later living, we turned left and continued to travel northwest for about another two hours through some very rough and hilly country.

Finally, we arrived at El Carrizal Grande. I was expecting that we would find only poor Indian people there, living in *covachas,* as was the case in Las Agujitas. To my surprise, there were a number of light-haired, blue and green–eyed, light-skinned people, living in very beautiful and substantial houses. The people could have been of German descent. I had read and heard that there are regions in Guatemala to where there had been considerable German immigration in the late nineteenth century.

Cesar had previously rented part of a large house to accommodate the store and our living quarters. Our rented quarters had only three rooms—a big room where the grocery store was located, the kitchen/dining room, and a big bedroom. A folding screen divided the bedroom, with Cesar sleeping on one side and the monster and I sleeping on the other. This arrangement did not offer much privacy. Outside the main door was a porch with an arcade and this is where people waited when they came for injections. The arcade continued around the house. To complete this pretty ensemble, the house was completely encircled with flowers, bougainvillea, camellia, and flowering shrubs.

One morning I heard some pieces of a conversation between Cesar and the criminal. I knew they were talking about me because I heard the criminal telling Cesar that he did not know what to believe about the pain I was experiencing during intercourse. He said that he thought my pain was solely due to my not loving him and that I was with him against my will. In a roundabout fashion he was confessing to Cesar that he had kidnapped me. I did not hear Cesar making any comments. He just stood, quietly listening.

Early one morning, during one of the monster's outings, Cesar seized the opportunity to ask me a question, "Do you love Jorge?"

I pretended not to hear and continued with my work. I did not want to lie, but I was afraid to tell the truth, suspecting that Cesar would tell his partner. After all, I was still amazed about how well the two of them got along. My eyes began to tear and I bowed my head, not saying a word, which, of course, indicated to Cesar that I did hear his question.

He sat down across from me and looked at me in a very pitiful way. Finally, he broke the silence and asked, "How did you lose the baby?"

"I fell off a horse," I replied weakly, with my head still turned away.

"Look at me," he said with a commanding but gentle voice, "How did you fall off the horse?"

I could not talk and started to cry.

"What did the doctor tell you in the hospital?" he pressed on.

Finally, I was able to say something in between my sobs. "He instructed me to return for an operation as soon as possible."

I found it easy to talk with him, but I still kept up my guard and did not give him much more information, certainly nothing about being kidnapped and raped by his brother-in-law. My greatest fear was that Cesar was going to ask me about my crying, complaining, groaning and moaning at night, but he never did and I was grateful for that. I think he realized he was getting into some very sensitive areas and did not ask any more questions.

We were in El Carrizal Grande no more than two weeks when my vaginal bleeding greatly increased, probably due to the activity the monster called sex. Every day I was becoming weaker. I thought that I had an extreme vaginal infection or a cancerous tumour. Every time the criminal raped me the pain and the bleeding increased. I was sure Cesar heard my moaning and cries. It was so painful when the monster was in me that all other feelings were completely blotted out; I could only see black. The criminal's penis felt like a blunt, coarse, dry object being forced into my vagina. He kept accusing me of crying to avoid giving myself to him.

"You're just making all that noise because you know that Cesar can hear everything, there's nothing wrong with you. You're up to your old tricks again, bitch."

"No, Jorge. It hurts so much. Something is terribly wrong with me. You can't imagine the pain I'm in right now. It hurts, it hurts; please have some compassion for me."

The sicker I became the more brutal and mean he was becoming toward me. He was now using every opportunity to torment me about my bleeding. He tried to make me feel guilty, accusing me of being the one who had killed his baby.

"What do you think people will say if they know you tried to kill me? What do you think people will say if they find out that it's your fault my baby died?"

I was now convinced that he was not going to take me to a doctor and was prepared to let me die. He had to see how sick I was. He could not have been that stupid. This little village was the perfect place to let me die—everybody would think that I had just died from natural causes.

When the monster had to go out to do errands I stayed behind doing the cooking and helping with the store. Cesar also stayed at the store because the little business was doing very well and was quite busy.

From the way Cesar kept looking at me I got a feeling that he wanted to ask me some more questions. I also wanted to talk to him, for I needed to talk to someone, to anyone whom I thought might have understanding and sympathy. I needed to confide in someone who could understand what had actually happened and who could possibly help me. He seemed to be a very kind, soft, understanding person. I even wanted to tell him about the time when I had tried to kill his brother-in-law. The desire to tell him my story was burning inside me and eating me up. I wanted someone to help me, although I was not sure what kind of help I was looking for. I had to tell him about my suffering. Now I wanted Cesar to ask me why I was moaning and crying every night. I wanted him to ask me why I was so ill.

Every day I was becoming weaker at a faster rate. More than ever I was feeling that if I did not get medical help soon I would probably never make it. I had been bleeding constantly and profusely for almost twelve days. A piercing and inexplicable abdominal pain accompanied this bleeding, a pain I knew could not have been the result of a normal menstrual flow. Even when there was some respite from the raping, the pain kept increasing in intensity and becoming more constant. I could not wait any longer, I had to take a chance and talk to Cesar soon; I had to do something to save my own life. The horrible pain had pushed me to overcome my usual feelings of embarrassment around the subject of sex and to overcome the fear of the troubles that disclosing to him might bring down on me. I was now determined to speak with him. I just did not know how to approach the subject.

⚓

One morning Cesar and the monster were talking about the monster's upcoming trip to San Pedro Pinula to buy more stock for the store. I did not hear them mentioning anything about me. I was tempted to ask the monster to take me to the doctor on this trip, but I did not dare.

On the following morning I got up very early to prepare food for the monster's trip. Cesar also got up early to give him instructions about what to bring back from San Pedro Pinula and of what quantity. I overheard the monster say that he was going to try to return that very evening or maybe the following afternoon. I was surprised that the monster trusted his brother–in–law to the extent of leaving me alone with him. I was beginning to trust Cesar too. Cesar did not say anything to him or to me, but I could sense that he was relieved that the monster did not want to take me with him.

After the monster had left, Cesar wasted no time and invited me to sit down. He sat down across from me and started to gently question me.

"Gabriela, I want you to tell me everything about how you ended up with Jorge. I want you to tell me everything. I want the truth."

This time I did not hesitate to recount my complete story, starting with my abduction on that horrible Good Friday. I even told him, without any prompting, about my attempt to kill the monster.

He kept probing, "Why didn't you stay with your father in Livingston when you went there for your convalescence?"

"I couldn't stay there," I answered. "My father told me to go with my husband. Besides, my brothers treated me so horribly behind my father's back and if I had told my father about this, I was not sure he would have done anything. He loves his sons more than me. I even think my father has seen how they treat me and chooses to ignore it. Besides, when we were in Livingston it looked like my father was trying to make this marriage work. He was friendly with Jorge and he never asked me once about what had happened to me. I don't think that Papá has any interest in helping me get out of this mess. I think that protecting his honour and his family's reputation is more important to him than protecting his daughter. I don't really want to think this," I said, shaking my head in denial. "Nobody wants to help me. Nobody has been honest with me. I don't know…I don't know anything for sure. I'm so…so confused."

Cesar looked at me for a few seconds, giving me time to compose myself and then asked softly, "Would you like to get away from Jorge if you could?"

My heart started to race, for I knew we were now venturing into new territory, into dangerous territory. But I also sensed that this was the chance I had been praying for.

"Yes…but…but where would I go?" I sputtered.

"Back to Livingston, to your father," he replied calmly, with a shrug of his shoulders.

When he said this I was shocked: *hasn't he listened to anything I have just said? Is he out of his mind to suggest that I go back to my father? Maybe he doesn't believe anything that I've told him?*

Cesar seemed to have read my thoughts very well. With his soft voice he continued, "I understand you're very angry with your father for accusing you of running away with Jorge. I believe all that you've told me and I don't approve of your father's actions. However, from what I have witnessed the past few weeks, nothing can be worse than the torture you are suffering with Jorge. I don't think you'll last very long in his hands. It's because I believe you—I believe everything you've told me—that I'm offering you my help. If you want my help, you have very little time to decide."

I was rapidly becoming less and less apprehensive and guarded around him. A long forgotten feeling was stirring in me. After a moment, I recognized it as hope.

I continued talking to him as if he had been my best friend for years. "What if Jorge tries to go to Livingston and take me back again? He has told me many times that if I leave him, he will find me wherever I go. His favourite words are, 'You're mine and nobody else's. If I can't have you, nobody will have you.' If I go to my father's and Jorge goes to Livingston and finds me, I don't know what will happen?"

"I understand your fears," Cesar continued, "but Jorge is broke and he has no friends to lend him money. I am his only friend and I would never lend him money to go anywhere. You told me that Livingston is accessible only by water and there are only two ferries a day that travel there from Puerto Barrios. It would be very difficult for him to get there undetected."

"But what will happen when he finds out where I am?" I replied with a voice of resignation mixed with fear.

"Jorge has no friends in Livingston, but you do. I'm sure they will protect you if he tries to go there."

As Cesar spoke I could tell that he had been thinking about helping me and had been devising a plan for me for some time. He talked with such confidence.

"Keep a very low profile," he continued instructing, "and hide as much as possible when you first get there. You must tell your story to people whom you trust and tell them that you need help. Don't be too shy or too proud to ask for help."

How Cesar could have been so knowledgeable was a mystery. He kept giving me ideas about what to do once I was free from the monster. He did not minimize the fact that I was about to decide to take one of the biggest risks of my life.

"Jorge will never try to harm you if your father is around," Cesar continued, "because he is very afraid of your father, I know he is. Jorge knows that your father killed someone years ago."

This news hit me like a bomb; I was speechless; I had never heard of this before. When he let this piece of information slip out I did not detect malice in his voice. From my puzzled, surprised and bewildered looking face he realized that he had just told me something that I had not known.

Before I could ask him what he was talking about he exclaimed, "Oh my God, I guess you didn't know. Gabriela, this is not a secret. The complete Folgar family knows about it. All your cousins know about it. Everyone in San Pedro Pinula knows it and I figured that you knew it too. Please forgive me. I feel awful and dumb. I hope you will forgive me. I did not mean to hurt you and please try to forget that I told you this. Please, don't hate me. I don't know what to tell you now; I only wish to ask you for forgiveness."

Is the monster afraid of my father? That can't be, but maybe that is why he was so anxious to leave Livingston.

I do not know how many times Cesar kept asking for forgiveness. Nobody had ever asked me for forgiveness before, especially a man. He sounded and looked so remorseful. I tried to reassure him, "Don't worry, I'm glad you told me."

Cesar returned to the topic at hand and resumed talking in a very serious and quiet voice, "The only condition I place on you for my help is that you never tell anyone—I mean this, anyone—that I helped you. Do you understand?"

I nodded that I understood.

"If you decide to leave," he continued, "I'll find a native from around here to take you to San Pedro Pinula. I will write a letter to your father and I will send a note to my parents, requesting that they keep you in their house until you get on a bus." He then added, "If you stay here, Jorge won't take you to see a doctor. I can see that he has no interest in doing that. He has no money anyway. I don't know what's wrong with you but it appears to be serious. You need medical attention and you need it now. If you stay here, you will die here. I want to help you and I don't see any other way out except for you to leave. You have to decide and this will probably be your only opportunity."

"But what about you when Jorge comes back? He's going to think that you helped me and question you."

"Don't worry. I'll tell him that I had to go and inject a sick person and when I came back you weren't here. Don't worry about me. I know how to handle him. Please remember, you have less than three years to turn eighteen and then you can leave your father's house and find work. Until then, you will have to toughen it out. With Jorge, you won't make it to eighteen. You won't even make it to sixteen. He is my brother–in–law, but I am not going to make any excuses for the way he is. I didn't know he had kidnapped you. He told me and everyone else that you had run away with him and I believed him. I want you to know that I now believe you. I know what Jorge is capable of and I know what he has done in the past."

I was crying again, this time from fear. With a trembling voice I stammered, "I'm...I'm afraid. What if he decides to return today and finds me on the road with this Indian you're going to hire? He will surely kill me, and probably the Indian man too. He will be returning to this place this afternoon and...and..."

Cesar put up his hand to interrupt, "Gabriela, please, don't worry, just trust in me. I'll give instructions to the man I hire to take you on a different route. These people here know many different ways to get to and from San Pedro Pinula. The note to your father will be short, just long enough to tell him that he must help you and take you to see a doctor as soon as you arrive in Livingston. You don't look well. You're not even the shadow of the girl I remember seeing in San Pedro Pinula at the beginning of the year. I hope your father will take care of your medical needs. I will tell him in the letter that you escaped from Jorge and that you want his protection, but you will have to tell him too. You have to tell your father everything you have told me, even if he doesn't want to hear it."

"But...but I wanted to tell my father everything before we went to the court hearing, but he didn't want to hear the truth. Before I could tell him anything he accused me of running away with Jorge. My father didn't even want to take me with him when he found out that I was pregnant. I'm afraid he'll tell me again that I must leave and go back to Jorge because he's my husband."

"Your father won't tell you that this time," Cesar asserted, "because in my letter I will explain to him that your life will be in danger the moment Jorge returns to El Carrizal Grande and finds out that you have escaped. If he tells you he doesn't want you after he reads my letter, find someone who will take you in, find a job, even as a maid for exchange of food and a place to live. Keep going ahead, keep your head pointed forward, don't turn back."

My crying had stopped and now I just listened in amazement as Cesar kept talking, "There must be stores in Livingston where you can work as a clerk. In the stores they hire minors at sixteen years of age. You will be sixteen very soon. Be glad you didn't kill Jorge. If you had done that, you'd be in jail right now. I am not a doctor, but from what I see and from what you have told me, you need medical attention. I don't have very much money here with me. I will ask my parents to give you some for travelling and for a visit to a doctor as soon as you get to Puerto Barrios. I will also ask them to give you enough money so you can stay in a hotel."

"My father might not accept me this time and what if nobody wants me? What am I to do then?" I said with a shaky and doubt-filled voice.

"I repeat," Cesar's tone turned even more insistent, "I know that Jorge may try to go after you and I don't know what he would do if he were to find you. In any case, if you stay here you will die without medical attention or you'll die from the way he treats you. Do you understand? YOU WILL DIE! You mentioned that you have an aunt, a lady you call Aunt Teco, in Livingston. Go to her and stay with her if your father refuses to welcome you in his house. Tell your aunt that you'll clean her house and cook for her if she allows you to stay. Above all, don't stay in Pinula or Jalapa. Those towns will be the first places Jorge will look for you."

Despite my growing trust in Cesar I still thought that maybe I was falling into a trap. "You're not just testing me on behalf of Jorge, are you?" I asked.

Cesar raised one of his eyebrows and with indignation in his voice he admonished, "Gabriela, I am a father, and if my own child were in the kind of trouble you are in, I would like for someone to do the same for him as I'm doing for you."

His words took away all of my doubts and fears. I would have liked to have a father like that. Cesar seemed so kind, soft, understanding and empathetic. It was hard to believe that there were men like him. But I was soon to learn that Cesar was not an exception.

Cesar had opened my eyes. I could now see some light in my

situation. He had opened a door and a fresh breeze was caressing my face. I had been so overwhelmed with all the stressful things swirling around in my mind that I had been incapable to think of even the simplest things that could be accomplished if I were to leave the monster and El Carrizal Grande. I could not believe that I had not been able to think straight, to the point of not being able to remember that I knew people who could help me. It was as if I had been enveloped in a cloud of stupidity. I felt lucid for the first time since the abduction. Warmth was radiating throughout my body. I even felt that I was already free.

I rose from my chair with my hands clasped in a prayer–like fashion in front of me. "Thank you, thank you, Cesar. Yes…please help me get away from here," I pleaded. "Please, please, I promise you that I will die before disclosing to anyone that you have helped me to get away. I give you my word that the only people who are going to know from my mouth are your parents and my father."

Now I was crying again, but this time from happiness.

Cesar immediately left the store to hire an Indian man to guide me and while he was gone his words started to sink deeper into my mind. Suddenly, all kinds of ideas were zooming around in my head like bees around a hive.

I could go to Doña Rome in Chiquimula and I'm sure she would give me a job in her grocery store or as a cook and kitchen helper. She liked me very much and I know she needs people to help around the house with all the boarders she has. And there are my uncles from my mother's side in Ipala. I can go there and I know they would welcome me, house me and feed me. The monster doesn't even know that I have relatives in that town.

I could not believe that I had not thought of any of this before; how could I had been so stupid; what had this horrible monster done to my brain? *Yes, I'm going to survive, I'm going to survive.*

Cesar's words and support were magic. I was so excited and happy. Although I was physically weak to the point of death, I now felt emotionally strong and I was determined that this new spirit was going to give me the strength to survive the next ordeal. I was seeing my future as a bright star in the sky. Fresh air was blowing on my face. Holy Saint Gabriel had sent another angel to my rescue and I was to find out that even more pleasant surprises were soon to come my way, and from some very surprising and unlikely sources.

ఴ

Cesar came back shortly with a middle–aged Indian man who spoke very limited Spanish. He took the Indian man into the room behind the little grocery store and gave him instructions. In the meantime, the only things I prepared were cloth sanitary pads, two or three undergarments, and an extra dress. I stuffed everything into one bag. Cesar gave me two envelopes, one for his parents and the other one for my father. I wanted to guard them very well and tucked them deep into my bra.

I thanked Cesar again and started my walk to freedom. At the bottom of the hill I stopped, turned, and waved good-bye to him once more. I knew that this was it. There was no turning back. On this trip, on this very day, I would either survive or die.

I did not know what time it was when the Indian man and I left El Carrizal Grande. It must have been before noon. The weather was warm and dry, for we were nearing the end of the rainy season. After walking for a short while, we came to a small river *(arroyo),* which we had to ford. In this region the amount of water in the creeks and rivers varies according to the season. There had recently been rain and the river was higher than usual and the current was very swift. The Indian man picked me up and carried me across. I do not think that I would have had the strength to fight the current on my own and I probably would have never made it across, possibly drowning, if he had not helped me.

We had walked for maybe an hour when we came across another small creek. My guide signaled for me to stop. At first I was very afraid because this creek reminded me of the one in Las Agujitas where the criminal first raped me. But my fears went away when the Indian man removed his *petate*, a mat woven from palm fronds, and unrolled it on the ground. Then he took his *morral*, a haversack woven from *agave* leaves, from his shoulder and placed it on top of the *petate*. He opened the *morral* and took out his *pishtones*, big thick corn tortillas, from his *bucul*. A *bucul* is a round pumpkin that has been dried and is used as a dish to store tortillas and to keep them moist and warm. He then unfolded the banana leaves that held his refried black beans and chopped dried chilis. He offered to share this food with me. I was very hungry and started to pick up my *pishtón* and beans when he grabbed my hands as a sign to stop. He then took his *pishtón* in his two hands and lifted his arms to the sky saying something I did not understand, but I knew that he was giving thanks to God. I watched

this wonderful Indian man in amazement, dressed so poorly, probably illiterate, having only these humble dishes and giving thanks to God for his daily bread. I, who at one time went to church two or three times a week, who studied the catechism and who wore a beautiful white dress for my first communion, did not practice this beautiful act of giving thanks to God for my food with the reverence that this man did. I tried to copy his actions, to pray and to give thanks to God. I put the *pishtón* in my hands and elevated my arms to the sky, but I could not say anything aloud—I could not because I still doubted the existence of God, the God who I thought had abandoned me.

After he had given thanks to God he told me to go ahead and eat. What a beautiful meal it was, such humble food served in

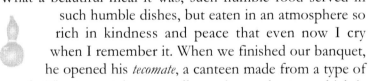

such humble dishes, but eaten in an atmosphere so rich in kindness and peace that even now I cry when I remember it. When we finished our banquet, he opened his *tecomate*, a canteen made from a type of squash. The *tecomate* has a small opening at the top, which is usually secured and closed with a piece of corncob. He poured water into two *guacales*. A *guacal* is a container made from the dried fruit of the *Morro* tree or sometimes from small round squashes.

As we were eating my guide offered me water. This was the very first time I made real eye contact with him and I thanked him. While sitting in front of him I paid attention to his chest. The top two buttons of his shirt were not fastened and I saw that he was wearing a necklace made out of seeds and dyed dried beans.

He put his hand inside his shirt, pulled out the necklace and with his broken Spanish asked me, "Do you like it?"

I look at the necklace and softly replied, "Yes, it is beautiful."

He pulled it over his head and took it off. He then bent forward toward me and still holding the necklace with his two hands he placed it over my head. As I bent my head down to take a better and closer look at the necklace he said, "It is for good luck and I made it myself. *Está bendito* (it was blessed in the church). This means you will always have food in your home." I have kept  this necklace with me to this day. These necklaces are not rare or precious in any material sense; Indian people make them to be sold on market day, mostly to tourists. But this one had now become very special to me. By witnessing this man's faith and by feeling his kindness I knew for certain that he was helping me along to a full restoration of my faith in God. Here I was, alone with a stranger in the woods. He was strong and he could have done the same or even worse things to me than what the monster had done. Nobody would hear me if I screamed, nobody would be a witness, and nobody would be there to save me. But yet, this man was protecting me, clearing all the weeds along the path with his machete, feeding me, guiding me to my freedom and even giving me a very humble gift, a gift that now had such a powerful meaning—that God existed and had sent another angel to guide and protect me.

The trip was long, tiring and frightening. My guardian angel stayed by the path every time I went deep into the woods to change my sanitary pad. I had to do this often, for the pads became saturated quite quickly. The arduous walk was aggravating the bleeding. My biggest fear was that we might suddenly come face to face with the monster. He had traveled to San Pedro Pinula by horse, which would have sped up his trip, and I was not the fastest walker due to my weakness. It was now late afternoon and he could be returning to El Carrizal Grande that very minute. Every time we heard the trotting of a horse or voices of people my guide grabbed my hand and led me into the bushes to hide me. The brush was very thick everywhere and provided excellent cover. My guide then went back to the path and sat down looking as if he were just resting.

The trail went up and down, very steep at times, and it was also very winding. I do not remember a flat surface for more than one kilometer during the complete trip. Several times the Indian man had to take my hand and pull me when we were climbing a particularly steep hill. We passed open fields with grazing cattle and mature cornfields, yellow silk tassels swaying in the breeze, waiting for the harvest crew. The trail traversed through several privately owned pieces of land and when we came upon a gate, the Indian man went ahead to open it. These gates were made from rough, hand-hewed wooden posts with barbed wire stretched between. In many areas of Guatemala farm plots form a patchwork and there is usually no road along the property lines to allow common access, which means that land owners have to allow people to use their land to travel from one area to another.

I was thinking and observing as I walked. I was constantly thinking about the two letters inside my bra. Cesar must not have written too much in the letters because it seemed to me that he had not taken that much time to write them. Besides, the letters felt quite thin, maybe one or two pages at the most. The letters were now all wrinkled and sweaty. I took them out several times during the trip for I was curious to read what he was telling my father, they were burning in my hand, but I did not dare open them.

I was also observing many things that I had never paid attention to before. As I walked behind my guide I kept looking at his feet. He was wearing thick sandals make out of car tires in the style of thongs. A leather string attached the thongs to the back of his heel. I looked at his cracked heels, a result of exposure to the weather, dirt and water. It looked like these cracks had healed and formed some type of callous. Still he walked as if the cracks in his heels did not hurt at all.

At times my guide whistled or sang a church song, an *alabado*. *Alabados* (praises) are very short hymns or sung petitions, similar to the *saetas* (arrows) that are sung in Spain, especially in Seville during Holy Week. I was very surprised when he sang an *alabado* that I knew. I can now remember only part of it, the chorus:

Perdón oh Dios mio,	Forgive me, O my God,
Dios mio, perdón,	My God, forgive me,
Perdon y clemencia,	Forgiveness and clemency,
Perdón y piedad.	Forgiveness and compassion.

This hymn is sung during the Good Friday procession when we recreate the funeral of Christ. I was singing this *alabado* with all the people in the procession right before the monster kidnapped me.

When I heard him singing hymns I felt guilty—very guilty for all the times I had doubted the existence of God. I felt ashamed and I became afraid that God might punish me with something worse than what I had experienced. I started to sing the words to myself asking for his forgiveness for having abandoned my faith. It felt good to remember and to repeat these words that my guide was singing. I think this was the first time that I gave thanks to God for not letting me die after the cruel monster had beaten me. At that moment I started to think about the Ten Commandments and the four words of one of the Commandments kept playing over and over in my mind: THOU SHALL NOT KILL. Now I was happy, extremely happy that the gun did not go off.

I still felt afraid, not with the same fear I had when the criminal and his accomplices surprised me that horrible night and kidnapped me, not with the fear I experienced in the jail cell, not with the fear I had when I saw the monster coming at me with a machete; it was a new and different type of fear—a fear of an uncertain future if my escape were successful. In addition, I still feared that I might soon die, either from my bleeding or at the hands of the criminal. We were in serious danger on this trail. I prayed to God with devotion and faith for my health and for a brighter future. I kept asking God for forgiveness and I promised him that I would never doubt his love for me again. I asked God not to let me die from cancer. I was still thinking that I might have cancer because of the agonizing pain and unusual symptoms I was feeling in my reproductive system. I was terribly afraid and I kept praying to God, "Please, let me live, I want to live." But most of all I prayed for my guide, "O Jesus, save him and keep him safe; thank you for sending an angel to save me. Amen."

I was so totally absorbed in my thoughts and prayers that I did not notice that we were approaching Pinula, not until my wonderful guiding angel announced, "We are almost there!"

We came across some big rocks that were hidden from the road by thick brush. The Indian man signaled to me to sit down. I did not understand everything he was saying, but from the movement of his hands and from the few words he spoke in Spanish, I knew he was telling me that we had to wait until it got really dark before entering Pinula. I sat down and he sat down too, close to me. By the look of the sky it was probably between five-thirty and six in the evening. It was already getting cool and I knew that it would not be long before the sun would disappear. I now had time to look around to see where we were and I noticed that we were near the main road to Jalapa, to the west of San Pedro Pinula. This meant that we had come by a completely different route than the one I had first taken to El Carrizal Grande (please refer to the maps on pages 308 and 309).

Night came and my guide carefully crept to the road, looked around and signaled me to follow him. I knew we were very close to the town. I could hear cars honking and dogs barking. We walked briskly along the side of the highway, through the hamlet of El Pinalito and on into San Pedro. It was so dark that I could not even see the outlines of the houses or the church in San Pedro. When we passed the first houses I noticed that their doors were closed. Even this close, the houses only looked like shadows on the landscape. A few very tiny points of light flickered from kerosene lamps, candles, or *ocote* torches, marking the windows of houses. The odor of burning wood from cooking stoves permeated the air. My guiding angel walked surprisingly fast and I did too in order to keep up with him. He was my *pillar of fire by night*, leading and guiding me along the dark road. I was tired, thirsty, hungry, and cold. I had blisters on my feet, but the fear of encountering the criminal or someone who knew him gave me the strength to walk as fast as I could. He kept saying, *"Puráte, puráte!"* I knew he was saying, "Hurry up, hurry up", although the words in correct Spanish are *apúrate, apúrate*. Indian people sometimes cut Spanish words in half or they place the accent on the wrong vowel. The closer to the town we came, the faster he walked, almost breaking into a run.

When we were on the edge of town my guide stopped in front of a house. He knocked on the door and an Indian lady who looked to be in her mid–fifties came to open the door. I had seen the house before from the time when I walked through the streets of San Pedro Pinula as a free person, but I could not remember having ever seen this woman before. My guiding angel made the sign that I should wait and I stayed behind as he got closer to the lady and whispered softly in her ear. In a hushed tone they both called and signaled to me to hurry and get in. I entered the house and the door closed quickly behind me. The lady went immediately to the kitchen and the Indian man motioned for me to sit down. After a not too long of a time the Indian lady came back with traditional Guatemalan food: beans, cream, cheese and tortillas. She even fixed dessert, fried plantain.

She looked at me and asked in excellent Spanish, "What is your name?"

"Gabriela Folgar," I replied. In the manner that she was examining me I could tell that she did not know me.

"I knew your father and mother. I remember that your mother was a very good seamstress. I also know your father's family very well."

She turned toward my guide and the two conversed for a long time in their own language. I knew they were talking about me or something related to me. I could also tell that the Indian man was giving her certain instructions. I heard my father's name being mentioned, then my grandmother's name, the monster's name and Cesar's.

The Indian lady turned back to me and said, "The man will be leaving now to alert Cesar's parents about your arriving, so that they will not be afraid to open the door. Please give me the letter that Cesar gave you to carry."

I retrieved the letter from my bra and gave it to her. She took it, quickly looked at the envelope, and handed it to my guide.

Up to that point I had hardly spoken a word, but I was feeling such gratitude toward these people I felt that I had to say something. I was finally able to utter, *"Dios se lo pague,"* (May God bless you and compensate you). That is the way the local Indian people say thank you. My guide quietly slipped out the door and the lady quickly closed and secured it behind him.

"I was not even able to tell that man how grateful I am. I feel awful," I said.

"It's quite okay. He knows you're very grateful," she replied with a kind and consoling voice, "and besides, he knows God will bless him for this."

I put my hands on the necklace and I said to her, "He gave me this souvenir and I think he told me that as long as I keep it I will never be hungry."

"He's a nice man," was her only reply.

"I don't even know his name."

She did not tell me his name or her name either. She just looked at me very seriously and said, "You're so young and young people just open their mouths without thinking. You could let our names slip out of your mouth and that could mean trouble for us. We know Don Jorge. He is not a nice man. I will take you to Cesar's parents' home and you have to promise me that you will forget this house and you will never remember you were here."

I nodded my head in agreement and did not ask any more questions. She was right, I was so young and it was difficult for her to trust me. I fixed my eyes on the kerosene lamp that illuminated the small room. I kept staring hypnotically at the quivering flame until I fell asleep.

The sleep was short. The Indian lady woke me up and said that it was time to go. She handed me a shawl and slowly gave me instructions: "It is cold outside, so put on this shawl. Cover your head completely, that way nobody will recognize you. You must walk with your head down, looking at your feet, and if we meet someone you know, pretend you don't see them and keep walking." She also wrapped a shawl around her shoulder and we silently left her house.

I knew where Cesar's parents lived. This Indian lady's house was on the west side of the town and Cesar's parents lived on the east area, along the road to Ipala. If I had gone by myself, I would have taken the most obvious route. I would have taken the main street toward the centre of the town, past the Municipal Building, past the plaza and the church, and then I would have continued on the paved street all the way to my cousin Rosa's house. From there I would have walked three blocks farther, almost to the river, where Cesar's parents' house was located. But that was not the route the Indian woman took. Her route was a darker and longer one around the edges of the town. We still had to pass by my Cousin Rosa's house; that was unavoidable because her house sits on the exit road from San Pedro Pinula to Ipala, the same road where Cesar's parents' house was situated.

While following this woman I was thinking: *the Indian man walked fast, but this woman can walk even faster.* I was running behind her. I do not think we met anyone on our way to Cesar's parents' home. It must have been very late. Cesar parents' house was built on a slope and we had about six stairs to climb before entering the living room. The couple was waiting for us. They were an older couple and I immediately recognized them. I remembered seeing the man at the front of his house swinging in his hammock and saying *hola* (hi) to everyone who passed by. When we were living in San Pedro Pinula, before my parents' separation in 1959, my mother and I used to pass by this house every time we went to the Agua Tibia springs to fetch drinking water, to swim or to wash clothes.

Cesar's mother immediately took me to a bedroom while her husband went somewhere with the Indian woman.

She asked, "Are you hungry, thirsty or cold?"

"No, all I want is to lie down and rest," I said, while looking around the room for the place where I was to sleep.

She left the room and a few minutes later returned, accompanied this time only by her husband.

"Where is the nice Indian lady who brought me here?" I asked. "What is her name? I haven't had a chance to even thank her."

"That lady knows how grateful you are," she answered. "You don't have to tell her."

Despite the assurances of the couple I felt guilty about receiving help from people I did not know and, in addition, not being in a position to express my gratitude to them.

Everything that had happened this day, from the time I had talked to Cesar in the morning in El Carrizal Grande to my being taken care of by his parents in the evening in San Pedro, appeared to be more of a dream than reality. It was as if I had been a guest in a five star hotel and all the employees knew what the guest needed. There were moments I had to tell myself::

Yes Gabriela, you are not dreaming, you are awake and what you see happening is actually happening to you.

The couple looked at me for a few minutes and then Mr. Sandoval said, "You will be getting on the first bus to Chiquimula tomorrow morning. You don't have to go to the plaza to catch it. That would be too dangerous for you, as someone will surely recognize you and possibly tell Jorge or someone in the Cárcamo family. The bus stops in front of this house and no one will see you get on. Do you know how to get to Puerto Barrios from Chiquimula and from there to Livingston by boat?"

"Yes, but I don't have any...."

And before I had finished my sentence he extended his hand and gave me fifty Quetzals. "With this money you should be able to get to Livingston with no problems," he said. "You'll even have enough money to go to a hotel if you miss the boat in Puerto Barrios. Tell your father to take you to see a doctor as soon as you get there. You don't look well at all. There are some recommendations I must give you: You must never tell anyone that you stayed in this house. You must never mention to anyone that my son Cesar helped you. You must be very careful because Jorge will be looking for you everywhere and lastly, you must see a doctor and take care of yourself."

When he mentioned the monster's name I broke out in a cold sweat and the old fears returned momentarily, but they immediately vanished when I looked around at the kind people in this house.

"Don't worry," I answered firmly. "I won't ever tell anyone. Oh, I will have to tell my father," I added, "because I have a letter for him from Cesar."

"That's fine," Mr. Sandoval answered. "Please say hello and give my regards to your father for me. And tell him that Gilberto Sandoval requests him to keep this very confidential."

Before the couple had left the room I asked Mrs. Sandoval, "Is it possible to wash up? I'm so filthy. Also, I need to wash my sanitary pads; they're all soiled. I'm bleeding really bad."

She took me by the hand outside to the washbasin (*pila*) and gave me soap.

"If you want to take a bath, I can heat up water for you," she said.

It was very cold now in the evening and in those days nobody had indoor showers. I accepted the offer of hot water and before I had finished laundering my sanitary pads and hanging them on the clothesline she brought hot water to me. We mixed it with some cold water and I took a lukewarm bath before going to bed. I felt like a new person.

The next morning, before sunrise, anxiety needled me awake. I was dressed and ready to go when Mrs. Sandoval came to knock at my door.

"Gabriela, you have enough time to eat. Come to the dining room for some breakfast."

In the dining room there was another lady sitting at the table, whom Mrs. Sandoval introduced as her daughter–in–in law. While we were eating breakfast and conversing I realized that Mrs. Sandoval's daughter–in–law was the mother of a boy named José Victor Sandoval, the boy I had always danced with at the elementary school dances. When I realized this, I felt embarrassed that she was seeing me in my horrible physical condition.

After breakfast I picked up my clean and dried but still stained sanitary pads and stuffed them into my bag. I said goodbye to everyone in the house once more, hugged them, and told them that they will always be in my thoughts and prayers.

It was six o'clock in the morning and I was standing alone by the road in front of the Sandoval's house. I covered my head from the cold and also, so as not to be recognized by anyone who might happen to pass by. All was deathly quiet except for the occasional cry of a rooster and the bark of a dog. The church clock rang six times. The sun was just appearing over the horizon when I heard the roar of the bus' diesel motor breaking the morning silence. My heart started to race. I was about to be free of the monster. I knew that I was entering a new and uncertain stage on my journey, for I had no firm plans. However, I now knew that I had friends who would surely help me, even if my father still refused. I was filled with optimism—I had endured the monster's mental tortures, survived the physical punishment of my captivity and withstood the pain of the difficult trek of my escape. The worst had to be over.

I was never again to meet Mr. and Mrs. Sandoval, Cesar, my Indian guide or any of the others who had risked their lives to save my life on this extraordinary day.

The bus from San Pedro Pinula at La Cumbre

Chapter 15
Restoration Through Love

My friends are my estate.
—Emily Dickenson—

As soon as the bus left town I felt a huge relief that I had made it this far without being detected. The morning was very cool, dry and crisp as the weather usually is in San Pedro Pinula in the mornings of October and November. The sun was rising from behind the mountains right in front of the bus, for we were traveling east toward Ipala. The mountains in this region, when viewed from a distance, always have a yellowish cast and in the early morning they take on an orange glow creating a beautiful impressionistic panorama. However, fear and pain prevented me from appreciating this scene on this particular morning. The road immediately climbed into the hills and as the bus twisted around one hill I could see the flat land below and the church in San Pedro in the distance. The town did not look so menacing, now that I was moving farther and farther away.

I knew that the first part of the trip was going to be very painful. The highway to Ipala was rough, narrow and unpaved. The buses that plied this route were school bus types that did not have good suspension systems. As the bus ascended to *La Cumbre* (The Peak) and again on its descent to San Luis Jilotepeque the road twisted around and around, hugging the sides of the mountains. The road was not wide enough to let two—way traffic pass and when the bus met another vehicle sometimes it had to back up to a place wide enough to park and let the other vehicle pass. And to make matters more interesting, there were no guardrails to prevent a drop of hundreds of meters into deep chasms. I was too ill this day to be concerned about any type of road danger. I had just survived a horrible six months where my life was in immediate danger every day from a gun or a knife.

I had traveled this road many times during the past four years and each time the trip was eventful, either in a good or bad way, and I was not sure what the outcome of this trip was going to be. What new adventure was waiting for me now? I really had no plans for the future. I was not even sure where I was going to end up today. Would my father have me in his house in Livingston if I go there? Would Doña Rome help me if I go to her in Chiquimula, especially after I had told her my story and predicament? How would I get money for the operation I needed? I now knew that I was no longer alone in the world and that there were friends that would help me, but to what extent? My clearer head and sense of freedom were now producing new and different worries, but at least I did not have to worry today that I might die at the hands of a sadistic maniac. The physical pain was so horrible I could only put my head down, close my eyes and try not to think, at least not until the bus had arrived in Chiquimula.

It was possible to travel from San Pedro Pinula to Livingston in one full day, but all the connections had to be on time. That meant leaving San Pedro Pinula on the first bus at six o'clock in the morning, arriving in Chiquimula at approximately ten o'clock, and then transferring to a bus going to Puerto Barrios on the Atlantic coast. From Puerto Barrios one had to take the six o'clock evening ferry to Livingston, arriving there at seven-thirty. The first leg of the trip, from San Pedro Pinula to Chiquimula, was not a terribly long distance, but the combination of bad roads and frequent stops made for a four–hour trip. When the bus reached Ipala, still at least thirty kilometers from Chiquimula, I knew that I was not going to be able to make it to Livingston in one day. Four hours on the bus was going to be enough.

When the bus arrived in Chiquimula, on time at ten o'clock, the pain in my body made it feel like I had already traveled a full day. As I stepped off the bus the crowd of bus drivers were singing a chorus advertising their destinations, "To Puerto Barrios, to Puerto Barrios, two Quetzals, one fifty, two Quetzals."

It was decision time. I was still thinking that I should get on one of the buses to Puerto Barrios in order to arrive at Livingston by evening. However, my body was telling me that I needed to see a doctor right away and Chiquimula was the perfect place to do it. I knew a doctor there—the one I was seeing when I was attending college at INSO. If I missed the last bus to Puerto Barrios, I could go to my old boarding house and ask Doña Rome to let me stay for a day or two; she surely would give me a place to stay. If not, I still had forty-nine Quetzals to pay for a hotel and food.

After a few more minutes of reflection, I finally made up my mind to stay in Chiquimula and headed to Dr. Conrado Balcarcel's clinic. In order to go to this clinic I had to cross Ismael Cerna Park in front of the two colleges. My thoughts immediately returned to the days when I used to go there with Canche on Thursdays and Sundays, holding hands and walking around the park while the local band was playing in the gazebo. Every inch of that park, every bench, every tree and every plant had some sort of a sweet memory related to Canche, my friends and my classmates. I paused by the Jacaranda tree. This tree was a witness to so many different moments I spent with Canche. I felt a heavy weight on my chest, crushing it and preventing me from breathing. Warm tears flowed down my cheeks, dropping onto my dress. People were walking past me, turning their heads toward me with looks of curiosity on their faces.

I restarted my walk as if I were in a trance. A thousand memories merged into a single force that slowed my pace and drained my little strength. The memories continued until I arrived at the door of Doctor Balcarcel's clinic. I rang the bell and waited. Dr. Balcarcel's wife came to the door and told me, "The doctor is at the public health clinic. He is the director there. If your matter is urgent, please go there or come back tomorrow."

I had to ask her to repeat what she had said, for the sweet and sad reminisces about my days at the school were still churning around in my head.

At the public health clinic my consultation with the doctor

was short. He gave me a prescription, told me not to travel for two days and to come and see him at his own private clinic. Although there was still time to catch the bus to Puerto Barrios, I decided to heed the doctor's advice and chose to stay.

I had to cross the park once more to get my prescriptions at the pharmacy. As I walked slowly through the park and around the gazebo the beautiful and vivid memories came flooding again back into my mind. However, when I passed close to the place where the buses stopped I remembered, to my horror, the events of a month ago, almost to the day, when the monster and I stopped here on our way back to San Pedro Pinula from Livingston. In my present state of health this was not a good thing to remember—his taunts, his cruelty. Anger welled up in me, quickly making me feel nauseous and dizzy. I sat on one of the benches for a few minutes. I shook my head trying to erase those painful memories and to allow the sweet ones to return. I glanced again at the Jacaranda tree and took a mental photograph of the various shapes of its branches, so as to never forget.

The pharmacy was just across from the central market, facing one of the corners of the park. I started to walk again, head down, my legs automatically taking me to where I had to go, for when I looked up I was standing inside the pharmacy, not being able to remember how I got there. I was so weak, almost delirious. The pharmacist took me inside, gave me an injection and told me that the bleeding should stop in less than twenty-four hours. Then he gave me the other part of the doctor's prescription, a bottle of capsules.

After leaving the pharmacy I was now left with thirty-nine Quetzals in my bra. I headed toward Doña Rome's house. Raw instinct was pushing me in that direction—the instinct of self-preservation since my mind was not making conscience decisions.

As I ambled through the park, passing once more in front of INSO and INVO, another wave of nostalgia wafted over me, and my eyes started to water. I suddenly saw an image of my father in front of me and I felt very angry and puzzled in regard to his decision to take me away from this place, this town and school where I have been so happy and successful. "Why, father?"

I was confused; too many things had happened so quickly. Only twenty-four hours had passed since I first began my escape with my Indian guide. Aside from being mentally drained, I was now really feeling the negative physical effects of the arduous trip from El Carrizal Grande; my ill body could not take any more abuse. I needed a rest. I had to find a place to stay.

A number of different feelings and emotions were coursing through my brain at the same time.

Will Doña Rome welcome me? Will she even recognize me now with my emaciated and sick body? How will I face my past classmates in the house?

I turned a corner and saw Doña Rome's house. It seemed like it had been ages since I walked this route. I stopped and did a quick inspection of my dress and shoes. I really did not look my best, I thought. I tried to regain my composure: *stand erect, shoulders back.* Disparate thoughts were still swirling around in my head:

What will they say when they see me like this? They won't even recognize me. Just take the bus to Puerto Barrios and forget about Doña Rome.

I was ready to turn around and run to the bus terminal. But then I remembered Cesar's words and thought that I must go through with this; that I must make connections with my friends to help me survive and to get my life back together; that I must keep moving forward.

Slowly, I approached the door, knocked once, not very loudly. I turned around, ready to run away, but the maid came immediately to open the door.

Yes, yes, it's still the same maid, Chabela (Isabel).

She took a quick look at me. A startled expression swept over her face. Her eyes widened, and she raised her hand to her mouth to stifle any noise of her surprise. She looked at me again, taking a much longer appraisal of me this time, from head to toe. "Come…come in Miss Gabriela," she gasped, "I…I'll get Doña Rome."

Doña Rome came quickly and stood before me. She paused, not saying anything. She pushed her glasses up to her eyes from the bridge of her nose, where she usually had them resting, and inspected me up and down, still not saying a word. Tears started to stream down her cheeks. She slowly came closer, silently took me into her arms and hugged me tightly, with more and more tears coming from her eyes. We were both crying now. She gently pushed me away by the shoulders, holding me there to have a second look and then embraced me again. "Oh Gaby, Gaby, did you come alone? Where is your husband? Is he with you?"

I did not know what to say. The words *your husband* did not register in my brain, they had no meaning at all; they never did. These words smelt like vomit and I felt like throwing up.

She asked again with a more insistent tone, "Are you alone or did you come with your husband?"

"No… I came by myself. I'm going to Livingston." I stammered, trying to show as little emotion as possible. I felt sick and was not very well coordinated with my words.

Holding me by my shoulders, she inspected me again, from head to foot. She then drew me near to her, hugged me once more and said, "Oh my God, look at you. What has happened to you? Come in and sit down. Are you hungry, thirsty?" She called to her maid, "Chabela, please bring a glass of juice for Miss Gabriela!"

I detected panic in her voice when she called to her maid. Chabela was back very quickly with juice and cookies. With the juice I swallowed my capsules as directed on the bottle. It was now almost noon and the students were just about to arrive for their lunch break. At that time I had no opportunity to ask her if I could stay at her house, for she had to get the maid going with serving lunch for the boarders, just as it was done when I lived there. I was so hungry and was hoping that she would ask me to stay for lunch—which she did.

I heard a knock at the door, "That must be the *Señoritas*," Doña Rome intoned.

As she started to walk toward the door I asked her, "Please let me open it."

As I approached the door I felt my heart was beating two hundred beats a minute. For a moment I thought it was going to jump out of its cavity. I opened the door and then there was silence. Nobody moved. Nobody walked inside the house. All of the girls were frozen, looking at me as if I were a creature from another planet. Finy (Serafina Aldana), one of my best friends and also my ex–roommate, was the first one to react. She started screaming and jumping up and down with happiness.

"Gaby, Gaby! It's you...it's you! Are you staying with us? Where is your husband? Can we meet him? Are you returning to school? Are you staying here tonight? How long are you staying in Chiquimula?"

After Finy came Elbia, Carmencita, Berta (the store clerk), and the rest of the students whose names I have forgotten over the years. They kept asking dozens of questions, all at the same time. I was not able to answer. I did not know which question to answer first or where to start. They kept looking at me, not so much with looks of surprise but more with looks of uncertainty and puzzlement.

Doña Rome clapped her hands and her voice chimed, "*Niñas,* lunch is served. It is getting late."

We sat together for lunch just like we had done at the beginning of the year and during previous years. It seemed so long ago, although it had been only a few months. Whether the emotions, illness, the medication, the food or the words *your husband* were the cause I am not sure, but while we were eating lunch the sickness in my stomach became worse and I had to run to the bathroom and throw up. After that, I felt much better. When I returned, some of the girls were already getting ready to go back to school, some had already left, and the few that were still around kept looking at me, in particular at my stomach, with curious and nervous looking smiles. Finy was one of them. I knew I needed to clarify the whole situation. It was going to be painful and embarrassing, but it had to be done.

I stammered, "No, it is not what you are thinking, thanks be to God." I noticed immediately that these words appeared to cause even more consternation, so I added, "We'll talk when you return this afternoon. I may have to go and find a hotel."

At that point Finy excitedly asked, "Doña Rome, can Gaby stay here tonight? Can we miss school this afternoon? Can Gaby sleep in my bedroom? Please Doña Rome, please."

Then Finy got her face close to my ear and whispered, "I want to know how it feels to have a husband. How does it feel to have sex?"

My body got very tense, but I did not think she noticed my reaction or if she did, she did not know why I had shuddered.

"No, you can't stay," Doña Rome interrupted, "you must return to school…all of you."

I knew that she would not allow anyone to miss school so they could socialize with me. Her values would not permit such a thing. Besides, I wanted time to talk to her privately, to see if she would have me back if things with my father did not work out very well.

After the girls had left, Doña Rome sat down with me and started the conversation. "Your father told me that you had run away with a man and decided to marry him because you were pregnant."

Doña Rome said this as a statement, but the slight rising tone of her voice and the quizzical look on her face told me that she had doubts and that she was also asking me a question. I knew that it was time to tell her the complete story.

I started by telling her about my abduction, captivity, forced marriage, illness and escape, but eventually the conversation got around to my parents' separation, re-union and all of the problems I was having with my father while I was living at her boarding house, problems that I had previously concealed from her. This was also the first time she heard the story of how I ended up under my father's custody and important details of my childhood. I got the impression that she already knew some things; however, I also got the sense that what she knew was only according to how my father had told the story, especially in relation to my mother. As I told my story I could see Doña Rome becoming more and more furious, at one point even cursing my father's name.

"Doña Rome," I said hesitantly, "I am afraid to go to my father in Livingston. Would it be possible to work for you so that I may return to school if my father won't have me?"

"First, I must tell you," she said, intoning her emphatic voice she always used when she was ready to talk about a serious matter, "I had various heated arguments with your father when he told me he was going to take you away from this city just because you were dating Canche. I could have fought harder on your behalf but your father told me that I was more concerned about the money I was receiving from the government for your scholarship than for your wellbeing. I'm sorry for what I am going to say; your father might be a very smart man, but his reasoning leaves a lot to be desired. Now, I don't want any more problems with him. If he knows that you stayed here without reaching his house first, who knows what his reaction will be. I cannot emphasize enough that I have to be careful. I'll repeat again, your father is not a reasonable and logical man. However, you can stay here for now, at least until you get well. You will sleep in Finy's room. Don't worry about paying for food or lodging. If you need money, I'll give you what you need. I prefer, however, that when you are well you go to your father. Try and see how it goes and if it doesn't work, then come back and you can stay here. We will find something that you can do so that you can earn money to support yourself and return to school. You can help around the house with some of the cleaning and cooking or help in the store. Besides, you are a very good little seamstress and you can make a lot of money from your classmates with your sewing."

I could not believe that I had even forgotten about my sewing skills. It was true that I had made lots of money by mending, hemming dresses, replacing buttons, and changing zippers for my friends in school and for the girls in the boarding house.

When the girls returned from college after the afternoon session Doña Rome took them aside and spoke with them as a group. She must have told them not to ask questions because nobody did, not even Finy, the one who wanted to know how it felt to have sex. Finy was my best friend in the house and that night we were sleeping in the same room. I took this opportunity to tell her everything that had happened to me.

"Gaby, my parents have money and if you need help I will ask them. I know that they will help you without any hesitation."

At one point in our conversations Finy asked me the question I did not want to hear, "Are you still in love with Canche?" My tears gave her the answer and she suggested, "Gaby, I think that Canche should be told what happened to you. He thinks that you ran away with this man. He thinks that as soon as you went to Jalapa you fell in love with this other guy. We must tell him. I will do it if you allow me."

"Oh Finy," I answered in a tired but anxious voice, "I don't think I've the strength to face Canche now. What if he doesn't believe you or me? I don't know."

We did not sleep at all that night. We just talked and cried about my misfortune and we sometimes laughed about some past reminisced event and then cried again. I was very tired and finally had to tell her, "Finy, I have to tell you that I'm very sick. You can't imagine how sick I am. I feel like I might die at any minute. I'll have to stay here a few days to see the doctor again because I can't travel."

She still did not seem to comprehend my situation, for she suddenly became animated and blurted out, "Let's go to the concert in the park this Thursday, just like we used to do. That'll cheer you up and help you get well."

I hesitated to give her an answer and it was then I saw her inspecting my torn shoes and ripped dress. "Your clothes, Oh my God!" she gasped. She went to her armoire, opened it and said, "Gaby, pick and choose. I know I have bigger boobs than you but I'm sure that if you select one of these skirts or pants one of the other girls will lend you a top."

She was right. The next day, after returning from school, all the girls helped to fix me up with a new beautiful wardrobe, starting with undergarments all the way to shoes. They gave me deodorant and make up. They all worked so hard to make me look my best.

"Keep everything, it's yours and take it to Livingston when you leave."

I do not think that I had said thank you so many times in such a short period of time during those few days at Doña Rome's house. I was overwhelmed with the kindness of so many people willing to help me.

When I went back to see Doctor Balcarcel I stopped at the church and prayed, "Thank you God, forgive me for doubting your power and your love for me. Thank you, Saint Gabriel and Holy Mary for your prayers. Our father who art in heaven…"

By Thursday I was no longer bleeding, I was feeling more optimistic and slightly stronger. I agreed to go the park in the evening. We all went together. We girls walked counter–clockwise around the circle while the boys walked opposite to our direction. It was there when I saw Canche walking with his best friends, Rubelio Gomez and Samuel Lam. Although the light in the park was in semi-penumbra, I saw his eyes locking onto mine.

Finy was holding my arm and excitedly whispered in my ear, "Did you see him? He saw you, I am sure of it and you look beautiful."

I really did feel beautiful that evening, but I did not answer, for I was too nervous, emotionally drained and scared; with every step pain shot through my body.

Finy continued, "I bet he'll come to talk to us. He always does when we come to the park."

I started to shake from the thought that he might come near me.

Finy babbled on, "Gaby, be strong. I know he still loves you. He needs to know that you love him too. If he knows what happened to you, he will want to start seeing you again, just as before. Besides, he is graduating this year and things can be different for both of you."

Finy was totally wrong. We walked around the park several more times but I never saw him again. His friends were there, for we saw Rubelio and Samuel, but it seemed like Canche had vanished. I learned sometime later that not only Finy, but Berta as well, tried to speak with him. However, he was so hurt and so angry that he did not want to hear anything related to me. I also found out from Berta, (Tita, we called her) that Canche had said something strange and obscure to her, something that sounded to her as, "I would never marry a woman who is not a virgin."

When it was time to leave Chiquimula toward the end of the week I had a new wardrobe, shoes, cosmetics, a small piece of luggage, and another twenty Quetzals that Finy had given me. I had to consult with Dr. Balcarcel once again before leaving. His recommendation was that I should go back to Dr. Carías in Jalapa, the doctor who treated me during the time of my miscarriage, or, as an alternative, I should stay in Chiquimula and get the needed operation there. I still did not know what was exactly wrong with me except that my uterus was damaged.

It was such a good feeling to be loved and I did not want this feeling to go away. Whatever was waiting for me in Livingston, it certainly would not be the warmth, love and concern I was receiving and enjoying in Chiquimula. But I could not stay; I had to return to my father. Besides, the thoughts of possibly crossing paths with Canche and the embarrassment and pain I would suffer if I had to explain things to him were becoming oppressive. My health, I thought, would not be able to hold up. I had to leave.

Time to say farewell had arrived. Once more I felt the same crushing and heavy feeling in my heart I was feeling when walking through the park and looking at the Jacaranda tree. We were all crying. Finy accompanied me to the bus terminal and it was only then I remembered that my father did not know that I had escaped from the monster and San Pedro Pinula. Before boarding the bus I stopped at the post office to send him a telegram:

PAPÁ, I WILL ARRIVE TODAY SEVEN-THIRTY BOAT.
—Anne-Sophie Swetchin—

Municipal Building–Chiquimula

Chapter 16
New Life—Old Problems

Our remedies oft in ourselves do lie, which we ascribe to heaven.
–William Shakespeare–

The *SANTA MARTA left Puerto Barrios at six PM* and there was still some daylight. Halfway into the trip night descended, surrounding the boat with blackness, broken only by the meager light provided by a few low-wattage bulbs hanging from the deck cover. The sea was glassy smooth, the only sounds were the water lapping against the sides of the boat, the soft murmurs of conversations, and the thump, thump, thump of the diesel motor. It was hot and muggy, as it usually is on the Caribbean coast. The night was dark, no moon, and there were so many stars in the sky. Off in the distance, I saw the twinkling lights of the freighters moored in the bay, waiting to enter the harbour. Those little lights, along with the beautiful stars, seemed to represent the little lights of hope that were now piercing through my own darkened existence. As I peered out into the blackness I kept wondering what was going to happen now? I had escaped, but my future was still so uncertain.

Will my father accept me? Will he pay for my needed operation? Will my brothers be civil with me? Will I be able to find my mother? At least, I'll soon be around some people who know me and who care for me, Aunt Teco for sure.

The boat docked in Livingston on time at seven-thirty in the evening. I was surprised to see my father on the pier collecting his bundle of newspapers, which usually arrive on the noon boat. We met, hardly greeted each other, and silently walked side–by–side up the long hill to his house.

The house was empty and dark. "Where are my brothers?" I inquired, skewing up my face with a surprised look.

"I told them to go out, so we can talk," he replied matter-of-factly.

That's good. We can talk freely about everything that was left unsaid on that horrible day before going to the court hearing in San Pedro Pinula.

"I must tell you that it was nice for you to send me a telegram. That gave me enough time to arrange for your brothers to go somewhere while we have some time alone. We must discuss how the situation will work with your returning home and what I'm willing to do for you…"

With these words I knew that my hopes for some clarification about my kidnapping were dashed. It was so disheartening. My father had his agenda and it definitely was not to find out the truth about what had happened to me, at least not from me.

"…Your brothers do not want you here, but I told them that I have to take this last step to help you."

"So, are you saying that my brothers are the ones to make the decisions in this house?" I inquired with a hardly concealed tone of sarcasm and anger.

He paused for a few seconds before responding, "Your brothers are the ones who faithfully stayed with me since the day your mother and I separated. Therefore, they have the right to have some say in it. Besides, you're now a married woman and I have no responsibilities toward you. However, we can both help each other. I need someone to help with the house chores and taking care of Eneida. In exchange, I will provide you with room and board plus five Quetzals a month as your salary…"

He paused again, maybe to judge my reaction and then continued,

…"I know you only have come here because your mother is nowhere to be found. If she were here, you would have run to her like you did in the past and you would not even come to this house."

"You're right! If my mother were here I would be with her. She would've welcomed me with opened arms. She would want to know what had happened to me. I could help her sewing and save money to return to school, which is what I want. You don't like it when I defend my mother. She's not the only one to blame for the mess between you two. I know more than what you think. I know my brothers stayed by your side faithfully and they show hate for our mother. You would like for me to do the same, but I can't. I love my mother as much as I love you. My brothers act the way they do toward her because you and your family have poisoned their minds in the same way all of you tried to poison mine. You never were happy with me because I'm a girl. Your favourite words before Eneida was born were: 'God punished me because he gave me a daughter.' Well, God has punished you two more times because now you have three girls."

I was so angry and could not be quiet but my father was perhaps even angrier; he was fuming. He looked at me with flaming eyes and threw at me his old favourite curse; "God should strike you with lightning and cut you in half."

I knew I was in a no–win battle. Once more I recalled Cesar's advice and started silently rehearsing it again: "First, you have to get well and after that start looking at other possible options, such as living with your Aunt Teco and finding a job at one of the stores or start doing some sewing."

Cesar was right. I needed to follow his wise advice and keep my mouth shut. I needed my father's help. I was sick, I had no job, and I had no other place to live. I composed myself and with a humble voice said, "I'm sorry for talking to you like that. I accept your conditions. However, I must tell you I am very sick. I've been bleeding from my vagina and Dr. Balcarcel in Chiquimula told me to go back and see Dr. Carías in Jalapa, and to do it soon."

We stayed quiet for a while. I finally broke the silence by saying softly, "Thank you for allowing me to stay here and I repeat, I won't be a problem and I'll do my best to keep the peace. I just need to ask you one final question and after that I will keep my mouth shut."

"Sure, go ahead," he said with a slight tone of exasperation in his voice and a look of annoyance on his face.

"I get the feeling that you blame me for what had happened to me. I heard statements in Chiquimula that you have been saying that I ran away with that man; even your words to me on the day before the hearing implied that. Do you really think I willingly ran away with him? Is that what you suspect? Is that what you believe? Is that what you've been telling people? Is that the reason you treat me like this?"

I had to try to break the blockage; I had to force my father to talk about what he knew about my situation and why he acted in the way he did. I had to bring this conversation back to my agenda.

He looked at me for quite some time before talking, "All I know is that a woman can scream, scratch, kick, bite and do many things to protect herself. I also believe that it would make it very difficult for a man to rape a woman if she's kicking and trying to fight back. Besides, what were you doing at that time in the street when I told you not to go to the procession? In fact, I found out in San Pedro that someone had even warned you that Jorge was threatening to kidnap you. Why didn't you take precautions?"

He said it; he said the word! He has never used the word "kidnap" before; he's always said I had run away with the criminal. What does this mean? Has he thought for a long time, or even known, that I was kidnapped? No use pursuing this. He'll only backtrack and defend himself.

I felt silly for asking him anything about my kidnapping. I just could not believe I was hearing correctly. I was now more confused than ever about what he thought had happened to me. Tears kept streaming down my face; I was so hurt. He just kept staring at me with a dispassionate look.

I abruptly grabbed the bottom of my dress and wiped my nose and eyes. I finally regained my composure and said, "You are totally right, Papá. I didn't fight back and I shouldn't have gone out without your permission. Everything that has happened to me has been my own fault."

I then stood up and walked over to my little suitcase, the one that was given to me in Chiquimula, with as an erect and strong posture as I could marshal. I took out the letter Cesar had given to me, turned around and walked back to him. With my head held high and with dignity in my voice I said, "This is a letter from Cesar Sandoval to you."

He took the letter from my hand, opened it and read it. It seemed short and I did not ask what it contained. Only my father's furrowed brow indicated that there was something of concern in the letter. His facial appearance softened as he folded the letter and shoved it into his pants pocket, without imparting its contents to me.

"As soon as the school term ends I will take you back to Jalapa to see Dr. Carías," he said quiescently.

That brought some comfort. I knew the trip was going to be soon because exams had already started, which meant that he would soon be free from his school duties to take me to Jalapa or Guatemala City.

"Does Jorge know that you're here?" he inquired.

"I don't know. Cesar helped me escape from him. I stayed with his parents and they gave me money. That's how I was able to see Dr. Balcarcel in Chiquimula and to travel here. Oh, I almost forgot, Cesar and his father told me to tell you that we are not to say anything to anybody about this. They don't want any trouble with the Cárcamos."

"Is Gilberto expecting that we pay him back?"

"I don't think so," I replied simply.

"Hum…well, you can stay here; just help around the house with as much as you can and take care of Eneida. By the way, she's at your Aunt Teco's house tonight. Don't worry about washing the clothes. I'll keep the same woman who has been doing it all this time for the time being."

I had now become the maid of the house again, this time having no rank or privileges as a daughter. The paltry five Quetzals he paid me was not the insult. It was his relegating me to the status of hired help that hurt. My father laid down strict rules for me to follow in all aspects of my life. I still had to ask permission to do certain things teenage children like to do, such as going to the movies or to another person's house. He retained all of his rights as my father, but now I had no rights as his child. In reality, not that much had changed at all. For years I was a child when it was convenient for him to treat me as a child, and I was an adult when it was convenient for him that I carry the responsibilities of an adult. The only real difference now was that I was a married woman and that meant he had absolutely no financial or legal obligations toward me, as he so dutifully kept reminding me.

I made a pledge to endure anything and everything until I had become well again and be able to leave the house to start a new life. I resigned myself to my miserable existence and swore that I would try to control my temper and not to get into any more trouble with my father. I needed his help, for my health was drastically deteriorating again and I was in as critical shape, if not worse, than I was in El Carrizal Grande. I was afraid that I was going to die very soon. I was so sick that I went to bed every night crying and praying. I feared that I would not awake the next morning.

While I was cleaning and rearranging furniture around the house I came across a notebook that was similar to the one my father kept when he was with my mother—the one I used to take to Mr. Ernesto Wong's store in San Pedro Pinula to buy things on credit. This notebook had my name on the front cover. It read: GABRIELA'S EXPENSES. I got very curious and opened it. I was shocked, for it contained a detailed list of things my father had purchased for me over the years, complete with dates and amounts, including the payments he made to the private hospital for my appendix operation. I could not believe that he had even written down the cost of the boots he had purchased for me so that I could participate as a majorette at INSO in Chiquimula for Independence Day. The only expenses missing were the ones for the recent medication he had been buying for me.

I did not know what to think about this. Looking at the recorded expenses, with the totals very well added up, the only thing I could think is that he wanted to know how expensive I was as a child. I was trying my best to heed Cesar's words, but I could not let go of this without an explanation. I had to confront my father about this notebook.

When he returned home, I took the notebook to him and asked, "Papá could you explain the meaning of this?"

His first answer was an angry retort, "What are you doing snooping around my private affairs? That's not part of your job in this house."

But I was insistent. "I need to know; why would you record the expenses of my operation and even the price of the boots I needed for my majorette uniform?"

He reflected and then replied calmly, "I'm a fair person and I want to give my children equal parts of what I have. In this way, I will know who should get more and who should get less at the time of my death. And by looking at this list, I can see that you have received more than your brothers and that's something I should take into consideration when I do my will. My other idea was that when you graduate and find work you would help your siblings with their education to level things off. Now, because of what *you* did, that hope is no longer a possibility but I still think that no child of mine should receive more than the other one."

"I'm not interested in your assets," I answered bitterly. "You can give them to whomever you wish. As far as my graduating and finding work in order to help my brothers and sister, how dare you talk like that when you always opposed my getting a good education, you've said this so many times. Papá, you're driving me absolutely crazy! You contradict yourself at every turn when you talk with me, and you always have. Nothing you say makes any sense at all…"

I could see that he was very angry; however, he stayed quiet.

"…And now you are giving me the message that if I want to get an education I'll have to do it on my own. And you know what? I will do it. I don't know how, but I will…"

My father's face was next to mine and still he did not say anything.

"...When you questioned me about what I had done," I continued on, "I guess you were referring to what happened to me on that Good Friday. Well, I told you before and I'll repeat it once more—I didn't do anything. I'm not the one who destroyed my career. I blame nobody else but you. You, with absolutely no logical reason, took me away from the school and town where I had been the happiest and where I was doing so well. This never would have happened if I had stayed in Chiquimula."

"I did that for your own good," he shot back.

"Maybe, and if that is the case, that shows how little you know me and trust me. That's very, very sad."

I could have said many other things in relation to the kidnapping and my suffering while in the hands of the criminal. The conversation, however, was getting too heated and I walked away.

I've to get out of this house as soon as possible. Oh God, oh Lord, please help me. Speed my healing. I'll do everything it takes to show him that I will succeed. I will show you father, I will show you.

This was probably the last major fight I had with my father, for whenever an argument was about to start I immediately applied the strategy I had mastered when I was in the hands of my captor: Be present, look attentive, pretend to listen, nod assent; but make sure that the mind is very far away. This worked.

Around two weeks or so after my arrival in Livingston the mailman delivered a letter to the house addressed to me. I saw the writing on the envelope and my whole body started to shake. It was the monster's scrawl. I paused. I did not know what to do. I knew that there would be nothing good in the letter and I was not interested in what he had to say. I thought about burning it or just dropping it in the outhouse latrine without opening it. I finally got the courage to open it and my fears were confirmed. The criminal scribbled only a few lines, misspelling almost every word, as usual. He ordered me to immediately return to San Pedro Pinula and he even gave me a deadline as to when I was to return. If I refused, he would come to get me.

I burnt the letter, but I told Aunt Teco about it. She thought that it would be a good step to be truthful and tell my father—advice I followed. When I told him he made only one comment, telling me to give him any future mail that would come addressed to me.

No more than a week had passed when a second letter from the criminal arrived. The contents of this letter were more frightening and threatening:

> *I am ordering you to come back right away. If you fail to do as I tell you I will come and get you myself, and nobody will dare interfere because I am your husband. If you think of refusing to come with me, just remember that if I kidnapped you once I will kidnap you again and as many times as I have to until you stop running away from me. Be reasonable and don't complicate things. I am saying this because your father may try to stop me when I come to get you. If that happens, I will have no choice but to get him out of my way at any cost. I mean, even if I have to kill him.*

This time I was hysterical with fear and I went to my father right away. He read the letter, quickly looked at his watch and said, "I'm going to Puerto Barrios this afternoon and file a complaint with the police."

And so he did. When he came back he appeared to be very happy and triumphantly announced, "I went to the authorities and presented the letter. There is an order to arrest Jorge for uttering death threats against me and kidnapping threats against you. They will notify us when he is captured."

"I hope they capture him soon and put him in jail. Will I be going to court again?" I asked apprehensively.

"No, you're a minor. I'm the one prosecuting him," he said, pointing to himself and putting special emphasis on the word *I*.

My father looked very happy and confident that the criminal was going to be captured and brought to trial, but another question was revolving around in my head:

Does my father believe me now; is he concerned about my safety? Has he finally realized how dangerous this criminal is? Or is it only the threat against him that has stirred him into action?

My father still did not ask me to tell him what had actually happened to me. I guess he still was not ready for that—too embarrassing now. I did notice, however, one big difference in his manner of speech—he never again used the phrases, "Why did you run away with him or why did you do this to me?"

My father traveled back and forth to Puerto Barrios quite often to find out if the criminal had been arrested. He returned one day quite dejected and said, "Jorge probably found out about the order for his arrest. The police in Puerto Barrios say that he is not to be found in San Pedro Pinula and that no one knows where he has gone. The police are not sure if he had fled San Pedro Pinula because he had been informed about his arrest order or if it is just a coincidence that he had left town when the warrant was issued."

Days and a few weeks passed and we had heard nothing in relation to his arrest. I was fearful that the criminal might sneak into Livingston and try to kidnap me again or kill me, along with my father. I was so nervous and anxious not knowing where this man was. I even avoided participating in one of the popular activities of the town, especially for young people, going to the pier to watch the arrival of the evening ferry. My father did not easily give up on his quest and kept traveling to Puerto Barrios to talk with the police, asking for any updates on the criminal's whereabouts, but there were no new developments in the case.

During these days I was no longer going anywhere; I was too weak. Although my father had offered to pay me five Quetzals a month to be the maid in the house, he was actually spending much more money by buying my medication. I was extremely grateful for that and I told him so. I was now resigned to stay at home, doing my chores and trying to ignore my brothers' ugly comments toward me and about our mother, trying to ignore my disgrace of being a maid to them. I had started to profusely bleed from my vagina again and the accompanying pain was as intolerable as it was in El Carrizal Grande. I was again getting weaker and weaker with each passing day.

᷃

Shortly after my arrival in Livingston I noticed that my sister Eneida was a good friend and playmate with the two children of Mr. Milton Wong, our neighbor. He was the owner of a bar/restaurant situated behind our house. His two children, Walter and Merle, were eight and seven years old respectively. Don Milton, as I called him, and I were acquainted with each other for some time, from the days when my father and mother had first come to Livingston four years earlier in the Spring of 1961. During the holidays I visited his house several times with Aunt Teco to practice the school dances, programs, and concerts she was organizing. Don Milton was the only person in Livingston who owned a modern hi-fi record player with good speakers and who had enough room in his house for the practices.

For my sixteenth birthday on November 7, 1964 Don Milton sent me a beautiful box of embroidered handkerchiefs. This was in gratitude for looking after his children when they came to play with my little sister. When my father learned about Don Milton's gift he became angry and said, "You are not to accept gifts from any man. Men give gifts to women because they want something in return and that's usually sex. Get that package and send it back to him immediately."

I had one of Don Milton's children take the package back to him and I attached a note:

I am sorry, it is a beautiful gift and I thank you for your nice gesture, but I cannot accept it.

Later, Mr. Wong apologized. "My daughter told me how furious your father was about the present I had sent you. I'm sorry; I had no idea that this would cause such a problem for you. Should I speak to your father about this?"

"No," I answered sadly. "It's already settled."

This was the first time I had spoken with Don Milton since arriving in Livingston and this encounter was the beginning of a wonderful friendship between the two of us.

My only other divertissement was going over to Aunt Teco's house and talking with her. She gave me moral support, clothing, cosmetics and some money during this difficult time.

In late November, about three weeks after the handkerchief incident, my health had deteriorated to the point that my father had to take me to Guatemala City. He left Eneida in Puerto Barrios with one of my mother's distant cousins and the two of us traveled by coach bus to see Dr. Labbé.

When we were in a hotel in Guatemala City we had some time to kill. I ventured to ask my father about what Cesar had told me in El Carrizal Grande. "Papá," I tentatively started, "I do not wish to fight or argue with you, but I have a question to ask you? It is very delicate and I am even afraid to bring this up."

"Echela a volar, señora," literally, "Let it fly," he replied eagerly.

He seemed to be in a good mood, which encouraged me to continue, "Cesar told me that you killed someone, is it true?"

"Yes it's true," he said with a sad voice. "I won't tell you where it happened, but it did happen...when I was thirty years old and when I was teaching in that town. It was in self–defense." His voice quivered and he sounded as if he were on the verge of crying. Slowly, he continued. "I was in love with this woman, you see. We had just become engaged to be married when a man from the same town returned after having been away for some time. Apparently, he had previously dated this girl for a long time and he wanted her back. Of course, he soon found out she was going to marry me. He approached me at the billiard hall and told me to leave her alone. My reply was, 'Don't talk to me, talk to her! If she prefers you, she will break the engagement with me and you can have her. If she decides to marry me, I will marry her.' After having said this, I left the billiards. He followed me outside and hit me on the head very hard with the butt of his gun, causing me to bleed. He told me, 'If you don't get away from her I will kill you!' He still had the gun in his hand and I took a small knife out of my pocket and started walking toward him. He lifted the gun and shot. I don't know if he shot the gun just to scare me or if his aim was not good. Anyway, the bullet did not hit me. I got closer to him and I stabbed him in the chest. My intention was just to make him leave me alone, but the wound was fatal. He fell to the ground, dead. I immediately went to the police and told them to arrest me because I had just killed someone."

"So, what happened? Did you have a trial?" I inquired.

"The declaration of the witnesses, along with my giving myself up voluntarily, helped me. I was charged with manslaughter instead of murder. I went to prison for five years and then I was on probation for another five years. When I was released I had a tough time getting a job as a teacher. The saddest part of this story was that my fiancée, the girl I was fighting for, never came to visit me in prison. I never saw her again. I have nothing to hide. I am not happy or proud of what I did, but I did it in self–defense and I served my time. Eventually, I was going to tell all of you about this."

After listening to his story I felt very sorry for him and started crying: *It's no wonder he never got married until he was forty–one years old.*

He told me many other details about his life in prison: how much he had suffered, how primitive it was, his becoming a teacher and tutor to other prisoners, and his witnessing other prisoners being beaten or tortured.

The next day I was taken to see Dr. Labbé. My father did all of the talking and the two discussed my case in private. When my father came out of he office he said, "Doctor Labbé told me that you need surgery as soon as possible. Your uterus and vagina don't look very good. He's writing a letter to Dr. Carías giving him his opinion."

My father used some medical terminology about my condition, which was a foreign language to me. One thing he said that I did understand was that bearing children in the future was going to be difficult, if not impossible.

"The operation has to be done in Jalapa. Dr. Labbe's clinic is too expensive and I can't afford it," my father continued. "In the meantime, the doctor will give you a prescription to stabilize the bleeding until we can travel there."

"Can't my operation be done in another hospital?" I asked. "Jalapa is too close to San Pedro Pinula. I'm terribly afraid. Please, I don't want to go there."

"I don't know why you keep going on about this?" my father said, clearly annoyed. "I told you that Jorge fled San Pedro Pinula." As soon as he had said this my father's face suddenly brightened up. "By the way, I've some excellent news for you. I was just talking about Jorge with my niece here in the City and she thinks that he's here, staying with his uncle Luis Cárcamo. She said that Luis and his family are living in the sixth zone only a few blocks away from where she's staying. And listen to this! She says that she's actually seen Jorge coming and going from Luis' house."

That same evening my father, his niece, and I went for a walk to snoop around the address given to him. He only wanted to make sure that it was the correct address. We did not see the criminal entering or leaving, but my father was adamant that he was in there. "Tomorrow I'll go to the police and as soon as they capture him we'll leave for Jalapa. Once this business is finished you'll have nothing to worry about." He was so excited. I do not think he slept that night and neither did I—not from excitement, but rather from fright.

The following day he notified the police about the criminal's suspected whereabouts and they came to talk with us. What the police had planned was frightening news for me.

"We will use you as bait," one of them told me. "We have no warrant to enter the house so we need you to help us lure him out. From what your father told us about the letters we think he wants you back and he will bite."

I did not know which fear was greater—the one I felt when the monster was rubbing his gun along my back when he kidnapped me, or the one I was feeling about this present dangerous and terrifying assignment.

"Papá, I'm scared and I don't want to do this," I pleaded. "What if Jorge grabs me and kills me before the police can save me?"

"You're just being uncooperative," he snapped. If you didn't willingly run away with him, as you told me, you must cooperate with us. If he's in that house, we can't waste this opportunity."

I had no choice but to follow orders.

That very same evening the police coached me on what to do and say once the operation was in motion. My father and I walked to the house to rendezvous with the police. Two unmarked police cars were waiting, one near the house and one across the street. The house was a combination house and small family grocery store; therefore, the front door was open to receive customers. I went inside the store—shaking—trying to remember the instructions I had been rehearsing all day.

"Is…is Mr. Jorge Cárcamo here?" I spluttered.

The lady behind the counter was inspecting me with a suspicious look on her face and finally replied, "Who are you? How do you know him?"

"I am his wife, Gabriela, and I would like to speak with him. Is he here?" Without waiting for a reply I handed her the short note the police had dictated to me:

Jorge, I love you and I need to speak with you. I will be waiting outside. Gabriela

"Please give him this note."

The lady took the note without saying anything and that led me to think that my father was right, the monster was indeed staying in this house. I immediately left and went outside, standing close to the unmarked police car as instructed.

The brief moment I spent inside the house was terrifying. I do not think I took a breath when I was in the store, for I was shaking and gasping for air when I got outside. I could not understand how my father and the police could have placed me, a sixteen–year old girl, in a situation like that. I was sure that the monster would not come out and the operation was going to fail. All in all, I thought that this was a really stupid plan; the criminal had to know that I did not love him.

Surprise of surprises, the criminal swallowed the bait and came out of the house looking for me. He looked different; wearing clothes I had not seen him wear before—more business, city–like clothes. He came very close to me. I made no movement. Those were my instructions. I did not see a gun or knife in his hand. I was not breathing. I was on the verge of peeing my pants. It seemed like an eternity before four police officers emerged from the cars and grabbed him. The criminal resisted and the police gave him a really good beating, right there on the street. They violently shoved him into the police car, banging his heard on the doorframe and then they sped away.

Yes, yes, do it…hit him, hit him! I was so happy to see the monster getting a beating. I have no words to explain my joy watching the police manhandle the detestable criminal. I was wishing that the beating had been a lot longer. I felt that finally there was some justice for me, not revenge, just justice.

My father complimented me for the good work and we left. The next day the police informed my father that the criminal had been taken to the Pavon prison in the city of Escuintla. In 1964, that prison had the reputation as the toughest and most fearsome in Guatemala. If my father received more information at that time about the fate of the monster, he did not share it with me.

Two days after the criminal's arrest we left for Jalapa and I immediately checked into the hospital. Dr. Carías was appalled when he saw my condition. He ordered five blood transfusions before he would perform the operation. To this day I do not know exactly what operation I had to undergo, for my father handled everything and I was just thankful that something was being done for me.

While I was recovering in the hospital Don Milton traveled all the way from Livingston to pay me a surprise visit. I did not know what to think about this, but he explained, "I found out from your brother Chus and my kids that you were hospitalized in Jalapa. I wasn't sure if it were true or not but I decided to venture and come to visit you. Merle has become very fond of you and she misses you a lot. It was not hard to find you because there is only one hospital in this city."

I was confused about this visit and I was so taken aback I

could not speak, but I thought it was a nice gesture.

"Please don't tell your father that I came here to see you," he said. "I remember how upset he was when I sent you a present for your birthday. I've only come to see you and wish you well because you have been so nice to my children."

He came twice to the hospital, each time bringing me flowers in the name of his children.

≈

I was in the hospital for almost six weeks and was discharged around the middle of January of 1965, barely three months after my escape. My father came to Jalapa to take me back with him to Livingston. I felt much better, but I was still very weak. The horrible pain I had been suffering for so many weeks was now gone and the bleeding had stopped. I also felt very safe knowing that the criminal was in prison. I never asked my father about him, and my father never volunteered any information either. It was as if nothing had happened—and that was just fine with me.

On the way to Livingston we stopped for one night in San Pedro Pinula for the inauguration of electrical service. Out of fear and sickness I sequestered myself in my cousin Rosa's house, only daring to go out when my father took me to the official ceremonies. The next morning we were on the early bus back to Livingston.

While in San Pedro several people told us a very strange story. Apparently Jorge rode into town one day on his horse perhaps the day after my escape, got really drunk at the bar, and started asking everybody if they had seen me. He kept checking the buses the whole afternoon. He then got on his horse and started circling the park, riding back and forth in front of my grand-mother's house, clattering up and down the stairs of the Munici-pal Building, trotting back and forth along its arcade, screaming all the time, "Where's my wife? My wife has left me!"

After hearing this story I was so happy that I had escaped. This event must have happened on the same day or on the fol-lowing day of my escape. Now I was sure the monster would have killed me if he had found me. The equestrian show around the Municipal Building was a display of intimidation—his way to show me, and anyone who had helped me, that he was boss and was to be feared and that someone had better turn me over to him. He probably thought that I was hiding in my grandmother's house that day. My father found this story amusing, but I did not. I could never forget how scared I was on the path from El Carrizal Grande to San Pedro that fateful day, afraid that the monster would come across my Indian guide and me and shoot us both.

The relationship between my father and me was now more settled. He was supportive and helpful during my convalescence. My brothers noticed my father's change in attitude and they became more careful with their nasty behaviour toward me. That was welcome. My father did not ask me to do very much around the house. I did eventually have to resume my duties as the maid in the house, but that was not until I had become healthier and stronger, and I did not mind this. I was very grateful to him for allowing me this time to recover my health. I became quite reclusive, at least compared to my previous extroverted character, and I especially avoided talking to anyone about what I had gone through. In fact, only Aunt Teco learned the true story of my ordeal.

The medicines Dr. Carías had prescribed were expensive and I did not want my father to have this financial burden. I wished to get well as fast as possible, to find work and be more independent. However, I was not letting these worries depress me at this time—they were nothing compared to what I had been through.

Courage is resistance to fear...not absence of fear.
–Mark Twain–

Chapter 17
Tranquility

The grand essentials of happiness are: something to do, something to love, and something to hope for.
–Allan K. Chalmers–

During my convalescence, which took more than six months, Mr. Wong and I got to know each other much better. He became my very good friend and eventually, another angel along my journey back to a normal life. Whenever I sat on my chair in the courtyard, to read or embroider, he came to talk with me from the second floor of his house, which overlooked my courtyard.

One day I asked him, "Where is your wife?"

"I have never been married," he replied. "Now, if you are asking about my ex-common–law wife and mother of my children, she is in Guatemala with her husband. I separated from her about four years ago. Now, what about you? I know you are married, where is your husband?"

With a lot of discomfort I related minimum details about the kidnapping and then requested, "Please don't refer to that man as my husband. I married him because I had no other choice. He is in jail now and I hope he stays there until he dies. I don't like to talk about him at all."

"I'm sorry, I promise you that I won't ever bring up that subject again."

One day, while sitting in the yard, I was whistling *The Theme from the Moulin Rouge*, which was a song we danced to in music class when I was at INSO. This song brought back many happy memories. I was also singing the songs, *Look For a Star* and *Green eyes.* I noticed that Don Milton was on the second floor of his house listening to me.

"I've been listening to your whistling and singing those songs a lot. I have all of those records. Would you like me to play them for you?"

"Why yes, of course." I answered enthusiastically.

He placed the speakers outside his house on the balcony so that I could hear the music. This was nothing new, for he had been doing this since I came back from the hospital. Don Milton had a great record collection of romantic and light classical music that I enjoyed very much.

While the song *Look for a Star* was playing I told him, "That song is the first song I danced to with my ex–boyfriend at the anniversary of my college in Chiquimula. I also like the song *Green Eyes* because his eyes are green and every time I hear the song it reminds me of him."

"Do you still love him?" He asked.

"Yes," I answered hesitantly.

"Why did you break up?"

"As I told you the other day there are parts of my life I don't wish to talk about," I answered sadly, not looking into his eyes.

We had conversations almost everyday with *Moulin Rouge* as background music. Eventually, I learned so much about him that it seemed that I had known him forever. He also learned many things about me, including my desire to go back to school and my desperate need to find work. Everyday I felt more comfortable conversing with him. I was no longer calling him Mr. Wong. I was now calling him Milton, as he requested.

One day I approached him to ask if there was a chance that he could give me a job.

"The only job I could give you is to look after my children. I could never employ you at the restaurant or the bar. That is not a place for a nice girl like you. If you take care of my children you could make enough money to go back to school, or… perhaps you and the children could all go back to school together?"

I did not pursue the matter because I was not sure what he

meant by this. Besides, my father's words were still with me, "Men only do favours for girls in exchange for sex."

Aunt Teco had been observing all of these interactions between Milton and me, for the kindergarten where she worked was just in front of Milton's house. One day she told me, "Hmm! I think Milton is interested in you."

"Are you crazy?" I replied with a look of disbelief. "He could be my father…he's thirty–seven years old. Milton is only a friend and he has never shown any signs of having any other intentions toward me except to be friends. He's just grateful that I'm nice to his children. I've told him several times that I'm in love with Canche and besides, he probably has a girlfriend anyway."

Aunt Teco was smiling and said, "Let me tell you something, my dear. The devil knows a lot, not because he is the devil, but because he is old and has lots of experience. I know I'm right about this. I'm going to tell you something else too. I know you're still in love with your Canche, but what I'm not sure about is if Canche is still thinking about you. Has he made any attempt to contact you? I should also inform you that I know that Milton doesn't have a girlfriend."

I was annoyed with her remark about Canche, but in my heart I knew that she was right.

Aunt Teco was also right that I did not know how to read men very well. One day in the summer of 1965, soon after my little talk with my aunt, Milton came to my house to speak with my father. They talked for about an hour while I played with Eneida and Merle outside. At first, I became concerned because I thought that my father had found out that Milton was secretly sending me food and treats with his children. Milton left and my father called me inside and invited me to sit down.

Oh boy, now what? Things have been very smooth for more than six months and here we go again.

"Gabriela, what do you think of our Chinese neighbor?" he asked in a genial manner.

I was not sure what he was up to by asking this question and I could only reply with another question, "What do you mean?"

"Well, you know… he was here to see me and we talked about

you... Well...what he really wanted was to ask me for your hand. I told him that I had to talk with you about this. When I told him about your desire to continue your studies and that you were married, he said that he would send you to college and pay for everything. He even said that he would pay for your divorce."

As my father talked I was becoming short of breath. I was in a state of panic, for I did not know what to answer. Many different thoughts were swirling around in my head. First, my father's preaching about how difficult it would be for a girl to find a husband if she were no longer a virgin came to mind. Then I started thinking about Canche. I was still holding on to the thin hope that he would come looking for me and ask me to marry him. I was also questioning about how could I marry a man I did not love and who was old enough to be my father.

"I must think about this," I replied quietly.

My father remained serene and with encouragement in his voice he continued, "He's financially settled, you know. He has his business, and people in town like him very well. You'll be able to finish your dreams of graduating from college if you marry him. He even has maids to do the housework. It seems to me that you would have a good life. My only objection is that he has two children, which will make you an instant mother."

Ha! As if I had not been already a mother of three children, my two brothers and sister. Playing this role is the least of my concerns.

My father continued talking, but I was not hearing anything, my mind was far away, thinking about the future. This reverie was short though. My father arose, pushed back his chair, and said, "Milton is coming to talk with you tomorrow."

I do not think I slept the whole night, thinking, trying to make my decision. My father's attitude toward Milton's request really surprised me, especially in consideration of his age. But then there was a twenty-four year difference between my mother and father. By morning, I had decided that I could not let this opportunity escape from my hands, at least not without further exploration.

That same day, in the late afternoon, Milton came to the house and I opened the door. "May I speak with your father? Is he home?"

I went to get my father. After the two had greeted each other, Milton asked him, "May I take Gabriela for a walk down by the pier?"

"Sure, go right ahead," my father replied encouragingly.

This answer really shocked me. My father had never before allowed me to be with a man without a chaperone.

Milton and I walked side–by–side, slowly past the *CAPITANIA* (the military and customs offices) and then down a hill to a very quiet area of the beach. The day was beautiful, warm and sunny with very little wind. We sat down close together on a fallen palm tree. My eyes were transfixed on the ocean, admiring the panoramic view. In one direction, off in the distance, I could see the faint outline of what appeared to be a blue mountain rising up out of the ocean. This was *Punta De Manabique*, a point of land far away across the bay. In the other direction there was only open sea, the water was so calm it looked like glass. Fishermen were sailing home since it was after four in the afternoon. Their boats were only part of the large flotilla in the bay because there were also small boats with outboard motors, sailboats and a tugboat pulling a supply barge. Children were swimming near the pier. The sky was filled with soaring sea birds—sea gulls *(gaviotas)*, pelicans *(pelícanos)*, and *tijeretas*. Palm trees were swaying in the breeze, their fronds making a soft rustling sound. The only other sounds were the muffled, distant burbling of outboard motors and the squawking of the seagulls gliding above our heads.

For a period of time we sat silently, not saying a word to each other. I was so nervous and excited, for I knew very well the purpose of this walk and what Milton was going to propose. There was no way, however, that I was going to be the first to speak.

Finally, Milton slowly turned his head toward me and said, "I asked your father for your hand. I'm sorry. I know that I should've asked you first, but I wanted to have your father's approval before I told you that I'm in love with you. We don't have to get married right away. I want to date you so you can get to know me first. I know you're still in love with your school sweetheart and you're not in love with me. I just want you to let me love you and I hope that maybe you'll learn to love me…"

I was having trouble digesting his words. I did not say anything and kept looking straight ahead at the ocean, leaving him no choice but to continue talking.

…"I will send you back to school in Chiquimula," he continued. "I have an idea about what happened to you and I want you to understand that nothing will happen between us that you don't wish to happen."

Am I dreaming? Should I turn this down when it's the door to my freedom, and future? How could there be a man on this earth with such a kind heart?

I kept repeating to myself his words, "I'm not asking you to love me. I just want you to let me love you," I then thought about Canche and tears came to my eyes. Milton must had read my mind and said, "If you get reacquainted with your old boyfriend while you're studying in Chiquimula you can change your mind and marry him, if that is what you both want. You won't have to fear anything. If that happens just let me know and you'll be free to do whatever you wish. I don't want to marry you until you decide that you are ready."

Milton's proposal instantly intrigued me. At that time I do not think that I was seeing him so much as a future husband, but rather, as another angel sent to rescue me from an uncertain and bleak future. I had suffered so much for so many years and I now wanted to have some happiness and security. I felt that this definitely was my chance. I just could not figure out how he could love and want me when he knew that I did not love him. After a few more minutes of reflection, I accepted his proposal. We became engaged in the fall of 1965, almost one year to the day from my arrival in Livingston.

When Milton and I started our courtship my father's rules were quite humourous. He treated us as if we were two teenage kids who had never had a relationship or had never been married. We were not to see each other unless it was in his presence. When we went to the movies we had to take him or one of my brothers along. Of course, it was very well stipulated that I was not to go unaccompanied over to Milton's house. The situation was absolutely hilarious; especially in view that Milton was thirty-seven years old. Needless to say, this did not deter us from doing what we wanted to do. Milton had a fast boat and when my father went to work we got into the boat and spent the morning cruising on the ocean or motoring to Puerto Barrios to do some shopping.

Life was so much fun now. Milton taught me how to water-ski. I was not very good at this and almost drowned. I played games with his children and listened to music at his house, especially the song that became our theme song, *The Theme from The Moulin Rouge*. Milton had several more LPs that contained different versions of this song. After our engagement my father's attitude changed and I was now allowed to be with Milton in private. According to the unofficial code of conduct this was still not proper, but I guess my father finally realized that he could no longer control me every minute of the day.

I immediately started taking steps to get re-admitted to INSO in Chiquimula. This was not as easy as I had thought it would be. Breaking customs and traditions in Guatemala was very difficult. *Señora* Lidia Luz Minera de Pinto, the same principal of the college, who in 1961 had kindly allowed me to leave the premises so that I could go to the park to talk with my mother, was still in charge at the school. When I appealed to her for re-admittance she firmly said, "I can't allow you to attend this college because you are no longer a *señorita*. You are a married woman and I believe you know that the title of this school is: *INSTITUTO NORMAL PARA SEÑORITAS (Misses) DE ORIENTE*. The name doesn't say *SEÑORAS* (Mmes.) and the college could become the talk of this town if I permit you to register."

There was no kindness in her voice and her words stuck into me like shards of glass, clear and cutting. She was right though—I was now a *señora* and my title did not fit with the college's name. I left her office devastated and went to visit my friend and ex-classmate Dora Galeano. She gave me some very good news. "Gaby," as she always called me, "just wait, this principal is leaving very soon. Come back when the new one takes over and maybe things will be different."

When the new principal, *Señora* Ana España de Catalán, took her position at the school a few weeks later I traveled back to Chiquimula to appeal my case. She was more approachable and told me, "I alone cannot make the decision to refuse or accept you as a student. I must admit that I have the same concerns as my predecessor. However, I have looked at your record and it tells me that you were an excellent student here. In fact, you were a leader. In that way you probably belong here more than some of the present *señoritas*. I'll tell you what I'm prepared to do. I'll bring your request to the faculty and advocate on your behalf."

Señora España de Catalán presented my petition to the faculty and each one of them, even the teachers whom I pestered the most when I was a brat in my first and second year at the school, voted in favour of my being allowed to return. I am sure that *Señora* España de Catalán's advocating for me influenced the faculty's decision. She was another one of St. Gabriel's soldiers, helping me in so many ways: advocating on my behalf to the faculty, giving me assistance during my school years, and recommending me as a teacher after graduation.

A big surprise took place prior to Christmas in 1965. My mother returned to Livingston and was staying with my aunt. She had disappeared from my life for almost two years. She learned from my aunt that I was in Livingston and got in contact with me. By this time I was mostly living at Milton's house, preparing for Christmas and for my move to Chiquimula with his children the coming January. Without going into great detail about my misfortune, I updated my mother about what had happened to me since I last saw her.

Then I asked her, "Why don't you come and live with us in this house, I will be going back to school next month and you could stay and help Milton with the restaurant. There is a big room where you can set up your sewing business."

She liked the idea and moved in with us.

Christmas was just around the corner and my mother, Milton's daughter and I were decorating the Christmas tree when he asked Merle, "What do you want for Christmas?"

"I would like a doll," she answered.

Then he looked over to me, "Gaby, what would you like for Christmas?"

I did not need or want anything. Milton had already bought me things that I never even dreamed I would ever own. He repeated his question and after reflecting a few seconds, I could think of only one thing, something that I had wanted so much when I was a child.

"I would like a doll too!" I answered excitedly.

Perhaps he thought he had not heard me correctly. His eyes opened as wide as saucers and slowly repeating each syllable he said, "You...want...a... doll?"

"Yes!" I answered with a huge smile on my face.

My mother saw the incredulous look on Milton's face and interrupted, "Milton, what she should get is a broom and a mop, you've spoiled her rotten, but if she says she wants a doll, she means it. Please, buy her a doll."

She then turned her head and gave me a knowing and understanding look.

Milton gave me a beautiful doll that Christmas. The doll had light brown curly hair, blue eyes that closed when I laid her down and opened when I sat her up. She had a button on her stomach that made her cry when I pushed it. I named her Little Gaby. I had never before seen such a beautiful doll and I knew that I could freely and happily play with it without making anyone upset. Milton made a nice bed for it and he watched with disbelief when I played with this doll like a little girl.

That Christmas of 1965 was the most wonderful Christmas I had experienced in my life up until then. We had a beautifully decorated tree and presents for every one. The children and I set off a ton of fireworks at midnight. In fact, we used up all the fireworks in Milton's store. Even my father was at our house for

that Christmas dinner. I had previously laid down the rules to
him about being civil to my mother in my house. I had never
been so happy.

‹❄›

In January of 1966 I returned to Chiquimula and took my
mother, my little sister Mimí, and Milton's children with me. My
mother eventually found a job and moved into her own place.
Milton paid for everything: food, clothing, my school expenses
and a house for his children and me. I was only able to return to
Livingston during school holidays, but Milton came to Chiquimula to see us quite often.

It was not too difficult going to school and taking care of the

children. Milton had given me enough money
to buy food at a restaurant if I needed to study
and did not have time to cook. For the first
time in my life I had enough money for
everything I needed, including the best medical
treatment.

It did not take long to get back into my old
activities at the school. The only difference
from before was that I was now taking care of
two children I therefore could not organize
and attend many of the evening activities, such
as the dances. I quickly re-united with my
student friends whom I had left behind two
years previously, and I made many new friends
too. My house was very close to the old
boarding house and I remained good friends
with Doña Rome. I was having as much fun at

*Studying at INSO-
age 18*

school as I did before—before my father forced me to leave.

Canche had graduated from INVO in October of 1964. Based
on the school's activity calendar, he would have been taking his
final exams and preparing for graduation when I stopped in Chiquimula after my escape. When I returned to college in the beginning of 1966 I heard that he was attending university in Guatemala City. It was a great relief to know that he was not in Chi-

quimula. Even though I was engaged to Milton I was still in love with Canche and I do not think that I would have been able to handle a face–to–face encounter.

When I married Milton at the end of 1967 I was the only married student in the school. An interesting fact here is that my being permitted to attend this school as a married woman opened the doors for other married women to be able to further their education in the public school system at this level. I am very proud of this accomplishment. I graduated from college on October 26, 1968, right before my twentieth birthday. The last three years at this school were as wonderful as the first three years.

The problems with my father never ceased to end. He still just could not let me enjoy my accomplishments without creating trouble. This time he became upset because the dedication on my graduation invitations read:

TO MY HUSBAND, MILTON WONG, WITH NEVER-ENDING LOVE AND GRATITUDE FOR TURNING MY GREATEST DREAM INTO REALITY.

Milton was my husband and had paid for all of my school expenses and it was only logical and right that his name would be first. My father's name and others were listed on the secondary list of contributors. My father became very angry and refused to travel to Chiquimula to attend the graduation ceremonies. The only thing I received from him was a generic telegram of congratulations—a type of congratulatory message one would send to anybody, except to one's own daughter. I could not believe it. Neither of my brothers would finish their secondary education and yet my father could not bring himself to be present at his oldest daughter's graduation from college because of his obtuse pettiness.

Shortly after my graduation I was able to secure a permanent teaching position in Livingston, teaching kindergarten, again through the help of *Señora* España de Catalán. She liked me so much; I still cannot adequately put into words my gratitude for her kindness and assistance.

ॐ

In 1967, one year before my graduation, Milton and I had one big problem preventing us from marrying—I was still legally married to the criminal, whose whereabouts was unknown. Milton had to hire a lawyer and arrange a divorce for me through the courts, which took time and cost him a lot of money. Finally, we were married on November 27, 1967. My father became upset over a very petty detail, just as he would a year later at my graduation. Milton and I had my mother's legal married name printed on the wedding invitations; that is, her name with the

 married addition *de Folgar*. My father wanted us to place only my mother's maiden name on the invitations and threatened not to attend the wedding if we did not change the printing. This would have been at Milton's expense, of

course. I did not bend and knowing my father, I was resigned that he would not participate in the wedding. However, on the day of the wedding I had one last card up my sleeve. I sent Merle to tell him that one of Milton's black employees, a person my father disliked only because we was black, had volunteered to escort me to the church and to represent him at the ceremony. It did not take my father more than two minutes to run to my house to escort me to the church. I guess I had learned a few manipulative ways of my own. The wedding was a huge affair, probably the social event of the year in Livingston, with practically the whole town attending the reception.

I eventually fell in love with Milton and we had some wonderful years together. Unfortunately, our marriage did not last and we separated, and then divorced. I might not have been the wife he deserved. I was too young and immature. I became capricious. When I look back upon this today, I think that I probably had not yet healed from the wounds of my past. I considered Milton more as a father figure than as a husband. He spoiled me as one would spoil a child and perhaps his extreme tolerance, understanding and patience, qualities that were wonderful and that I appreciated, were not the qualities I most needed at the time to overcome the ghosts of the past. During our relationship we never discussed my Calvary in San Pedro Pinula or the other problems from which I had been suffering since I was a small child. I never brought up these subjects and he never pressed me to discuss them with him. Milton never learned any of the sordid details of my past. Some professional counseling at the beginning of and during our marriage could have helped heal my wounds and possibly have saved the marriage. However, post-traumatic and marriage counseling were unheard of in my country in those days.

Milton and I have continued being very good friends up to this day. He will always have a special place in my heart. It was Milton who made it possible for my health to recuperate. It was Milton who made it possible that I could return to school and pursue a professional career. It was Milton who brought happiness back into my life and who helped me regain trust in men. He is even admired by my second husband and they have remained the best of friends. Milton was a great husband and a wonderful father.

In 1972, Dalila Cárcamo, one of my kidnapper's first cousins, was teaching in Livingston at the school where I was teaching. We were colleagues and friends. Surprisingly, the subject of her cousin had never been brought up between the two of us, that is, until the day she broke the following news to me. "I went to San Pedro Pinula for a visit and found out that Jorge had been killed. Some people say that he received the *Ley Fuga,* but we aren't totally sure."

The *Ley Fuga* (Fugitive Law) is not a law; it is rather a sarcastic, euphemistic expression used to describe the way some prisoners are unofficially done away with. The police or prison guards would *accidentally–on purpose* leave the cell door unlocked, thus encouraging the prisoner to escape. When the prisoner tries to escape they shoot him dead, probably as close as possible to the fence.

I had previously heard that the criminal had been in and out of prison since his first capture in late November of 1964. I knew little else or wanted to know anything else about his activities since then. It did not surprise me at all that he might have been killed in this manner.

"Oh, now I feel much safer," was the only thing I said to her.

"Why do you say that?" She replied with a look of puzzlement.

I did not know if she was pretending ignorance or if she really did not know what her cousin had done to me. I answered her *why* with another saying, *"A cada cerdo se le llega su Sábado* (Every pig has his Saturday). Saturday is the traditional slaughtering day in rural Guatemala."

She appeared uncomfortable with my answers and I changed the subject. This conversation, even with my terse answers, did not cloud our relationship and we remained good friends.

A few days later, my father came to my house to tell me essentially the same story. But his version had some added details. He said that people in San Pedro Pinula had told him that the criminal was buried without any ceremony and that the only people accompanying the body to the cemetery were his mother, two police officers and four prisoners carrying the coffin.

The Spanish saying: *El que mal empieza, mal acaba* (that which starts badly, ends badly) flashed in my mind—a horrible death was the natural consequence of the pain the monster had inflicted on me and on other people. The news of his death was what I needed to at last bring closure to my ordeal. Although I had been leading a normal and happy life since 1965, I knew that I would always be in danger as long as the monster was alive. I did not let this bother me to any great extent or stop me from doing what I wanted to do, but it was always present in the background. Finally, I had a feeling of total freedom, peace and safety.

Municipalidad de Escuintla
Departamento de Escuintla, Guatemala, C. A.

CERTIFICADO DE DEFUNCION

EL INFRASCRITO REGISTRADOR CIVIL DE LA CIUDAD DE ESCUINTLA, DEPARTAMENTO DE ESCUINTLA

CERTIFICA: _____

Que al Folio ___125___ del Libro ___109___ de defunciones se encuentra el Acta

No. ___250___ en la cual consta la defunción de: ___Jorge Arturo___

___Carcamo Portillo.-___ de ___27___ años de edad, Estado Civil:

___Soltero___ con ___"___ ___"___ ___"___ ___"___

hijo de ___Manuel Antonio Carcamo.-___ y de ___Hortencia Portillo.-___

Originario de ___San Pedro Pinula.-___

Según informe de: ___Dr. Juan Rafael Minera.-___

Falleció el ___veintisiete___ de ___julio de mil novecientos setenta y dos.-___

A las ___-10-___ horas ___-45-___ minutos en ___Ingreso muerto___

del I.G.S.S. Esc.-

A consecuencia de ___Hemorragia intracraneana masiva, con destrucción tejido___

___cerebral producido por proyectil de arma de fuego.-___

Firmaron el acta:

(F) ___Ilegible.-___   (F) ___Tono A. Solis.-___
El Compareciente   Registrador Civil

ANOTACIONES: ___ninguna.-___

Se extiende la presente en la ciudad de Escuintla, Departamento de Escuintla, a _____

___tres___ de ___diciembre___ del año dos mil ___cuatro.-___

Honorarios: Los de Ley Q1.00 Decreto Leg. 111-96

Hecho por: ___Blanca___
___Blandina Teresa Escobar___

Confrontó: ___Noemi Hernandez Solorzano.-___

N° 000205   Registrador Civil

Death   Certificate

In the year 2004 I was able to secure the criminal's **death certificate** through channels in Guatemala. The certificate does not say where he was killed or the circumstances. It states that death was a "consequence of a massive intracranial hemorrhage, with destruction to brain tissue, caused by a projectile from a firearm." The certificate was issued in the town of Esquintla where the infamous Pavon prison is located. The photograph is from the monster's national identity paper *(Cédula de Vecindad)* and superimposed onto the death certificate.

Wedding-1967

It was nearly impossible to get my parents to sit together for this photo.

Graduation-1968 with Zoila Guerra

Zoila was a very good friend during my second time at INSO.

Epilogue

The diagnosis of Dr. Carías and Dr. Labbé were very accurate. I indeed had difficulties bearing children. I had five miscarriages, and a stillbirth. In addition, the child from my first full–term pregnancy lived only four days. There were times when I thought that I was being punished for having wished the death of the baby. But God had mercy on me and blessed me with three healthy children.

In the course of writing this book I have traveled twice to San Pedro Pinula in order to try to clear up some of the mysteries that were still bothering me. I did not find answers to all of my questions, but here is what I learned: People in San Pedro Pinula confirmed what my father had told me—that when I was kidnapped no one in town knew what had happened to me. It is rumoured that it was not the police or prison guards who shot Jorge, but rather it was one of his numerous enemies avenging the crimes he had committed. I also learned that his brothers, Erasmo and David, had also been killed, separately, and not in relation to my case

I was able to find out where the Cárcamo's farm was located. My husband prepared the maps in this book from this information and from the clues and descriptions I was able to provide. Up until then I had no idea where I was held captive.

Cesar and his parents, Mr. and Mrs. Sandoval, and all of the other angels who came to my rescue are now deceased and while they were alive I kept my promise to them to never reveal to anyone, except to my father, that they had helped me.

In 1989 my father begged me to sponsor him to come to Canada. He was eighty-four years old, frail and blind in one eye. His reasons for wanting to come to Canada were to iron out all the wrinkles that made our father-daughter relationship so turbulent. He said that he was not going to be able to die in peace if we did not resolve our differences. I was previously resigned to leave the past sealed and undisturbed for the rest of my life.

It was a painful process for both of us and our conversations lasted until late unto the evening over several days. I questioned him about his actions toward my mother, his taking the children away from her, and his preventing us from having any contact with her. He told me he did that because he was very angry with her due to her unfaithfulness. His only desire was to seek revenge and to destroy her. He said that he had realized that his actions not only destroyed her but also destroyed his children and himself. He had also realized that his vengeful actions toward my mother prevented him from enjoying many years of happiness together with her—"I never stopped loving her."

He expressed his love for me and thanked God for having given him three daughters. "I wish now that I'd had two more daughters, instead of the two sons who have disappointed me." He praised me and thanked me saying, "you're very kind, you've never forgotten about me since moving to Canada. You always made sure to send me a card and a gift for my birthday, Christmas, and Father's Day despite our rocky relationship. All of the negative comments I said about your being a girl were nothing but bad jokes and I never really meant it."

When I told him what had happened to me when I was kidnapped, for once he did not interrupt. I was reliving each one of those horrible moments in my life and many times I had to take a break in order to regain my strength and composure. He just listened and sobbed.

When I asked him why I was put in jail along with Jorge, he said that it was the law—the couple had to be put in jail until it was established if the girl went with the boy willingly or not. How my father could have suspected that I had run away with Jorge will remain a mystery to me.

My father also admitted to his mistake of taking me away from Chiquimula and away from my education and from he man I loved. When I started to bring up the subject of his mishandling of my case before the court hearing (Chapter 10), the look on his face told me that the strain might end his life.

With much difficulty he said, "I could not take you with me because I was too ashamed to face the world with a daughter who was going to be an unwed mother and who possibly would never find a husband because she was not a virgin. I was also embarrassed to face everyone who had told me and had pleaded with me that I should have left the children with their mother. I fought your mother for your custody and look what happened to you."

Suddenly, he took my hands into his hands and started to kneel, but I did not let him. He then placed my hands into his and pulled them close to his face and said, "It is difficult for me to give explanations for my actions, actions that I don't even understand myself." Tears were flowing from his eyes as he continued, "Please forgive me for all the wrong things I did as father. I just wanted the best for you, even if you don't believe me. I will do anything to have your forgiveness. If you do forgive me, please promise me that you won't ever bring up the subject again. It's just too painful."

His remorse was enough to deter me from pursuing any more questioning, even if his logic and many of his explanations still did not make much sense to me. I told him, "Papá, I forgive you and the past will be buried. And please forgive me for the many mistakes I have made as a daughter."

We stood up and hugged each other. His last words before going to bed that night were, "Now, if God wants to take me with him, I can die in peace."

My father lived almost three more years and died at the age of eighty-seven. Those were the best years we had as father and daughter. A few days before his death he said to me, "If I had taken this step a long time ago our happy time together would have been much longer. I shouldn't have waited until I'm near death to make amends." My father also told me that he now wanted to go back to Guatemala to ask forgiveness from my mother in person. Sadly, he was not able to do this—time had run out.

On a recent trip to Guatemala in 2006 I consulted with a lawyer about my kidnapping, my going to jail and my father's explanation about the law. The lawyer told me that it had never been written in the law that a girl had to be held in jail until it was established whether she had really been kidnapped or if she had eloped. He said that sending the kidnapped girl to jail was a local custom—just part of the coercion process a family used to force her to marry her abductor and therefore, save the family's honour. This custom of kidnapping girls for marriage, especially minors, is called bride kidnapping and it disgracefully still happens in certain regions in Guatemala.

Papá–1990, and Mamá with her sewing machine–1993.

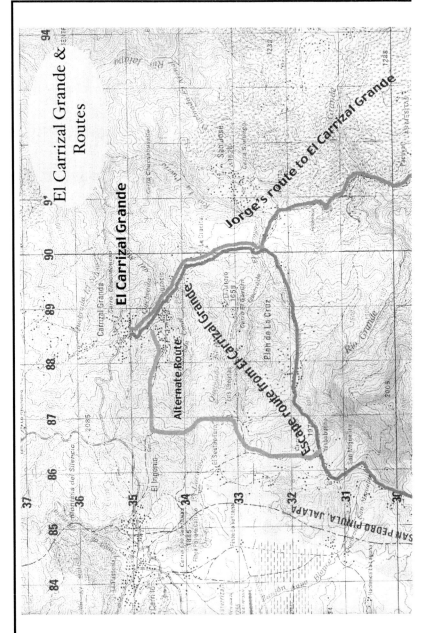

El Carrizal Grande—Showing the route to the village and the possible routes of escape (Chapter 14).

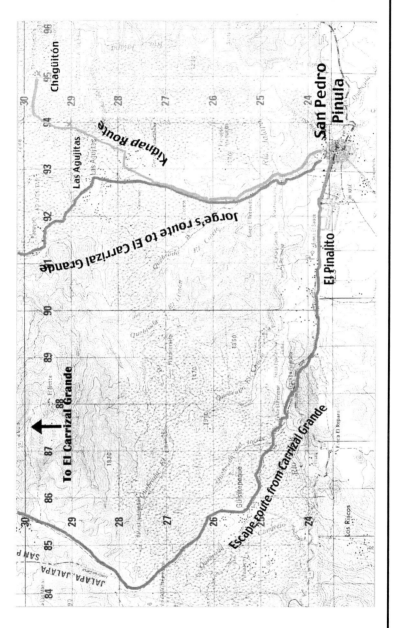

El Carrizal Grande to San Pedro- a continuation of the previous map-showing the routes to and from San Pedro Pinula.

About The Author

Gabriela A. Folgar de Shea was born in the town El Progreso Guastatoya in Guatemala on November 7, 1948. Her arduous and at times painful childhood and adolescence is very well described in this book. However, by the age of twenty she had overcome most of her difficulties, was married and had become a schoolteacher in the coastal town of Livingston, Guatemala. Although there were other setbacks after her escape from her terrible ordeal as a teenager: a divorce, many miscarriages and the death of an infant child, she did not let these events hold her back. She has been married for over thirty years to her second husband.

In 1974 Gabriela immigrated to Canada and settled in the city of Edmonton, Alberta. As with many immigrants possessing little knowledge of English she had to work, at first, in entry–level jobs: janitor, assembly line worker, and waitress. She enrolled in school to learn and eventually master English and was able to move back into professional life.

Gabriela has been working for the City of Edmonton since 1988, first, as a family resource worker and later, as a social worker in assessment and short–term counseling. She feels fortunate to be in a position to help people with their problems that quite often resemble her troubles from forty years ago.

Gabriela's next project is to translate her story into Spanish and have the book published for the Latin American market.

ISBN 141209656-1

9 781412 096560